THE LIVING DEAD
ECCLESIASTES THROUGH ART

Of making many books there is no end [...].

Ecclesiastes 12:12

Ecquid Sunt aliud
quam breve gaudium?

THE LIVING DEAD

ECCLESIASTES THROUGH ART

Edited by Corinna Ricasoli

museum of the Bible

Ferdinand Schöningh

The Living Dead: Ecclesiastes through Art is an exhibition of Museum of the Bible,
November 17, 2017–April 30, 2018.

Exhibition Catalog and Curator
Corinna Ricasoli, PhD, *Curator of Fine Arts*

Exhibition Design
Jeff Baxter, *Director of Exhibits*
Tetmura Amira Rasayon, *Graphics Technician*

Editors
Corinna Ricasoli, PhD, *Curator of Fine Arts*
Audrey Nicholls, PhD, *Independent Scholar*
Stacey L. Douglas, *Manager of Research, Editorial, & Publications*
Jared N. Wolfe, PhD, *Senior Writer & Editor*

Cover Design and Layout
TYPO85, Rome (Italy)

Published by
Verlag Ferdinand Schöningh
Ein Imprint der Brill Deutschland GmbH
Jühenplatz 1-3, 33098 Paderborn
Deutschland
www.schoeningh.de

Printing and Binding
AZ Druck und Datentechnik GmbH
Heisinger Straße 16, 87437 Kempten
Deutschland

The views expressed in this work are those of the authors, editors, or contributors and do not
necessarily represent, reflect, or have the endorsement of Museum of the Bible. The various views
presented in this work published by Museum of the Bible are the writers' own, and are intended to
further the engagement of all people with the Bible.

Unless otherwise indicated, all Bible quotations are from *New Revised Standard Version Bible*,
copyright © 1989 National Council of the Churches of Christ in the United States of America.
Used by permission. All rights reserved.

Artworks not on display in the exhibition are marked by an asterisk (*).

ISBN 978-3-506-73276-7

Printed by Ferdinand Schöningh in Germany

The Living Dead: Ecclesiastes through Art

Museum of the Bible
November 17, 2017
April 30, 2018

Essays

Fr. Luca Mazzinghi, Full Professor of Old Testament at Gregorian University, Rome, Italy

Eric S. Christianson, Independent Scholar

Msgr. Timothy Verdon, Director of the Museo dell'Opera del Duomo, Florence, Italy

Entries

Oriane Beaufils, Curator, Château de Fontainebleau, Fontainebleau, France

Magali Briat-Philippe, Curator, Monastère royal de Brou, Bourg-en-Bresse, France

Quentin Buvelot, Senior Curator, Mauritshuis, The Hague, the Netherlands

Philip Cottrell, Lecturer, University College Dublin, Dublin, Ireland

Zsuzsanna Dobos, Curator, Szépművészeti Múzeum, Budapest, Hungary

Donatienne Dujardin, Curator, Palais des Beaux-Arts, Lille, France

Pippa Mason, Johnny Van Haeften Old Master Paintings, London, England

Audrey Nicholls, Independent Scholar

Beata Purc-Stepniak, Curator, Muzeum Narodowe w Gdańsku, Gdańsk, Poland

Corinna Ricasoli, Curator, Museum of the Bible, Washington, DC, United States

Virginie Spenlé, Kunstkammer Georg Laue, Munich, Germany

Lea van de Vinne, Curator, Mauritshuis, The Hague, the Netherlands

Peter van der Ploeg, Director, Huygens' Hofwijck, Voorburg, the Netherlands

Wendela Wagenaar-Burgemeister, Salomon Lilian Dutch Old Master Paintings, Amsterdam, the Netherlands

Registrar

Stephen Gorman, Lead Registrar, Museum of the Bible, Washington, DC, United States

Co-operating Registrars

Karien Beijers, Frans Hals Museum, Haarlem, the Netherlands

Katalin Borbély, Szépművészeti Múzeum, Budapest, Hungary

Louise Crossley, Bradford Galleries and Museums, Bradford, England

Lisa M. MacDougall, Shannon Schuler, National Gallery of Art, Washington, DC, United States

Amalia D'Alascio, Maria Adalgisa Ottaviani, Vatican Apostolic Library, Vatican City State

Anna Maria De Gregorio, Accademia di San Luca, Rome, Italy

Richard Harris, Richard Harris Collection, Chicago, IL, United States

Andre Jordaan, The Kremer Collection, Amsterdam, the Netherlands

Silvia Lucantoni, Galleria Borghese, Rome, Italy

Janneke Martens, Rijksmuseum, Amsterdam, the Netherlands

Sabine Schiewer, Staatliches Museum Schwerin, Germany

Sona Lisa Shaboyan, Kunstkammer Georg Laue, Munich, Germany

Kelli Sohanpaul, Tomasso Brothers Fine Art, Leeds, England

Mirosław Szwabowicz, Muzeum Narodowe w Gdańsku, Gdansk, Poland

Romuald Tanzilli, Monastère royal de Brou, Bourg-en-Bresse, France

Patrizia Tarchi, Gallerie degli Uffizi, Florence, Italy

Patricia Truffin, Palais des Beaux-Arts, Lille, France

Margherita Viola, Polo Museale della Toscana, Florence, Italy

Wendela Wagenaar-Burgemeister, Salomon Lilian Dutch Old Masters, Amsterdam, the Netherlands

Main Shipping Coordination

Alessandra Brocca, Janet Lloyd,
Masterpiece International, United States

Italian Shipping Coordination

Barbara Panduri, Arteria, Italy

Shipping Partners

Masterpiece, United States

Arteria, Italy

IKON, United States

Constantine, England

Hasenkamp, Germany

Crown, the Netherlands

Hizkia, the Netherlands

Hungart, Hungary

LP Art, France

Renesans Trans, Poland

Insurance Brokers and Facility Assessment

Linda Hale, Taylor Hargrave and Rose
Proby, Marsh & McLennan Agency LLC

Michael Watters, McLarens

Installation Service for Temporary Exhibitions

ARTEX Fine Art Services

Couriers

Karien Beijers, Frans Hals Museum,
Haarlem, the Netherlands

Dirk Blübaum, Staatliches Museum
Schwerin, Schwerin, Germany

Magali Briat-Philippe, Monastère royal de
Brou, Bourg-en-Bresse, France

Diego Cauzzi, Galleria Nazionale di Parma,
Parma, Italy

Cordelia Hattori, Palais des Beaux–arts,
Lille, France

Jill Iredale, Bradford Museums and
Galleries, Bradford, England

Andree Jordaan, The Kremer Collection,
Amsterdam, the Netherlands

Anna Koves, Szépművészeti Múzeum,
Budapest, Hungary

Catia Lamerton Viegas Wesolowska,
Muzeum Narodowe w Gdańsku, Gdańsk,
Poland

Lisa McDougall, National Gallery of Art,
Washington, DC, United States

Marina Minozzi, Galleria Borghese, Rome,
Italy

Laura Mori, Gallerie degli Uffizi, Florence,
Italy

Ambrogio Piazzoni, Vatican Apostolic
Library, Vatican City State

Lorenzo Sbaraglio, Museo della Natura
Morta, Poggio a Caiano, Italy

Catalog Design

TYPO85 s.r.l., Rome, Italy

Table of Contents

Foreword

Although the original Hebrew has only 2,987 words, less than 1% of the 305,441 words of the Hebrew and Aramaic Bible, this "booklet" has stimulated and troubled many centuries of theology, art history, philosophical reflection, and exegetical analysis. In a short essay from 1909, at the dawn of a period of the most refined critical research, A. S. Kamenetszky did not hesitate to define Qoheleth/Ecclesiastes as a *Rätsel*, an elusive enigma with its multiple styles and fluidity of thought.

Our author, hidden behind a pseudonym and sometimes vested with the sumptuous apparel of King Solomon, is not afraid to weave into his message both a sense of emptiness and the brightness of serene enjoyment; the marked coldness of the sayings are united to a subtle anxiety, such that no one can read these pages and remain unmoved. He has no fear of being both conservative and a surprisingly innovative critic who shows up the fragility of traditional wisdom. His understanding of history rhythmed in repeating circles where "there is nothing new under the sun" is exemplary, contradicting the linear and progressive vision of Messianic biblical history.

The rich and emotionally charged series of artistic works in the exhibition offered by the Museum of the Bible, that can now be admired in the following pages, is held together by four cardinal points which are like a free and creative map of the thought of Ecclesiastes. Here, above all, we see the cyclical flux of historical time that unceasingly reiterates construction and destruction. Here, too, we see the mystery of human existence in all its coarseness with its limitations of knowledge, the scandal of social injustice, and the inconsistency of happiness and wellbeing.

Here, also, the further experience of the transience of things and the frailty of life that quickly slips away from youth to the ruins of old age and the arrival of death, such as to seal the famous motto of the Latin version of Ecclesiastes, *vanitas vanitatum*, as a hallmark that has dominated the pessimistic worldview of humanity. Here, finally, following again the representation offered by the collection of images in this catalogue, there is the appeal made by the "wise elder" to enjoy those rare moments of happiness that are scattered through human existence. The emptiness that deeply marks reality will return soon enough.

The modernity of Ecclesiastes, witnessed in the constant resurfacing of his message throughout the history of Western civilization is clear to the reader of these pages. As the commentator Daniel Lys wrote, "Ecclesiastes is a lucid analysis of the human condition, it is a book full of questions which ultimately puts into question traditional doctrine and one's self and culture."

Cardinal Gianfranco Ravasi
President of the Pontifical Council for Culture

Preface

The people of long ago are not remembered, nor will there be any remembrance of people yet to come by those who come after them. Ecclesiastes 1:11

In popular understanding, the Bible stands for truth that never changes, that gives direction to the human experience from the moment we are born to the moment our lives come to an end and something new, less defined will welcome us. Everything has a purpose, a plan that is bigger than we can see.

The book of Ecclesiastes, however, sets a counter point. Life does not make sense. What we do, we do in vain. There is no reward for good behavior and no punishment for moral failure. And nobody has power over death.

Nevertheless, this bleak outlook becomes a source of joy. If all is in vain, why not explore the moment? Why not explore the divine mystery that is in all and over all?

Despite the book's lament that "the people of long ago are not remembered" by the "people yet to come", Ecclesiastes has spoken to its readers through millennia who find their own experience of life in almost every sentence, foremost artists and courageous thinkers.

It is with great pleasure that Museum of the Bible, as one of its inaugural exhibitions, presents this piece of ancient literature as it is reflected in the imagination of visual artists.

David Trobisch
Director of Collections

Acknowledgements

This exhibition and catalog would not have been possible without the help of many individuals and institutions. I wish to express my gratitude to the following institutions and collectors and their staffs for their help in making this exhibition possible:

Bradford Museums and Galleries, Bradford, England
Frans Hals Museum, Haarlem, the Netherlands
Galleria Borghese, Rome, Italy
Galleria dell'Accademia Nazionale di San Luca, Rome, Italy
Galleria Nazionale di Parma, Parma, Italy
Gallerie degli Uffizi, Florence, Italy
Kunstkammer Georg Laue, Munich, Germany
Palais des Beaux–arts, Lille, France
Monastère royal de Brou, Bourg-en-Bresse, France
Museo della Natura Morta, Poggio a Caiano, Italy
Muzeum Narodowe w Gdańsku, Gdańsk, Poland
Rijksmusem, Amsterdam, the Netherlands
Richard Harris Collection, Chicago, IL, United States
Richard Green Fine Paintings, London, England
Salomon Lilian Dutch Old Master Paintings, Amsterdam, the Netherlands
Staatliches Museum Schwerin, Schwerin, Germany
Szépművészeti Múzeum, Budapest, Hungary
The Kremer Collection, Amsterdam, the Netherlands
The National Gallery of Art, Washington, DC, United States
Tomasso Brothers Fine Art, Leeds, England
Vatican Apostolic Library, Vatican City State

My acknowledgements also extend to the great help and support provided by Museum of the Bible and its staff.

Corinna Ricasoli

Introduction

Who has not come across *Vanity Fair*? How many women have not owned a *vanity* table or a *vanity* case at some point in their lives? How often have we thought of ourselves or others as *vain* after too much time spent looking in a mirror, leaning over a *vanity* washbasin? What about *vanitas* paintings—which speak to us of our own mortality—in museums and galleries all over the world? *Vanity, vain, vanitas* are familiar words, but how many know that their meaning and place in Western culture today is derived from the biblical book of Ecclesiastes?

One of the goals of Museum of the Bible is to illustrate the impact of the Bible on culture, namely on literature, music, the visual arts, and—more generally—on many aspects of daily life that we are no longer aware have been in some way influenced by the Bible. Through permanent and temporary exhibitions, such as *The Living Dead: Ecclesiastes through Art*, Museum of the Bible also strives to fulfill its aim to be a global institution that is open to all, regardless of their faith or worldview. Indeed, this exhibition addresses themes that are universal, transnational, and cross-cultural, and these concerns for diversity and inclusion are the foundation on which Museum of the Bible has been built and operates every day.

Why an Exhibition on Ecclesiastes?

When the time came to choose a theme for the Museum of the Bible inaugural fine-art exhibition, my thoughts first turned to the remarkable book of Ecclesiastes—one of the most important and intriguing books of all time. Its influence has been felt since late antiquity, throughout the early modern era, and into our own time. Ecclesiastes tackles many of the most essential questions regarding the purpose and meaning of life. The book explores what it means to live knowing that we must die, what are the unwritten rules that can lead to a happy life, and indeed a happy death. It questions what is truly important and what is not. Traditionally, the book is thought to be written by Solomon, and is considered to be one of the 'Books of Wisdom' found in the Old Testament. Although this is no longer agreed to be the case, the concept of deep wisdom remains strongly linked to the text, an issue explored in greater depth in Luca Mazzinghi's erudite essay *The Book of Ecclesiastes*, in this catalog. Ecclesiastes's influence on Western culture is inestimable, and reference to it is found in literature, philosophy, music, and the visual arts.

Today, in a world of considerable distractions, the book no longer enjoys widespread popularity. Mention of its name and of the intention to create an exhibition that centered upon its influence frequently led to polite but somewhat blank expressions. Only when quoting its famous opening lines "vanity of vanities! All is vanity" or mentioning the international hit song *Turn! Turn! Turn! (To Everything There Is a Season)* by the well-known 1960s rock band The Byrds awoke a slumbering recognition that these words were related to Ecclesiastes. In other words, the verses had transitioned into popular culture without an awareness of their original source or context.

These considerations, coupled with an awareness that an exhibition entirely devoted to the book of Ecclesiastes had yet to be undertaken, convinced us of its merit. Although there have been a number of exhibitions devoted to the topic of *vanitas* still-life painting, none have made Ecclesiastes its central component. Exploring the multifaceted themes raised in Ecclesiastes is a major focus of this exhibition.

Exhibition Structure

The book of Ecclesiastes was not written using a narrative format, no story unfolds, rather, it follows a series of thoughts, questions, and considerations on the meaning and purpose of life. It asks what is the point of human existence and human achievements if nothing lasts, if in the end, through death and decay, everything vanishes. What is the point of amassing knowledge if the educated must die like the illiterate? Why do the poor suffer? Why do they exist at all while others are blessed with wealth and power? What is the point of being wealthy if 'you can't take it with you'? What are the advantages and disadvantages to being born into one or the other category? What are the responsibilities that come with privilege, if any? Ironically, humanity's only certainty in this world is that everything passes, that we all die. Nothing lasts forever—material possessions, youth, life—all experience the same inevitable fate.

One of the aims of the exhibition is to help visitors understand the main themes of the book of Ecclesiastes. The display is intended to guide visitors through the fascinating, yet somewhat meandering, composition of the verses, employing the powerful visual aid of art. From a curatorial perspective, this was a challenging remit. The wide scope of topics encountered in Ecclesiastes ensured that it would not be possible or desirable to attempt to illustrate the numerous individual verses. In addition, ideas and themes addressed at the beginning are resumed and readdressed later in the book. Therefore, the themes and ideas that recur most frequently were chosen to best demonstrate the overall thrust of the meaning of the book.

The exhibition is divided into four rooms, each focusing on one main theme. Room 1 explores the idea that history repeats itself, Room 2 the mystery of existence, Room 3 the impermanence of earthly things, and Room 4 the deceptiveness of earthly pleasures. In addition, each room addresses sub-themes that are linked to the main theme of each room: Room 1, the cyclical nature of time and the worthlessness and transience of human endeavors; Room 2, the limitations of knowledge, social injustices, and the futility of wealth; Room 3, the unpredictability of one's fate, the transience of things, the transience of youth and beauty, the inevitability of death, and the fragility of life; Room 4, the earthly pleasures of life and the deceptiveness of earthly pleasures.

Timeframe and Geographical Origins of the Artworks

For historical reasons, the timeframe of the artworks on display is the early modern era. This is when the influence of Ecclesiastes on the visual arts was at its peak due to particularly violent events (including almost two centuries of religious wars), which had a significant impact on the cultural mentality of Europe, the continent in which these artworks were all originally carried out. The famine and plague that accompanied war made people particularly keen to meditate on transience and on the fleeting nature of life, of material possessions, and earthly pleasures, as clearly shown by the ubiquitous presence of the symbols and allegories of death, often expressed through *vanitas* still-life paintings. Themes of transience have been addressed innumerable times in art, and artists, as well as intellectuals, have been particularly sensitive interpreters of this general awareness.

Because of the abovementioned historical and social events, and because of the themes addressed by Ecclesiastes, early modern readership understandably considered this book, and its ideas, particularly relevant and topical. For this reason, Ecclesiastes played a significant role in the arts of the time, and it can truly be seen as one of the most relevant biblical books of the early modern era. Writers, musicians, and artists quoted and illustrated its verses—but especially its celebrated Latin translation of the opening verse, *vanitas vanitatum* "vanity of vanities"—countless times, either to criticize contemporary society, or to offer a chance for reflection on transience and the unpredictability of human life and endeavors, or simply to encourage the viewer to seize the moment since life is short.

Museum of the Bible does not focus on, or have, many paintings, prints, drawings, and sculptures in its permanent collections. Therefore, this exhibition has been possible thanks to the extraordinary generosity and collaborative spirit of a number of museums and galleries worldwide, whose contribution to this project has been crucial.

In four instances, in which the loans were not possible, the decision was made to include the catalog entries related to these artworks such is the relevance of the inclusion of these images to the overall theme.

It is also important to note that not all of these artworks were directly inspired by Ecclesiastes. The aim of the exhibition is not to suggest that this was the case, rather it aims to highlight the manner with which the themes that pervade the book of Ecclesiastes also pervade artworks of the early modern era. In this way, viewers are invited to explore connections that heretofore may have escaped their notice.

The panels that introduce each room and theme quote the relevant verses in Ecclesiastes so that the visitor may better understand the connection between the artworks and the verses. The New Revised Standard Version of the Bible has been used throughout the exhibition because its modern adaptation allows for ease and speed of understanding. Older editions, such as the King James Version of the Bible, first published in 1611, would have provided a contemporary context but at the price of straightforward comprehension.

About the Catalog

The catalog has been devised with ease of accessibility in mind, and with technical terms and complex themes explained as fully as possible.

The catalog is divided into two sections, the first of which contains three introductory essays written by eminent academics that include biblical scholars and art historians: Luca Mazzinghi, Eric S. Christianson, and Timothy Verdon. The essays move progressively from a general outline explaining the overall context of Ecclesiastes to a more detailed focus of its impact on the cultural mentality of the early modern era. Thus, Luca Mazzinghi's essay provides an outline of the book of Ecclesiastes—the historical background in which the book was written, its place in the Bible, its content, and its exegesis. Eric S. Christianson's paper narrows the focus to the early modern era by providing an insightful reception history of Ecclesiastes during that period. He analyzes some of the philosophical and literary work *on*, or inspired *by*, Ecclesiastes during the timeframe in question, as well as how this biblical book was used by authors such as Bacon and Montaigne. Finally, Timothy Verdon's essay addresses the core of the problem—Ecclesiastes's impact on society and therefore on the European artistic scene.

The second part of the catalog, concerning the entries, has been organized in a way which reflects the exhibition display. It is therefore divided into four sections (equivalent to the four display rooms), each divided into its respective sub-themes mentioned above. In order to better translate the display to the catalog, each thematic section is introduced by the same text used throughout the exhibition to provide more context and explain why the artworks in that segment are relevant to the theme. To facilitate the reader, we decided to present the entries in each thematic section ordered alphabetically by artist.

In the catalog, emblems feature strongly. This is because emblems had a significant role in the success of certain *vanitas* symbolism. Emblems were an exquisitely intellectual divertissement of Renaissance and early modern scholars, especially until the mid-seventeenth century. As may be seen in George Wither's *Book of Emblems* of 1635 (from which the emblems displayed here are taken), the topics emblems address are countless, spanning love, morals, life, religion, and more. In many instances, because they combine an image with a motto, they aim at expressing some teaching—generally concerning morals—in a simple, straightforward, and intelligible way, at least as far as seventeenth-century emblems are concerned; sixteenth-century emblems are, on the other hand, often quite impenetrable. This concise, yet powerful, way to teach and offer pause for reflection on morality made emblems particularly successful among preachers and religious congregations (such as the Jesuits)—and in this respect, it should be noted that there is a substantial number of emblems illustrating *vanitas* subject matter, such as the fleetingness of life. Similarities may therefore be found between emblems and *vanitas* imagery, as in both instances there is a particularly strong connection between the image and its meaning.

In order to avoid interrupting the flow of the text, the dates of birth and death of the persons mentioned throughout the catalog are provided in the Index of Names at the back, together with a brief description of who each person was. Additionally, to further assist readers, this catalog provides a list of entries at the front of the catalog to ease the locating of images. Although rarely included in exhibition catalogs, we hope readers will find these lists a useful addition.

Lastly, this catalog has benefitted from the knowledgeable contributions of a number of scholars. In order to provide the reader with information on who they are and their affiliation, a list of contributors may be found in the front matter.

It is our hope at Museum of the Bible that this exhibition and catalog will contribute to the knowledge and understanding of the book of Ecclesiastes, and that it may enable visitors and interested parties to (re)discover the book and appreciate the extraordinary topicality and timelessness of its reflections on the purpose and value of life.

In a world ever replete with what Ecclesiastes refers to as 'earthly vanities', *The Living Dead: Ecclesiastes through Art* seeks to offer a moment of reflection in which visitors can contemplate the fleeting nature of "all the deeds that are done under the sun" (Ecclesiastes 1:14). Ecclesiastes's reminder not to be preoccupied with 'worldly vanities' is a warning that concerns everyone, because, regardless of whether faith is a feature of life or not, 'earthly vanities' will continue to be irrelevant at the point of death; and that is an incontrovertible, universal truth.

Corinna Ricasoli

Essays

The Book of Ecclesiastes

Luca Mazzinghi

Introduction

The book of Ecclesiastes is one of the books of the Hebrew Bible (or, from a Christian perspective, of the Old Testament). It is part of the so-called Wisdom Literature, which includes the books of Proverbs, Job, Sirach, and Wisdom. "Wisdom" is in those books not something intellectual, but something very close to our concept of "experience"—the sage is the one who knows in a very realistic way how to live with joy, peace, and justice. But for the biblical sage, that is possible only if we understand that every human experience of the world is in some measure an experience of God. Finally, biblical wisdom is also a matter of education: How can I learn? How can I help young people to live their life?

Generally considered to have been written around the third century BCE, the book of Ecclesiastes, as it is called in the Christian Greek and Latin traditions, is an extremely intriguing text. Readers, old and young, know the famous opening statement: "Vanity of vanities, says the Teacher, vanity of vanities! All is vanity."[1] But did the writer of Ecclesiastes really say that? Or were his readers responsible for putting these words into his mouth? And what is the real message of a book whose meaning, even now, seems something of an unsolved riddle? Was the author a pessimist, a skeptic and possible atheist, or was he a "fearless lover of life" (Robert Gordis), or even "a preacher of joy" (Norman Whybray)?[2] Or was he something else entirely? Perhaps, as the scholar Robert Gordis suggested, the historical Ecclesiastes "would have been shocked, even amused, to learn that his notebook was canonized as part of Holy Scripture".[3]

The book of Ecclesiastes may be considered as having three main themes. The first, and perhaps the main theme of the book, is that everything is ephemeral and absurd (*hebel*). The second theme is the possibility of real joy, in spite of everything, and the third theme is that at the core of every human experience there is the discovery that there is a God.[4]

History of Interpretation

According to an ancient Jewish tradition, the book of Ecclesiastes was written by the aging King Solomon. We now know that the book was most likely written at some point in the third century BCE. Passages such as Ecclesiastes 5:7–8, for example, reflect the period when the whole region of Judea was under the rule of the Egyptian dynasty of the Ptolemies, who introduced a new style of bureaucracy and a new kind of economy based on a class of small-time money-making landlords.[5] Indeed, Ecclesiastes says, "The lover of money will not be satisfied with money; nor the lover of wealth, with gain."[6] However, a main question of the book is: "For who knows what is good for mortals while they live the few days of their vain life, which they pass like a shadow?"[7] This is a question that is better understood against the background of Hellenistic culture—a period conventionally dated from Alexander the Great to the beginning of the Roman Empire (31 BCE)—

which in the third century BCE explored ideas related to what constituted "the Good" for human beings. But what does the author mean by "the Good"? It refers to what is fruitful, efficacious, of lasting value. The theoretical questions about human life (i.e., about the soul and body, the immortality of the soul, etc.) raised by Plato and Aristotle turned into practical and ethical questions in the main post-Aristotelian schools at the end of the fourth century BCE when Greek culture discovered a bigger world with the conquests of Alexander: the Stoics, the Epicureans, the Skeptics, the Cynics. The main philosophical problem in those schools is exactly the same for Ecclesiastes: What is good, what is fruitful for human beings in a life that so often appears to be incomprehensible?

However, the real problem about the book of Ecclesiastes is not the date of its composition, but the book's interpretation.[8] For ancient Jewish readers, Ecclesiastes was undoubtedly the famous King Solomon, who invited his readers to follow the Torah.[9] The old Aramaic translations of the Hebrew Bible (the *Targumim*) and the ancient Hebrew rabbinic commentary of the whole book of Ecclesiastes, the *Midrash*, are also along these interpretative lines. For ancient Christian readers, starting with Jerome, who translated the book into Latin, this was essentially *the* "Ecclesiastes", meaning that he is a man of the congregation, namely a preacher. In the opinion of these authors, this book's main theme is that everything is meaningless. According to various ancient church fathers, the book teaches its readers to despise this world and its attractions. Jerome, in particular, reads the book as an introduction to ascetic life. All is meaningless in this world except that which lasts forever. So, Ecclesiastes teaches us to put our hope only in God and in the world that is to come. This negative interpretation has heavily influenced the Christian world, as we can see in the fine arts, as well as in literature and music. At the dawn of the seventeenth century, artists saw in this book a reflection of the futility of human life, which in spite of its riches cannot escape the inevitability of death.

Modern readers have increasingly stressed this negative aspect of the book, and Eric S. Christianson will address this in the following essay. Not only did Ecclesiastes have a pessimistic view of human life, his faith in God was not recognizable as a faith in the God of the Bible. To many readers, the God of Ecclesiastes seems to be a distant, incomprehensible, and even anonymous deity (see **section 6**).[10] During the sixteenth century, the Protestant Reformer Martin Luther was one of the first early modern scholars to read the book through a more optimistic lens:

> [...] the point and purpose of this book is to instruct us, so that with thanksgiving we may use the things that are present and the creatures of God, that are generously given to us and conferred upon us by the blessing of God. This we have to do without anxiety about the things that are still in the future. The important thing is that we have a tranquil and quiet heart and a mind filled with joy, that is that we are content with the Word and the work of God.[11]

Human Experience as Ecclesiastes's Method of Research

To better understand Ecclesiastes's message, we must first illustrate his methodology.[12] Many readers of the book are only able to see the negative side of Ecclesiastes's message, that life is short, meaningless, and full of sorrow, and that God seems to be responsible for this. To grasp the full meaning of the book, we have to be aware of the methodology that Ecclesiastes employed. We get a clear glimpse of his approach at the end of the first chapter where he says, "[I] applied my mind to seek and to search out by wisdom all that is done under heaven; it is an unhappy business that God has given to human beings to be busy with."[13]

What do seeking and searching by wisdom mean? Here, wisdom is the instrument of Ecclesiastes's research. He applies himself to what is already known ("to seek") and to what is unknown ("to search"), but always within this worldly realm ("under heaven"). This is precisely the task that God has given to humanity, which is an "unhappy business", because—as Ecclesiastes says in the following verses—human wisdom can never fully reach its goal. No sage can claim to have fully understood the meaning of the cosmos and of life because God's works are unfathomable and too far removed from human understanding.

At this point, we should note that Ecclesiastes's method is fully rooted in the wisdom tradition of ancient Israel. Comparable with the sages who wrote the book of Proverbs, Ecclesiastes, too, is a realist, not an idealist or a dogmatist. Looking at this world, at human reality "under the sun", as the world really stands, is the "unhappy" but necessary task that God has given to human beings.

The sage is not like a prophet. Although he believes that he has received the word of God, he does not aim to change the world. Given that everything that comes from God's hands has a meaning, the sage is convinced that his main task is to understand reality as it stands.

In chapter 3, Ecclesiastes talks again about this human task but in more optimistic terms:

> I have seen the business that God has given to everyone to be busy with. He has made everything suitable for its time; moreover, he has put a sense of past and future into their minds, yet they cannot find out what God has done from the beginning to the end.[14]

For Ecclesiastes, the problem is not God's action in the world as he has made everything as it should be, beautiful (or *suitable*). The real problem is the inadequacy of human knowledge to fully understand God's ways. We do understand that there is a time and place for everything, but we are not able to uncover the mystery, because time is in God's hands.[15] As Ecclesiastes says:

> When I applied my mind to know wisdom, and to see the business that is done on earth, how one's eyes see sleep neither day nor night, then I saw all the work of God, that no one can find out what is happening under the sun. However much they may toil in seeking, they will not find it out; even though those who are wise claim to know, they cannot find it out.[16]

Humanity strives to find a meaning of life; we don't even sleep for that quest. We can try to understand that there's a God acting in this world, but we are unable to find out God's project. The first result of Ecclesiastes's research is for that reason surely a negative one and he declares that all is *hebel*. But what does this mean? What is the meaning of this mysterious word, *hebel*?

A History of the (Mis)understanding of the 'Negative' Side of Ecclesiastes

From the fourth century onward, hundreds of Ecclesiastes's translators have used the expression "all is vanity". The word *vanity* first appears in the ancient Greek translation of the Bible, known as the Septuagint, made in Alexandria of Egypt by Greek-speaking Jews, approximately between the third and first century BCE. In the Septuagint, the Hebrew word *hebel* was translated into the Greek ματαιότης (*mataiótês*), namely *vanity*. This term had a moral connotation, and it could even mean *folly*. In accordance with the Greek translation, Jerome—the most important ancient Latin translator of the Bible—translated *hebel* into the well-known Latin expression *vanitas vanitatum,* "vanity of vanities". This translation gave a strong ethical sense to the word *hebel*: everything is vanity. Striving after money or success is, in Jerome's interpretation, ethically wrong (Ecclesiastes would simply say it is unwise); vanity points also to human pride and self-satisfaction. Everything is vanity, so says Jerome, except what will come in the afterlife, in the kingdom of God (but Ecclesiastes does not speak about an afterlife).[17]

But we must first note that Ecclesiastes is not referring precisely to "vanity". The Hebrew word *hebel* literally means *vapor, wind, breath*. As we read in the Psalms, human beings (Hebrew *'adam*) are but a mere breath.[18] By using this word—*hebel*—Ecclesiastes wants to emphasize that human life is short, ephemeral, and that nobody can avoid death.[19] Not only is life short, but every human effort toward wealth and success is "chasing after wind".[20] This is not an ethical judgment, just a realistic one. There's a clash between expectation and result; that's another nuance of *hebel*, close to our concept of *absurd*.[21]

If we look at nature (the earth, the sun, the wind, the rivers, the sea, etc.) we see phenomena that seem to be governed by a perpetual and meaningless movement. In the beautiful poem that opens the book, the sun rises, the sun sets, the wind blows, the rivers flow to the sea, but human words are "wearisome" and incapable of explaining the sense of a universe in constant movement.[22] If we turn to human history, we also see that "there is nothing new under the sun".[23] So not only is everything in this human realm merely a breath "under the sun", but life itself can be viewed as meaningless.

If, from observations of nature, we turn to observations of human life we discover that, according to Ecclesiastes, humanity only strives after money, power, violence, and oppression, and in the end there is only death.[24] "This is an evil in all that happens under the sun, that the same fate comes to everyone. Moreover, the hearts of all are full of evil; madness is in their hearts while they live, and after that they go to the dead."[25]

By wearing the mask of the aging King Solomon, the richest and the wisest of kings in Israel and all around the world (at least according to a well-known biblical tradition), Ecclesiastes wants to show his readers the failure of every human illusion about the possibility of a life full of delight.[26] Death is the only and final certitude of humanity.[27] In that sense, the word *hebel*, employed so many times by Ecclesiastes, can also be interpreted as *absurd*, meaning that there is an ugly gap separating how humans hope and see life, compared to what it really is.

Again, the statement that all is a breath and a chasing after the wind becomes a refrain that goes through the bitter reflections of old King Solomon. At the end, life seems to be hateful:

> [...] How can the wise die just like fools? So I hated life, because what is done under the sun was grievous to me; for all is vanity and a chasing after wind. I hated all my toil in which I had toiled under the sun, seeing that I must leave it to those who come after me—and who knows whether they will be wise or foolish? Yet they will be master of all for which I toiled and used my wisdom under the sun. This also is vanity.[28]

"For everything there is a season" says the sage, "and a time for every matter under heaven".[29] There is "a time to be born, and a time to die; [...] a time for war, and a time for peace."[30] But nobody knows when and if this is the right time, and the conclusion is a negative one: "What gain have the workers from their toil?"[31]

By reading the entire book, we understand that death is the ultimate reason for Ecclesiastes's statement that all is like a breath. The thought of death reveals to us that there is really no hope for humanity; a harsh destiny seems to await us:

Whatever your hand finds to do, do with your might; for there is no work or thought or knowledge or wisdom in Sheol, to which you are going. Again I saw that under the sun the race is not to the swift, nor the battle to the strong, nor bread to the wise, nor riches to the intelligent, nor favor to the skillful; but time and chance happen to them all. For no one can anticipate the time of disaster. Like fish taken in a cruel net, and like birds caught in a snare, so mortals are snared at a time of calamity, when it suddenly falls upon them.[32]

We should note that when Ecclesiastes strongly denies any possibility of an afterlife, comparing human beings to beasts, we are not really outside the biblical tradition. Suggesting that we must return to dust is simply a quotation of the famous "you are dust, and to dust you shall return" from Genesis.[33] Moreover, Ecclesiastes is arguing against a new perspective that was developing in Judaea at the end of fourth century BCE, and especially during the third century BCE, in the apocryphal book of Enoch: the oldest parts of this book were composed probably in the fourth century BCE; the composition of this book ends only at the beginning of Christian era. Here we find the first clear tendencies of Jewish tradition concerning faith in an afterlife of joy for the just and of eternal punishment for the evil. But, as Ecclesiastes says, "who knows whether the human spirit goes upward and the spirit of animals goes downward to the earth?"[34] Ecclesiastes strongly adheres to the older biblical tradition that seems not to believe so openly in the afterlife.[35] By showing that human beings are nothing but beasts, death puts an end to any human illusion.

But Ecclesiastes is not a moralist. To him, saying that everything is *hebel* is not a means to call his audience to a good and ethically correct way of life—and it should be highlighted that Ecclesiastes is not a preacher of immorality either. He never speaks about following God's law, except in the epilogue which, in all likelihood, is the work of a faithful disciple of his.[36] Instead, besides the statement that everything is in vain, like chasing after the wind, and that death awaits everybody, in the book we discover an unexpected call to joy.

Joy or Pleasure? The 'Positive' Side of the Book of Ecclesiastes

In any case, according to Ecclesiastes, there are good things in life:

> Two are better than one, because they have a good reward for their toil. For if they fall, one will lift up the other; but woe to one who is alone and falls and does not have another to help. Again, if two lie together, they keep warm; but how can one keep warm alone? And though one might prevail against another, two will withstand one. A threefold cord is not quickly broken.[37]

Inside a historical context where the lack of solidarity was a bitter reality, Ecclesiastes stresses friendship first as a matter of cooperation and mutual help. In a world of oppression and competition, Ecclesiastes recommends unity and solidarity among human beings.[38]

Seven times Ecclesiastes announces that in life there are things that are not necessarily in vain and a chasing after the wind, but rather are moments of joy.[39] The possibility of enjoying one's life does exist. The secret to joy is, for Ecclesiastes, to receive life as God's gift, and not look at joy as the fruit of human effort. Rather, he says, working very hard to gain an advantage will lead to empty hands very quickly. At the very beginning of his book, Ecclesiastes asks if there is a profit for man under the sun.[40] It clearly is a rhetorical question, but the answer is easy: there is no advantage at all for man under the sun. But this is not Ecclesiastes's final word.[41]

Of the abovementioned seven passages on joy (see endnote 39), Ecclesiastes does not speak about spiritual, religious, or even intellectual joy. He finds joy in very simple things, such as eating and drinking: "I know that there is nothing better for them than to be happy and enjoy themselves as long as they live; moreover, it is God's gift that all should eat and drink and take pleasure in all their toil."[42] Everything is a gift of God, eating and drinking included!

> This is what I have seen to be good: it is fitting to eat and drink and find enjoyment in all the toil with which one toils under the sun the few days of the life God gives us; for this is our lot. Likewise all to whom God gives wealth and possessions and whom he enables to enjoy them, and to accept their lot and find enjoyment in their toil—this is the gift of God. For they will scarcely brood over the days of their lives, because God keeps them occupied with the joy of their hearts.[43]

Here Ecclesiastes refers to joy as "our lot". If in human life there is no advantage, no gain at all for those who are toiling hard, there is still a "lot" given from God, if one is able to accept it.[44] The difference lies between those who try to find joy at any cost with all their strength and effort (and will eventually find no advantage at all), and those who accept life as a gift of God. So, Ecclesiastes is really speaking about joy, something that one cannot buy or achieve with human effort; joy is received as a gift. Ecclesiastes does not speak just about "pleasure", something that one can buy with money or obtain as a result of one's activity; for many modern scholars, something like a drug, a narcotic that a far away (and perhaps cruel) deity gives to human beings to keep them calm.[45] While joy can include pleasure, pleasure does not necessarily know joy. The rich, old King Solomon who speaks in chapter 2, experienced a lot of pleasure, but not always as joy.[46]

The real problem for Ecclesiastes is that he believes God gives joy, but not according to the retribution theology that ancient Israel's theology had in mind: God rewards the just and the good ones in this life and punishes the wicked, as hundreds of Hebrew Bible texts say. So, joy is not necessarily connected to human behavior; it is not true that joy is given only to the good, and that it is denied to the evil.[47] God's criteria are not human criteria.

God keeps humanity occupied with joy; and we could also translate this as God "answers them with the joy of their hearts".[48] In this sense, joy is the means by which God makes himself present in human life; a small but real form of revelation.[49] This is not the joy of paradise, of course, but the joy of everyday life, if lived as a gift. There is also the joy of love: "enjoy life with the wife whom you love".[50] It should be noted that Ecclesiastes's feelings toward women is a matter of debate.[51] Is Ecclesiastes a real champion of misogyny, or is he here polemicizing against the traditional views of the time, which were in some measure misogynistic?[52] The sentence of Ecclesiastes 7:26 ("I found more bitter than death the woman who is a trap, whose heart is snares and nets, whose hands are fetters; one who pleases God escapes her, but the sinner is taken by her") is not representing Ecclesiastes's thoughts, but what he found in the (male) tradition of his time, usually very negative about women. "See what I found", says Ecclesiastes, "One man among a thousand I found, but a woman among all these I have not found".[53] That is to say that perhaps there are a few human beings ("one among a thousand") more bitter than death, because they are full of evil and unjust, but nobody can say that only women are to be blamed as "bitter than death". Moreover, Ecclesiastes adds that a woman among all these, that is, among humanity, "I have not found"; perhaps women are, in the end, better than men! As this text ends, we read: "See, this alone I found, that God made human beings straightforward, but they have devised many schemes."[54] The answer lies, for Ecclesiastes, in the fact that God created both man and woman "straightforward", or, as we can also translate, 'upright'. For that reason there is no room, according to Ecclesiastes, for a misogynistic theology.

There is a final passage where Ecclesiastes, right at the end of the book, speaks again about joy. It is useful to read in full this intriguing and certainly wonderful—albeit difficult—poem:

> Light is sweet, and it is pleasant for the eyes to see the sun. Even those who live many years should rejoice in them all; yet let them remember that the days of darkness will be many. All that comes is vanity. Rejoice, young man, while you are young, and let your heart cheer you in the days of your youth. Follow the inclination of your heart and the desire of your eyes, but know that for all these things God will bring you into judgment. Banish anxiety from your mind, and put away pain from your body; for youth and the dawn of life are vanity.[55]

> Remember your creator in the days of your youth, before the days of trouble come, and the years draw near when you will say, 'I have no pleasure in them'; before the sun and the light and the moon and the stars are darkened and the clouds return with the rain; in the day when the guards of the house tremble, and the strong men are bent, and the women who grind cease working because they are few, and those who look through the windows see dimly; when the doors on the street are shut, and the sound of the grinding is low, and one rises up at the sound of a bird, and all the daughters of song are brought low; when one is afraid of heights, and terrors are in the road; the almond tree blossoms, the grasshopper drags itself along and desire fails; because all must go to their eternal home, and the mourners will go about the streets; before the silver cord is snapped, and the golden bowl is broken, and the pitcher is broken at the fountain, and the wheel broken at the cistern, and the dust returns to the earth as it was, and the breath returns to God who gave it. Vanity of vanities, says the Teacher; all is vanity.[56]

In the first part of the poem, Ecclesiastes speaks to young people, inviting them to rejoice in all the years that they will live, and to remember that life will in any case be short: rejoice, and remember! At first glance, Ecclesiastes seems to speak here exactly as a Greek poet, inviting young people to take out all the pleasure of life they can, because life is short and full of sorrow. This message, coming from Greek and Roman philosophy, continues until the Renaissance: life is short, youth even shorter, so rejoice while you can.[57]

But suddenly, the tone changes: "but know that for all these things God will bring you into judgment."[58] What does this mean? Rejoice, but do not sin against God? Rejoice, but with moderation? Rejoice, but remember that in the afterlife God will judge you? But Ecclesiastes does not believe in an afterlife, nor is he a moralistic preacher.

God's judgment of which Ecclesiastes is speaking here is simply our death. God gave us life and the possibility to rejoice in it. If you do not catch in this very moment the little sparks of joy that God has put in your life, when darkness comes and times get rough, when old age reaches you and when death takes you forever from this earthly world, you will not have another possibility: that is God's judgment. If you are not able to rejoice in your life as a gift from God, in the end you will lose everything. As the ancient rabbinic tradition says, "You will one day give reckoning for everything your eyes saw which, although permissible, you did not enjoy".[59] God will judge you one day on the gifts that he gave you and that you refused to accept. As is written on George Gray's gravestone, in Edgar Lee Masters's *Spoon River Anthology*:

I have studied many times
The marble which was chiseled for me
A boat with a furled sail at rest in a harbor.
In truth it pictures not my destination
But my life.
For love was offered me and I shrank from its disillusionment;
Sorrow knocked at my door, but I was afraid;
Ambition called to me, but I dreaded the chances.
Yet all the while I hungered for meaning in my life.
And now I know that we must lift the sail
And catch the winds of destiny
Wherever they drive the boat.
To put meaning in one's life may end in madness,
But life without meaning is the torture
Of restlessness and vague desire
It is a boat longing for the sea and yet afraid.[60]

But let us turn back to the second part of Ecclesiastes's poem, which begins with a mention of God with a new title: "your creator".[61] Ecclesiastes invites young people to remember God before old age comes. In the following verses, Ecclesiastes is describing with lots of metaphors (the guards of the house, the women who grind, the doors on the street, etc.) a rich home in which something terrible happened: he seems to be referring to us—to our death, and our funeral, when "the mourners will go about the streets".[62] Old age came, with all its sorrows and illnesses; for example, the old person will rise up early at the birds' song, but will not be able to hear their melody because he is deaf. The almond tree blossoms; spring came at last, but for him there is only winter. The grasshopper (perhaps a sexual allusion, see footnote 63) drags itself along; (sexual) desire fails; old age is destroying human beings and only death awaits, with no hope of return, as a golden bowl that crashes, or a broken pitcher, or a wheel broken at the cistern.[63]

But is death really the last goal of human life? Just a dark hole? A blind alley? If dust returns to the earth, says Ecclesiastes, breath returns to God who gave it. If God is the creator, he is at the beginning of your life; better still, he is the beginner of every life, so he is also at the end. Ecclesiastes does not even dare to say that there is another life—he only says that everything is in God's hands. If we accept the risk of living, we will not lose joy.

The Image of God in the Book of Ecclesiastes

Ecclesiastes knows very well that if life "under the sun", that is, in this earthly world, can really seem a breath and even absurd; over the sun, that is, metaphorically in the heavenly realm, there is God.[64]

Ecclesiastes never speaks of the Tetragrammaton, YHWH (pronounced as *adonay*, the Lord), the sacred name of God as it appears in the Hebrew Bible. God is mentioned in the book of Ecclesiastes thirty-eight times always as *'elohîm* (with a further two references of *'elohîm* in the epilogue), a Hebrew word meaning "God," as many times as the other keyword, *hebel*.[65]

For Ecclesiastes, God is above all the maker: God makes everything beautiful at the right time.[66] However, his way of acting in the world is incomprehensible to human beings.[67] It seems that God makes the good and the bad day at the same time; human beings have to rejoice in the good day, and think about the bad day, only to conclude that they will not understand the ways of God at all.[68] But our sage says that God has made humanity straightforward (see above); so the problem is on humanity's side, not God's.[69] Toward the end of the book, Ecclesiastes compares the actions of God—the one "who makes everything"—to the growing of the human fetus in a woman's womb.[70] When God makes something, it is life. At the end, the God of Ecclesiastes is really the creator, "your creator", as we read, even if just once, in the final poem of the book.[71]

Not only is God the maker, but also the giver. God gives life to humanity—even though it is a short one—and imbues human beings with the spirit that is life.[72] God also gave us—so says Ecclesiastes—the task of exploring and searching for the meaning of life, even though this is "an unhappy business".[73] But God also gives joy to human beings, and joy is a true gift of God.[74] The problem, once again, is that human beings cannot understand the criteria of God's giving. In giving and in making, God is absolutely free to do whatever he wants, including even the traditional theological criteria of a divine retribution that God would give joy to the righteous ones and sorrow and punishment to the wicked.[75]

In view of such a God, present and active in the world but at the same time distant, unfathomable, and incomprehensible, what can humanity do? Ecclesiastes suggests that if you want to go to the temple (the temple of Jerusalem), be careful not to offer sacrifices as the fools do; instead it is better to listen (to obey), so prefer the silence and do not waste many words in your prayer.[76]

In four different texts, Ecclesiastes suggests that humanity can only "fear God", respect him, and believe in him; an old biblical tradition to which Ecclesiastes gives a completely new shape.

Ecclesiastes says: "I know that whatever God does endures forever; nothing can be added to it, nor anything taken from it; God has done this, so that all should stand in awe before him."[77] To be in awe (or fear) of God means respecting his mysterious ways of acting in the creation; keeping our place as creatures without pretending to be "God" as the snake suggested to humanity in Genesis 3:5.

At the end of the abovementioned passage, Ecclesiastes invites humanity to first keep silent before such a God; second, he suggests guarding oneself against going into the temple too lightly; and third, he counsels one not to believe in one's dreams and visions. He concludes: "With many dreams come vanities and a multitude of words; but fear God".[78] Fearing God is listening to him, not presuming that our ritual acts can achieve any results, if taken as human efforts to reach God; in that sense, cult is completely useless. An intriguing and even ironic passage reads:

> In my vain life I have seen everything; there are righteous people who perish in their righteousness, and there are wicked people who prolong their life in their evildoing. Do not be too righteous, and do not act too wise; why should you destroy yourself? Do not be too wicked, and do not be a fool; why should you die before your time? It is good that you should take hold of the one, without letting go of the other; for the one who fears God shall succeed with both.[79]

Again, Ecclesiastes is not a moralistic preacher: do not be too righteous; do not act too wise! And do not be too wicked, but do not be a fool! Between righteousness and evil there is a middle path, a grey zone. But between wisdom and folly, no: too much wisdom will harm you; but you must exclude folly from your life. The true ethical suggestion given by Ecclesiastes is: fear God. Believe in him, accepting him as he really is, and you will find success in your life.

A similar text reads:

> Because sentence against an evil deed is not executed speedily, the human heart is fully set to do evil. Though sinners do evil a hundred times and prolong their lives, yet I know that it will be well with those who fear God, because they stand in fear before him, but it will not be well with the wicked, neither will they prolong their days like a shadow, because they do not stand in fear before God.[80]

At the end of the book, an anonymous disciple tries to summarize the entire teaching of Ecclesiastes: "The end of the matter; all has been heard. Fear God, and keep his commandments; for that is the whole duty of everyone."[81] In reality, Ecclesiastes does not say anywhere in his book that you have to keep the commandments of God and is very cautious about God's judgment. Perhaps the epilogist wanted to protect Ecclesiastes from the possibility of being accused of being a teacher opposing God's law, the Mosaic law. In any case: fear God, says Ecclesiastes, because that is everyone's duty—or, as it can also be translated, for this is every man—the substance of every human person.

In conclusion, Ecclesiastes does not describe God as an absent divinity or as an unjust or even violent God. He is simply beyond all possibility of comprehension: the absurdity of evil and the ephemerality of life are a strong demonstration of the human incapacity to decipher the will of God. Certainly, in the book of Ecclesiastes, there is an unresolved tension between the experience of life, which leads our sage to reflect on the absurdity of oppression, and faith in God, who should be claimed as the comforter of this same oppression.[82] What makes the book of Ecclesiastes still fascinating today, and, in many aspects, contemporary, is the success with which he maintained a strong position between the two extremes: on the one hand, the experience of humanity itself, and, on the other hand, the fear of God and faith in the one who allows human beings to reclaim the little joys of daily life, joys that are limited but real signs of his presence.

Ecclesiastes: An Ancient Book for Modern Times

Ecclesiastes is certainly an ancient book which has a strong validity for modern times. The author is a sage whose aim is to explore our human world and to search for the meaning of life accepting reality as it stands. According to Ecclesiastes, even if life is pain and toil, inconsistent, even absurd, it also involves a labor of seeking and exploring, which God himself has given to humanity.[83] In this laborious search, the human explorer undoubtedly experiences the darkest side of life and even the dark side of God, but at the same time discovers that God is the giver of life and joy, and that in fearing God, eating, and drinking, the daily joys of life can be rediscovered as those signs of a presence which is certainly limited and mysterious, but nonetheless always real and not necessarily negative.

According to the American biblical scholar Michael V. Fox, "[The book of Ecclesiastes] tells us how to make the best of a bad situation, where to find 'portions' and 'good things'. [Ecclesiastes] hardly knows the way to happiness, but he does point to some things, including pleasure, that can take us a bit further away from unhappiness".[84] Whereas, according to the scholar Robert Gordis, "[Ecclesiastes] does not claim to have penetrated to the secret of the meaning of life. Nor, strictly speaking, does the author of *Job* [...]. But they have done far more. They have demonstrated that it is possible for men to bear the shafts of evil that threaten the human condition if they cultivate a sense of reverence for the mystery and miracle of life [...]".[85] Indeed, the German biblical scholar Norbert Lohfink points out that for "many modern agnostics [the book of Ecclesiastes] is the last bridge to the Bible. Some Christians today find in [Ecclesiastes] a kind of back door—at once sinister and highly esteemed—through which their minds can admit those sceptical and melancholy sentiments that would be refused entry at portals where cultivation of virtue and belief in the afterlife are inscribed on the lintel".[86]

Human beings do not have everything under control, and Ecclesiastes teaches us that life is a serious problem; but joy, even if short and limited, is not impossible. Despite all possible negative experiences, hardships, and challenges that we have to face in life, for this ancient sage of Israel, the king and the wise Ecclesiastes, life is always worthy to be lived—as a gift of God: "Likewise all to whom God gives wealth and possessions and whom he enables to enjoy them, and to accept their lot and find enjoyment in their toil—this is the gift of God."[87]

[1] Eccles. 1:2. For an alternative translation of the term *vanity*, see p. 21 *et seq.* It should be noted, however, that all Ecclesiastes's quotations are taken from the *New Revised Standard Version*, with changes indicated and explained in the footnotes.

[2] See WHYBRAY 1982. In this article, the traditional Greek name of the book, *Ecclesiastes*, (instead of the correct Hebrew *Qohelet*) is used for the book, the book's writer, and the book's main voice or character, even though in other contexts these may be examined and treated separately.

[3] GORDIS 1978, p. 131.

[4] The author's use of gendered language when referring to God is based on Ecclesiastes.

[5] "With many dreams come vanities and a multitude of words; but fear God. If you see in a province the oppression of the poor and the violation of justice and right, do not be amazed at the matter; for the high official is watched by a higher, and there are yet higher ones over them." Eccles. 5:7–8. See CRENSHAW 2007. With strong irony, this text clearly shows the consequences of a widespread social injustice raised by the new Ptolemaic bureaucracy.

[6] Eccles. 5:10.

[7] Eccles. 6:12.

[8] See the relevant writings of HOLM-NIELSEN 1975–1976; CHRISTIANSON 2007, and DELL 2013.

[9] See Eccles. 12:13.

[10] See for example, under two different perspectives, the studies of CRENSHAW 2007 and LAVOIE 1995 for the issue of God seeming like a distant deity in Ecclesiastes. See also ELLUL 1990 for a more positive approach to the book's content.

[11] LUTHER 1972, p. 15.

[12] MAZZINGHI 2009a, p. 176–188.

[13] Eccles. 1:13.

[14] Eccles. 3:10–11. The Hebrew word *yapheh*, translated by the NRSV as *suitable* can also be translated as *beautiful. A sense of past and future* is a possible translation of a single Hebrew word, *'ôlam*, that refers to a time without beginning and end, but that can be also a wordplay with *'elem* (same Hebrew consonants), *mystery*; so an alternative translation could be *the mysteriousness of time.*

[15] See Eccles. 3:1–9.

[16] Eccles. 8:16–17.

[17] SCHOORS 2013, p. 40–47.

[18] Psalm 62:9.

[19] See Eccles. 6:12.

[20] Eccles. 1:14; 2:11, 17, 26; 4:4, 6; 6:9.

[21] For the term "absurd" see FOX 1999, p. 27–50; but BARTHOLOMEW 2009, p. 104–106, prefers translating *hebel* with "enigmatic".

[22] Eccles. 1:8.

[23] Eccles. 1:9.

[24] See Eccles. 5:8–10, and 4:1–3.

[25] Eccles. 9:3.

[26] See 1 Kings 3–4, and Eccles. 2.

[27] See Eccles. 9:2–6.

[28] Eccles. 2:16–19. The reader should keep in mind the literal meaning of *vanity—breath.*

[29] Eccles. 3:1.

[30] Eccles. 3:2–8.

[31] Eccles. 3:9.

[32] Eccles. 9:10–12.

[33] Gen. 3:19.

[34] Eccles. 3:21.

[35] MAZZINGHI 2002, p. 157–168.

[36] See Eccles. 12:13.

[37] Eccles. 4:9–12. Verse 12 is one of the so-called 'better-proverbs', a kind of proverb where the sage compares two different things suggesting that one is better than the other. As for the meaning of "lie together", probably, the author does not refer to a married couple (as the old Jewish tradition thought), but to a couple of friends travelling in the cold desert nights. Whereas, according to some ancient readers, the "threefold cord" is an image of God who binds friends together.

[38] See Eccles. 4:1–2, 4.

[39] See Eccles. 2:24–26; 3:12–13; 3:22; 5:18–19; 8:15; 9:7–9; 11:7–12.

[40] See Eccles. 1:3, but also 3:9.

[41] See GIANTO 1992, p. 528–532, and PINÇON 2008 for a full analysis of the theme of joy in Ecclesiastes. See also MAZZINGHI 2009a, p. 389–408.

[42] Eccles. 3:12–13.

[43] Eccles. 5:18–20.

[44] See again Eccles. 1:3; 3:9.

[45] "Does Qohelet think the deity afflicts them [i.e., humanity] with thoughts of unattainable pleasure?"; see CRENSHAW 1987, p. 28.

[46] For a different interpretation concerning Ecclesiastes and pleasure, see FOX 1999, p. 121–131.

[47] See Eccles. 2:24–26.

[48] Eccles. 5:17–19.

[49] LOHFINK 2003, p. 85.

[50] Eccles. 9:9.

[51] See Eccles. 7:26–29.

[52] See the warnings about the danger of women contained in many wisdom texts, such as Prov. 2:16–19; 6:20–35; 22:14; 23:27–28; Sir 9:1–9; 26:22–27. Classical Greek literature is also full of misogynistic texts.

[53] Literally: one *'adam*; one human being. Eccles. 7:28.

[54] Literally: *many war machines*. See Eccles. 7:29. See SCHWIENHORST-SCHÖNBERGER 2004, p. 400–410.

[55] Eccles. 11:7–12. Remember that "vanity" is not an appropriate translation of *hebel*; for instance, "all that comes is vanity" sounds as "all that comes is a breath".

[56] Eccles. 12:1–8. On the issue connected to the meaning and translation of the term "vanity", see footnote 28.

[57] This notion has come to be expressed in modern Western cultures as the essentially hedonistic, existential acronym and saying, YOLO! / "You only live once!".

[58] Eccles. 11:9.

[59] See Talmud Yerushalmi, *Qiddušin*, 4:12 in *THE JERUSALEM TALMUD* 2008, p. 414

[60] MASTERS 1992, p. 146.

[61] Eccles. 12:1.

[62] Eccles. 12:5.

[63] Eccles. 12:4b–5. The grasshopper can be viewed as a kind of delicious food that elderly people cannot afford anymore, because it's too heavy for them. Or, according to a well-known ancient tradition (both Jewish and Christian interpreters) as a metaphor of sexual desire; the caperberry was a well-known aphrodisiac in ancient times. If we think to a real grasshopper, the text would rather speak about an ecological disaster. See VÍLCHEZ LÍNDEZ 1994, p. 409; MAZZINGHI 2009b, p. 294–296; SCHOORS 2013, p. 808–810.

[64] See Eccles. 5:2: "God is in heaven, and you upon earth".

[65] See SCHOORS 2013 and MAZZINGHI 2009a.

[66] See Eccles. 3:11.

[67] See also Eccles. 3:14.

[68] See Eccles. 7:13–14.

[69] See Eccles. 7:29.

[70] See Eccles. 11:5.

[71] Eccles. 12:1.

[72] See Eccles. 11:5; 12:7.

[73] See Eccles. 1:13.

[74] See Eccles. 2:24–26; 5:18–19, and 3:12–13.

[75] See again Eccles. 2:24–26 and the negative conclusion at the end of the sentence: "to the one who pleases him God gives wisdom and knowledge and joy; but to the sinner he gives the work of gathering and heaping, only to give to one who pleases God. This also is vanity [literally, 'a breath'] and a chasing after wind".

[76] See Eccles. 4:17–5:6 and especially verse 5:2.

[77] See Eccles. 3:14. The term *awe* is, more literally, *fear; fearing God*, in biblical language, points to an attitude of awe, respect, and even faith.

[78] Eccles. 5:6–7. For the translation of the term vanity, see footnote 28.

[79] Eccles. 7:15–18. The term "vain" could also be translated as *fleeting, ephemeral*, or even *absurd*.

[80] Eccles. 8:11–13.

[81] Eccles. 12:13. The whole epilogue is in Eccles. 12:9–14.

[82] Eccles. 4:1–2.

[83] See Eccles. 1:13; 3:10–11.

[84] Fox 1989, p. 77.

[85] GORDIS 1978, p. 129.

[86] LOHFINK 2003, p. 1.

[87] Eccles. 5:19.

Reading Ecclesiastes in the Early Modern Era

Eric S. Christianson

> [...] *we sometimes feel that*
> *there is something ominous in the changes*
> *rung on Ecclesiastes during the sixteenth century.*
> Michael Hattaway[1]

As we will see, the themes of Ecclesiastes suited thinkers in this period tremendously well. Indeed, Renaissance thinking (particularly skepticism) and the book of Ecclesiastes enjoyed (if that is the right term) a terribly complex relationship.[2] As a rough overview, Michael Hattaway's comments on the significance and appeal of Ecclesiastes (and other "books of Solomon") to Renaissance learning in the early to mid-1500s (and beyond) provide a useful starting point:

> Humanist writers did not go to Ecclesiastes merely because the doctrine it contained was particularly suited to their theological quarrels with the schoolmen. At a time when the reading of the Bible was by no means unrestricted, the books of Solomon were, it was felt, texts that could safely be put into the hands of a young man to teach him moral philosophy and eloquence [...]. Sir Thomas Elyot [who moved in the circles of Sir Thomas More and Henry VIII in the 1520s–1530s] prescribed them along with the Ethics of Aristotle and the works of Cicero and Plato, they were studied and annotated by Henry VIII, recommended by his Tutors to Edward VI, and by James I to his son Henry. William Lily in his Grammar cited them as suitable texts to turn into Latin, and generations of schoolboys must have absorbed Solomon's proverbial learning in class.[3]

As well as for these reasons, Ecclesiastes, with its empirical form of skepticism, seemed to fit the cautious yet energetic approach to the new sciences embodied in humanist and reform thinking. Indeed, the long-acknowledged personal approach to knowledge exemplified in its pages would resonate with a new critical change, "when the evidence of observation came to be accepted as more compelling and credible than inherited wisdom and authority: when natural philosophers quite literally insisted on believing the evidence with their own eyes."[4] This appeal to Ecclesiastes was bound up with the quest to legitimize the pursuit of the new human sciences.

Rosin's in-depth survey of Renaissance skepticism in relation to the Ecclesiastes commentaries of Luther, Brenz, and Melanchthon notes the energetic bundle of attitudes toward skepticism dominant at the start of the Renaissance revival:

> Skepticism [...] was nothing extraordinary. As the reformers viewed skepticism, it grew from a common human problem [...]. Viewed thus, classical skepticism did not differ from more spontaneous radical doubt in the 16th century. Natural, garden variety doubt could multiply, questioning order and direction in the world and eventually challenging divine purpose and providence in life. Interest in skepticism emerged with the burgeoning Renaissance, resurrecting from classical

antiquity a philosophical approach not simply to epistemology but to life. In general, the 16th-century understanding of 'skepticism' echoed the original precept: philosophical non-dogmatism refused to make assertions and shied away from definition, disputing the ability to attain certain knowledge and allowing only a suspension of judgment [...]. Broad tributaries contributed to a skeptical revival [...]—philosophers with their striving for lofty anthropological heights, some common, popular attitudes, plus thinkers with their misgivings on the darker side of man's nature—fostered a natural interest in skepticism.[5]

Ultimately it was to the implications of this epistemological relativism that Luther, Brenz, and Melanchthon felt compelled to respond. But it was not only the Protestant Reformers who would engage with Ecclesiastes. A broad range of humanist thinkers would recognize the same dangers but would also see in Ecclesiastes a safe bridge from the sacred world of the Bible to the intoxicating danger of the new sciences. The luminous figure of Solomon, one who had experienced the heights of learning and of royal authority, would enliven this capacity of the book to connect, making his judgment regarding the great sorrow brought on by the increase of knowledge simultaneously a humanist battle cry and lament.[6]

A significant and sustained engagement with Ecclesiastes comes from a towering figure of Renaissance learning, Michel de Montaigne, who has frequently been compared to Ecclesiastes.[7] The themes of the limits of human knowledge, of vanity, of the role of wisdom in the formation of the self—all appear throughout his *Essays*, composed between 1580 and 1592, and often keenly resonate with Ecclesiastes.[8] Just as quotes from Ecclesiastes adorned his personal library (e.g., a loose paraphrase of chapter 9:2, "Of everything which is under the sun, fortune and law are equal, Eccl. IX"), so they are peppered throughout the *Essays*, sometimes elusively.[9] In the course of his most lengthy and carefully argued essay, *An Apology for Raymond Seybond*, he writes, "A line of ancient Greek poetry says 'There is great convenience in not being too wise' [Sophocles, *Ajax*, 554] [...]. So does Ecclesiastes: 'In much wisdom there is much sadness, and he that acquireth knowledge acquireth worry and travail.'"[10] A few pages later comes the familiar Renaissance lament that so echoes Ecclesiastes: "It is so far beyond our power to comprehend the majesty of God that the very works of our Creator which best carry his mark are the ones we least understand."[11] At least part of his solution comes when he summarizes Ecclesiastes's thought while giving the impression of citing it: "Ecclesiastes says: 'Accept all things in good part, just as they seem, just as they taste, day by day. The rest is beyond thy knowledge.'"[12]

At a deeper level, Montaigne's contradictory and querulous approach as articulated in his essays mirrors Ecclesiastes's own style, a feature that Harold Fisch recognized when he suggested that Ecclesiastes could say with Montaigne, "It is my portrait I draw [...] I am myself the subject of my book."[13] Theodore Anthony Perry goes as far to suggest the fundamental influence of Ecclesiastes's rhetorical form on the genre for which Montaigne is famous, the essay: "This was perhaps the only new literary genre that the modern age had ever produced, alongside the novel."[14] Perry goes on to argue that Montaigne mines Ecclesiastes to forge his distinctive style of writing, which would produce the modern essay. "When [...] the author writes, 'I, Kohelet ...', he gives to the literary world the first instance of the genre that Montaigne was about to discover."[15] Montaigne gives notice to his self-aware approach throughout the *Essays*, and one can recognize the imprint for which Perry has argued. So, for example, in *On repenting*, Montaigne anticipates philosopher Ralph Waldo Emerson's famous dictum that "foolish consistency is the hobgoblin of little minds" (in his own *Essays*!):

> Constancy itself is nothing but a more languid rocking to and fro. I am unable to stabilize my subject: it staggers confusedly along with a natural drunkenness. I grasp it as it is now, at this moment when I am lingering over it [...] I must adapt this account of myself to the passing hour [...] This is a register of varied and changing occurrences, of ideas which are unresolved and, when needs be, contradictory, either because I myself have become different or because I grasp hold of different attributes or aspects of my subjects. So I happen to contradict myself, but [...] I never contradict truth.[16]

If Perry is right, Montaigne anticipates far more than Emerson's insight, but more significantly (if indirectly) that growing pool of scholars who have recognized that what holds together Ecclesiastes's disparate sayings is nothing less than the thread of his consciousness. And even though, as for Montaigne, Ecclesiastes's consciousness is cohesive, it may also be seen to stagger along "with a natural drunkenness."

The appeal of Ecclesiastes to Renaissance thinkers relates in part to a social malaise. Rosin traces the Renaissance obsession with misery, death, and contempt of the world, as well as the mass experiences of war, famine, and pestilence.[17] We might further note the contribution of Pope Innocent III's *De Contemptu Mundi sive de Miseria Condicionis Humane* [i.e., *On the Contempt of This World, or the Misery of the Human Condition*], published nearly 400 years previously (1195; it was adapted and translated in the Renaissance by George Gascoigne as the first section of *The Droomme of Doomes Day* in 1576). As Robert Lewis has shown, the extensive influence of *De Contemptu* is difficult to understate. It is quoted, referred to, translated, and adapted in hundreds of works through the Middle Ages.[18] To this we can add works that propound the general theme of the "vanity" of the world, suspicion of material wealth and wisdom, such as the numerous "vanity poems" in one of the most popular collections of verse in the sixteenth century, *The Paradise of Dainty Devices*, which went through ten editions between 1576 and 1606.[19] Further, Hattaway surveys a range of Renaissance humanist scholars and poets who saw in their own work some affinity with Ecclesiastes. For example, Cornelius Agrippa von Nettesheim published his influential *Of the Vanitie and Uncertaintie of Artes and Sciences* (*De vanitate et incertitudine scientiarum et artium*) in 1530, a work that explored the limits and perceived superstitions of occultism and other sciences (i.e., common and concurrent means of accounting for human experience). The book further served the Renaissance revival of skepticism, and because it was reprinted in his day, skepticism's champion, Montaigne, drew heavily on it.[20] On its title page, *Vanitie* bore the words of Ecclesiastes 1:1: "All is but most vaine Vanitie: and all is most vaine, and but plaine vanitie." As Hattaway comments,

> Their discontent with contemporary ways of recording experience had provoked the desire of the earlier humanists to explore the learning of the ancient world, which had in turn given rise to the flowering of arts and sciences we associate with the Renaissance. But as the skepticism of Solomon had been applied to the wisdom of the schools, now it was applied to the wisdom of the humanists themselves.[21]

Other figures of the period would use Ecclesiastes to critique the endeavor of human learning especially. In this regard, we might note Antonio de Corro, a Spanish-born reader in divinity at Oxford, who in 1578 published *Solomons sermon of mans* [sic] *chief felicitie* (so the English title, published 1586), a commentary on Ecclesiastes (which would become very popular) in which he "denied that human knowledge could bring truth or felicity":

> Either for that [man] cannot attain to the ful & absolute knowledge of things, because they are lapped & inwrapped in so manifold knots & marveilous difficulties, & beside the things themselves be so infinite in number: or for that there happen so many perverse, crooked, and overthwart chances in the life & doings of men, which by no reason can be ordered or amended.[22]

A similar spirit of intellectual critique can be noted in the *Treatie of Humane Learning* by Fulke Greville, a philosophical poet and courtier.[23] While the vanity of knowledge-oriented endeavors is a key theme of the poem, he makes no *direct* reference to Ecclesiastes. However, as an expression of the age it helps further to understand the broad appeal of Ecclesiastes's themes. One verse in particular suggests Ecclesiastes as its subtext:

> *Salamon* knew nature both in herbes, plants, beasts; [...]
> Let his example, and his booke maintaine:
> Kings, who have travail'd, through the Vanity,
> Can best describe vs what her visions be.[24]

It is, however, Francis Bacon who sheds perhaps the brightest light on Ecclesiastes's significance to Renaissance thinkers and their concerns in his monumental and unprecedented (in English) *Of the Proficience and Advancement of Learning, Divine and Human* (1605). His overarching treatise on the sciences of knowledge begins with extensive reflection on the themes of Ecclesiastes. After a lengthy dedication to the king, Bacon sets out to correct the manner in which the "dignity of learning" has been woefully mishandled by divines, politicians, and "sometimes in the errors and imperfections of learned men themselves."[25] He takes issue with those who say that "knowledge hath in it somewhat of the serpent," and who would cite Solomon as giving "a censure, *That there is no end of making books, and that much reading is weariness of the flesh* [Ecclesiastes 12:12]: And again in another place, *That in spacious knowledge there is much contristation, and that he that increaseth knowledge, increaseth anxiety* [Ecclesiastes 1:18]."[26] He then sets out to "discover [...] the ignorance and error of this opinion" and makes immediate recourse to Ecclesiastes, but this time in support of his view, that

> *Solomon* speaking of the two principal senses of inquisition, the eye and the ear, affirmeth that the eye is never satisfied with seeing, nor the ear with hearing [Ecclesiastes 1:8] [...] so of knowledge it self, and the mind of man, whereto the senses are but reporters, he defineth likewise in these words, placed after that kalendar or ephemerides, which he maketh of the diversities of times and seasons for all actions and purposes; and concludeth thus: God hath made all things beautiful or decent in the true return of their seasons: Also he hath placed the world in man's heart, yet cannot man find out the work which God worketh from the beginning to the end [Ecclesiastes 3:11]: declaring not obscurely, that God hath framed the mind of man as a mirrour of glass, capable of the image of the universal world, and joyful to receive the impression thereof, as the eye joyeth to receive light [...]. If then such be the capacity and receipt of the mind of man, it is manifest, that there is no danger at all in the proportion or quantity of knowledge, how large soever [...] but it is merely the quality of knowledge [...]. And as for that censure of Solomon, concerning the excess of writing and reading books, and the anxiety of spirit which redoundeth from knowledge [...] let those places be rightly understood, and they do indeed excellently set the true bounds and limitations, whereby human knowledge is confined and circumscribed.[27]

What is so crucial and telling here is that Bacon uses Ecclesiastes exclusively (though he somewhat superficially cites Paul's warnings as well that *we be not seduced by vain philosophy* and that *knowledge bloweth up*) to defend his approach to knowledge, knowing that it is in the framework of Ecclesiastes that many of his readers, divines, and learned men, have formulated their 'erroneous' epistemology. Ecclesiastes, then, set the terms for what many regard to be the first significant work of philosophy in English.[28]

English statesman William Temple echoes these themes as well in his essay *Upon the Gardens of Epicurus, or of Gardening in the Year 1685*, in which he suggests that Solomon's "natural philosophy" has not been improved upon:

> How ancient this Natural Philosophy has been in the World, is hard to know [...]. The first who found out the Vanity of it, seems to have been Solomon, of which Discovery he has left such admirable strains in Ecclesiastes. The next was Socrates, who made it the business of His Life, to explode it, and introduce that which we call Moral in its place, to busie Human Minds to better purpose. And indeed, whoever reads with Thought what these two [...] have said, upon the Vanity of all that mortal Man can ever attain to know of Nature, in its Originals or Operations, may save Himself a great deal of Pains, and justly conclude, That the Knowledge of such things is not our Game; and (like the pursuit of a Stag by a little Spaniel) may serve to amuse and to weary us, but will never be hunted down.[29]

The Solomon of Ecclesiastes can by this time with ease be spoken of in the same breath as "Socrates", and together they are seen to stand as a stalwart warning to not exasperate oneself in the fruitless pursuit of "Knowledge". Indeed, one might as well chase after wind.

Literary *Vanitas* Readings

Ecclesiastes's influence on the theme of *vanitas* in the Renaissance period is the result mainly of the prolific output of one man who lived centuries earlier: Jerome. Jerome's framework for understanding the book is in his articulation of its main theme, of vanity as representative of what is to be despised of the world—*contemptus mundi*. There is no doubting the outstanding and lasting influence of Jerome's commentary, which is well captured by biblical scholar Roland E. Murphy, who finds in it "fairly liberal interpretation [...] erudite philology, command of the ancient Greek versions, lessons from his Jewish tutor, Bar Aqiba, etc."[30] His translation of Ecclesiastes for the Vulgate (which reportedly, *along with* Proverbs and Song of Songs, took only three days to complete) itself wielded its influence through, among other things, its reading of the key term of Ecclesiastes, *hebel* (in most English translations "vanity" or "meaningless"), as *vanitas* (the reader should refer to Luca Mazzinghi's essay in this volume for an in-depth analysis of this matter). Indeed, Jerome's preface, "since it became one of the standard prefaces to the book in medieval Bibles, was probably the most widely read exegetical help on Ecclesiastes in the middle ages."[31]

In the introductory words of his preface concerning "virtuous Blesilla's book of Ecclesiastes", that he "taught her to think lightly of her generation and to esteem futile everything that she saw in the world", Jerome makes his own theme clear in his commentary on Ecclesiastes's first words, worth quoting here at length:

> *Vanity of vanities* [*vanitas vanitatum*] said Ecclesiastes, *Vanity of vanities, all is vanity*. If all things that God made are truly good then how can all things be considered vanity, and not only vanity, but even vanity of vanities? [...] [H]eaven, earth, the seas and all things that are contained within its compass can be said to be good in themselves, but compared to God they are nothing. And if I look at the candle in a lamp and am content with its light, then afterwards when the sun has risen I cannot discern anymore what was once bright; I will also see the light of the stars by the light of the setting sun, so in looking at the world and the multitudinous varieties of nature I am amazed at the greatness of the world, but I also remember that all things will pass away and the world will grow old, and that only God is that which has always been. On account of this realisation I am compelled to say, not once but twice: *Vanity of vanities, all is vanity* [...]. All things are and will be vain, until we find that which is complete and perfect.[32]

Here Jerome shows his nuanced development of the *vanitas* theme. It is echoed in a later letter (ca. 394) to Pammachius: "But if all things are good, as being the handiwork of a good Creator, how comes it that all things are vanity? If the earth is vanity, are the heavens vanity too? —and the angels, the thrones, the dominations, the powers, and the rest of the virtues? No."[33]

This qualified approach to *vanitas*, which ironically mirrors Luther's reasons for rejecting Jerome's reading (see below), is found in numerous Christian commentators, such as Augustine in his *City of God*, John Chrysostom in *Homilies on Ephesians*, and the later commentary of Gregorius of Agrigentum, who "agrees with Ecclesiastes that all is vanity, but says that nothing can be totally useless, since God made everything. Gregory even says that the ideal person is one who has experienced reality and still chosen the good."[34] It also appears, with little modification, in the *Glossa ordinaria* (ca. 1100), and the writings of Rupert of Deutz and Hugh of St. Cher.[35] Hugh of St. Victor, in discussing the idea that *omnia* is *vanitas*, marks out his own approach:

> If everything is vanity, then he himself who says this is vanity. And how can what vanity says concerning vanity not be worthless? Because if it is true that what he says is worthless, he ought not to be heeded, but rather rejected [...]. What lives in the flesh is worthless. What lives in God is not worthless, but is true, since it comes from truth.[36]

The sixteenth-century Protestant reformers held up *contemptus mundi* as an exemplary target. In his preface to his lectures on Ecclesiastes (1532), Luther addresses the *vanitas* tradition and relates it directly to Jerome. Here he calls "noxious" the

> influence of many of the saintly and illustrious theologians in the church, who thought that in this book Solomon was teaching what they call 'the contempt of the world', that is, the contempt of things that have been created and established by God. Among these is St. Jerome, who by writing a commentary on this book urged Blesilla to accept the monastic life. From this source there arose and spread over the entire church, like a flood, that theology of the religious orders or monasteries. It was taught that to be a Christian meant to forsake the household, the political order, or even the episcopal [...] office, to flee to the desert, to isolate oneself from human society, to live in stillness and silence; for it was impossible to serve God in the world. As though Solomon were calling 'vanity' the very marriage, political office, and office of the ministry of the Word which he praises here in such a wonderful way and calls gifts of God![37]

Luther exaggerates the approach of Jerome himself (which is far more nuanced) and, of more interest here, regards Jerome's commentary as causing the *contemptus* reading to "spread over the entire church, like a flood". Luther's own approach to *vanitas*, which he develops throughout his lectures, is to identify "the vanity of the human heart, that it is never content with the gifts of God that are present but rather thinks of them as negligible".[38] The *contemptus* reading is also rejected by two of Luther's Protestant colleagues at roughly the same time: Johannes Brenz (1528) and Philip Melanchthon (1550). This veritable onslaught complemented Luther's own strategy to "overthrow the principles of monasticism and transform theology out of recognition".[39] Yet the *contemptus* reading did manage to survive, evidence that reading paradigms rarely fall into neat periodization schemes.

Luther and the Reformers close to him are neither the only humanist-minded thinkers to be drawn to Ecclesiastes, nor the only ones who will take issue with the monastic reading (which will continue to be understood in exaggerated terms). Skepticism's champion, Montaigne, engaged frequently with *vanitas*. As Rosin points out, vanity "is only one of Montaigne's many themes, but it represents an important step in his intellectual odyssey."[40] Note Montaigne's opening remarks in one of the longest of his essays, *On Vanity*:

> Perhaps there is no more manifest vanity than writing so vainly about it. That which the Godhead has made so godly manifest should be meditated upon by men of intelligence anxiously and continuously. Anyone can see that I have set out on a road along which I shall travel without toil and without ceasing as long as the world has ink and paper.[41]

It immediately becomes clear that for Montaigne, "vanity" is largely about the unchecked proliferation of knowledge: "What can babble produce when the stammering of an untied tongue smothered the world under such a dreadful weight of volumes [as the "six thousand" books on philology of Didymus]? So many words about nothing but words!"[42] Indeed, for Montaigne, understanding the true nature of vanity ensures awareness of human limitation and compels one to live *hic et nunc* [i.e., *here and now*]. Montaigne recognized, suggests Perry, the "textual absence" of God in Ecclesiastes, an absence of the kind of religious commitment that might impede critical reflection and living in the world. In practical terms, this is embodied in skepticism and is set against authoritarian law and religion, namely as represented by the *contemptus mundi* tradition.[43] In a different way than Luther, then, Montaigne has the monastic readings in his sights.

By all accounts the *contemptus mundi* approach to Ecclesiastes dominated Christian exegesis through the Middle Ages (one can see its influence in Thomas à Kempis's fifteenth-century *Imitation of Christ*) and survived the age of reform, particularly in moral discourse. A few examples will help to flesh this out.

As the seventeenth century progressed, the reading faded in poetry but was still typical in the work of pious commentators who closely adapt Jerome's reading as a framework. So, in his *A Commentary, upon the Whole Booke of Ecclesiastes* (1639), under the heading, "The generall scope of the Booke", Michael Jermin writes:

> It is a mistake, as some thinke, of the meaning of *Epicurus*, to imagine that he [God] placed the chiefe good of man in a sensuall pleasure; but that he intended the sweet delight of vertue [...]. Now much more are they mistaken, who thinke that in this booke a luxurious pleasure is commended to us: seeing it is from a discommendation of worldly things, in respect of the vanitie of them [...] as St. *Hierome* speaketh, that the Preacher laboureth to make us to deny the world.[44]

As well as Jerome, Hugh of St. Victor features prominently in such *contemptus mundi* commentaries.

Certain portions of Ecclesiastes held a special interest for the skeptical humanists, particularly 1:9: "There is nothing new under the sun." For Francis Bacon, the truism of 1:9 can only complement the wider Renaissance exposition of the dangers of philosophy. So, in the enlarged version of his *Essays* (*The Essays or Counsels, Civil and Moral*, 1625), Bacon begins his *Of Vicissitude of Things*, as follows:

> Salomon saith, there is no new thing upon the earth: so that as Plato had an imagination, that all knowledge was but remembrance: so Solomon giveth his sentence, that all novelty is but oblivion. Whereby you may see, that the river of Lethe runneth as well above ground, as below.[45]

He then concludes the essay: "But it is not good to look too long upon these turning wheels of vicissitude, lest we become giddy. As for the philology of them, that is but a circle of tales, and therefore not fit for this writing."[46] In other words, there is an implicit judgment in Ecclesiastes's observation that only further serves to underscore the perilous pursuit of knowledge. The poet John Collop makes a similar point some thirty years later in a popular tract on religious tolerance entitled *Medici Catholicon* (1656, reprinted in 1658 and 1667 as *Charity Commended*). In his (second) preface, "To the Romanist", Collop addresses the circuity of learning, understood in a manner not unlike Bacon's "circle of tales":

> Error is of a teeming Constitution, this Hydra's heads multiply by amputation, there is no end of writing of Bookes the wisest of men dead said, and the wisest of men living lament. Study is a wearinesss [sic] to the flesh, I wish most mens studies were not onely a wearines [sic] to their own but all flesh [...] while there is nothing new under the Sun, not onely bookes but men are transcribed, men are liv'd ore againe: the Pythagorean Metempsychy is verified: the revolution of planets reduce the same constitutions, same errors: hence Learning is in the circle and not in the Progresse: error hath alter'd her modes and garbs with times, someties more gaudy, better painted, trim'd and drest to become more tempting, but still hath carried her old rotten body through all her veils and disguises discoverable to a curious inquirie.[47]

The French Calvinist Pierre du Moulin published his *Heraclitus, or, Mans Looking-Glass and Survey of Life* in around 1605.[48] The work as a whole is a "Meditation upon the Vanitie and Miserie of Mans Life", which opens with the *vanitas* theme in order to undertake a fairly morbid form of self-examination:

> The distracted diversity of the affairs of this World mangles our time in an hundred thousand pieces; every business snatcheth away some part of our life; No time is ours but that which we steal from our selves, robbing some hours to examine our selves apart, and confer with God; there is work enough to be found in these solitary Meditations: But the first work to be considered of is the vanity and misery of our life, not to perplex us for it, but to prepare us to leave it [...] for worldly pleasures nigh at hand dazle & distract the judgement. Now if we would enquire of any that hath trod this path, *Salomon* in the beginning of his Ecclesiastes entring into this Meditation cryes out *Vanity of Vanities all is Vanity.*[49]

The end goal is soon identified: "taking the Razour from their hand [i.e., from David and Solomon, who have modeled such reflection], let us Anatomize our selves."[50] Like so many others, du Moulin highlights in the language of Ecclesiastes the perceived dangers of the pursuit of knowledge:

> Now a dayes Vnderstanding consists in the Knowledge of Tongues—the Learned busie themselves to know what the Women of *Rome* spake 2000 years since, what Apparell the *Romans* did wear, in what ceremony Stage-play's were beheld then among the people, and to new furbish over [...] this is to rake a Dunghill with a Scepter, and to make our Vnderstanding [...] a Drudge to a base Occupation [...]. *Philosophy* and the *Arts* as they are somewhat higher, so they are somewhat harder [...] so they perplex more; *He that increaseth Knowledge* (saith *Salomon*) *increaseth Sorrow* [Ecclesiastes 1:18]. Ignorance hath some commodity; and when all is done, this Knowledge goes not far: For no Man by *Philosophie* can clearly tell the nature of a Fly, or an Herb, much less of himself; our Spirits travell every where, and yet we are strangers at home, we would know all, but doe nothing, for (to speak properly) our study is no labour, but a curious laziness which tires it self, and goes not forward, like Squirrells in a cage, which turn up and down, and think they goe apace, when they are still where they were; we learn little with great labour, and that little makes us little the better, nay, many times worse; a drop or dram of divine Knowledge is more worth than all humane whatsoever [...]. What are we the better [...] by *Astronomy* to learn the motions and influences of the Heavens, and know not how to come thither? [...] *This is also Vanity and Vexation of the Spirit* [Ecclesiastes 1:14].[51]

Here there is a hint of the feature many later interpreters of Ecclesiastes will recognize: his exasperation with the circular and existentially frustrating nature of knowledge. While the end of the sixteenth century sees a fairly abrupt cessation in the attack on (a caricature of) monastic readings of Ecclesiastes, it is perhaps not an exaggeration to say that readings of the *vanitas* theme between 1500 and 1600 signify an allegiance for or against the monastic reading and the religious authority it signifies—a sort of political badge of piety.[52]

Scores of poems in the early modern period are framed and often bound by the language of traditional *vanitas* readings. Notable exceptions inversely grow in number in this period, and include the poetry of William Neville, Edmund Spenser, John Donne, Francis Quarles, George Herbert, and Anne Bradstreet. Their work marks an engagement with the theme of *vanitas* outside of the politicizing context of *contemptus mundi*.[53]

One of the most popular works of verse in the seventeenth century in England was Francis Quarles's *Emblemes* (1635), a series of engravings with accompanying verse. The images are mainly allegorical, in reference to divine love. The relationship between word and image here is subtle and not simply a matter of text "commenting" on image: "the emblem was understood to embody a language *in rebus* mutually interchangeable with the language *in verbis* of the accompanying text."[54] *Emblemes* and *Hieroglyphikes* (the 1638 'sequel') appealed to moderate Catholics as well as Protestants because of their concern for the "general tenets" of the Christian life as opposed to the detail of doctrine.[55] In Embleme VI, *All is vanity and vexation of spirit*, Quarles reflects on a delicate and transitory world, the vastness of which cannot be measured and which provokes human restlessness:

> How is the anxious soule of man befool'd
> In his desire,
> That thinks a Hectick Fever may be cool'd
> In flames of fire? [...]
> Whose Gold is double with a carefull hand,

His cares are double;
The Pleasure, Honour, Wealth of Sea and Land
Bring but a trouble;
The world it selfe, and all the worlds command,
Is but a Bubble. [...]
It [the world] is a vast Circumference, where none
Can find a Center.
Of more than earth, can earth make none possest;
And he that least
Regards this restlesse world, shall in this world find Rest. [...][56]

The accompanying image shows an angel who, untroubled and serene, holds the world, an orb on an embroidered table, perhaps suggesting how hopeless would be humanity's attempt to do the same. Clearly writers leading to the modern period had in place a tradition of *vanitas* to mine for rich reflection on human experience.

Vanitas Readings in the Arts

Another medium that deals with *vanitas* explicitly in the Renaissance period, and which further exposits the scrutiny of human endeavor especially, is the *vanitas* fine art movement. I will discuss this only briefly and refer the reader to Timothy Verdon's essay in this volume. Hans J. van Miegroet suggests that *vanitas* painting is concerned with human fragility, desires, and pleasures in the face of the inevitability and finality of death.[57] Others note the relationship between the words of Ecclesiastes and the *vanitas* paintings, but this link is subtle rather than overt.[58] The paintings themselves are largely symbolic representations of a zeitgeist, which, although the themes are present as early as Hans Holbein's celebrated 1533 painting *The Ambassadors* (The National Gallery, London), with its widely acknowledged theme of the futility of human endeavor, is felt most profoundly by the Dutch of the seventeenth century.

The dangers of an abundance of the good things in life were all too apparent to the Dutch, and to prevent its good citizens from going astray the teachings known collectively as "the Wisdom of Solomon" were utilized as corrective guides for moral behavior. Specially published editions of Proverbs, Ecclesiastes, and Ecclesiasticus were placed in houses of correction, for the edification of those who had gone astray.[59] It is reasonable to conjecture that the Ecclesiastes was a particularly appealing guide to a life that could hold great riches and great misery.

Directly from or alongside the *vanitas* painting tradition emerged *vanitas* choral and string music. In a 1995 recording entitled *Vanitas Vanitatum*, Tragicomedia, a group specializing in seventeenth-century music, performs eleven such pieces, all Italian and dated between 1620 and 1677.[60] The sleeve notes, by Tragicomedia co-founder Erin Headley, place the works in their context:

Nearly every native and foreign artist looked to Rome for inspiration, and it was the Roman more than any other European who was confronted daily with the *memento mori* of the past. It is no surprise then that Roman poets, painters and composers of the 17th century should have adopted the *vanitas* theme so ardently and so fruitfully [...]. Both in the north and in the south of Europe, artists interpreted the *vanitas* theme according to their own temperaments and traditions. In the north it provided painters with an excuse to detail and classify nature, and through what better vehicle than the still life? [...] [M]usic here proves itself to be the ideal medium for symbolising the *vanitas* theme, since it is an art that disappears as soon as it is articulated.[61]

The music indeed captures the complexity and inherent incongruity of *vanitas*: haunting melodies set alongside Ecclesiastes's words (some of the lyrics are direct renditions of chapters 1 and 2 especially, with long choruses of simply *vanitas vanitatum*), or which could have emerged from the mouth of Ecclesiastes: "The healthy, the sick / the brave, the defenceless / must all come to an end / We all must die" (from Stefano Landi's *Homo fugit velut umbra*, also known as *Passacaglia della vita*, translated in the sleeve notes).

It is clear that the *vanitas* theme had widespread and enduring appeal. *The Web Gallery of Art*, for example, which archives about 14,500 European fine art works, returns over 100 examples of *vanitas* paintings, and Haak mentions a dozen more.[62] Cavalli-Björkman mentions not only Dutch painters but also German, French, Italian, and Spanish artists who painted *vanitas*.[63] The impact of the theme continued, with artists such as Vincent Van Gogh (*Skull with Burning Cigarette*, 1886/1887, Van Gogh Museum, Amsterdam) and Paul Cézanne (*Nature Morte au Crâne* [*Still Life with Skulls*], 1895–1900, Barnes Foundation, Philadelphia, PA) producing paintings clearly reminiscent of the *vanitas* still-life. The *vanitas* theme, broadly understood, can still be found in the visual arts. In the summer of 2000, the Virginia Museum of Fine Art held a major exhibition entitled "*Vanitas*: Meditations on Life and Death in Contemporary Art." The accompanying book has as its epigraph the opening verses of Ecclesiastes 1:2–4. John Ravenal sees the *vanitas* theme as universal and culturally relevant.[64] Also, it is worth noting that a Google image search of "vanitas" yields some extraordinarily rich and diverse results, ancient and modern. The appeal of the *vanitas* painting tradition lies in its successful capture of the subtle balance between transient and joyful modes of living, so vociferously endorsed by Ecclesiastes.

Conclusion

The extent of the unabated influence of *vanitas* is impossible to map accurately. This was brought home to me on a visit to the Tate Modern museum in London. It was with some disbelief that I took in the room I had just entered, entitled *Memento Mori*. It began with a late but perfectly classical *vanitas* painting by Edwaert Collier (see **cat. n. III.4**) (a Dutch artist who painted *vanitas* works for the English market, and who anglicized his name from Edwaert Colyer), *Still Life with a Volume of Wither's 'Emblemes'* of 1696 (London, Tate Britain), the display caption of which read,

> This seventeenth-century work is a typical *vanitas* painting. The skull and hourglass, which symbolise the inevitability of death, are joined by musical instruments, wine and jewels, representing the fleeting pleasures of life. A book by the English poet George Wither is opened at the title page, where a brief poem emphasises the theme of mortality. The Latin inscription in the top left corner is a celebrated quotation from the Old Testament book of Ecclesiastes, from which the term *vanitas* was derived: 'Vanity of vanities, all is vanity.'[65]

The room had a range of modern work that articulated the themes of mortality inspired by *vanitas*.

In the end, comprehending the influence of *vanitas* itself requires imagination. For Renaissance thinkers, *vanitas* provided a skeptical line of inquiry weighted with the disquieting authority of the Bible, as well as a polemical language to be voiced against the monastic tradition that had permanently fixed *vanitas* in the intellectual life of Europe. *Vanitas* fired the imagination of artists, musicians, and poets from the Renaissance to the present day. Part of the enormous appeal of Ecclesiastes's theme lies in its radical openness. In Ecclesiastes, *hebel* has no reference but itself and the troubled observations that Ecclesiastes attaches to it, and the superlative construct *hebel* of *hebels* is infamously self-defining (as many exegetes have pointed out, the "all" of "all is vanity" also lacks a semantic reference, one that must be provided by readers). These yield meaning only in a discourse that provides their terms of reference, only as poets and moralizers fill them with a host of experientially bound ideas. This non-referential quality also hints at a transgressive power, a power to wrest free from the cultural conditions of its performances. Where it appears to succeed (even if it necessarily fails), *vanitas* often encapsulates the entirety of Ecclesiastes's story, his sense of failed quest and the yearning of the older Ecclesiastes to redeem it.[66]

Two typical examples of reading Ecclesiastes from the Renaissance period will help round out and conclude this essay. In 1576, the poet and "literary innovator" George Gascoigne closely adapted Pope Innocent III's abovementioned *De Contemptu Mundi sive de Miseria Condicionis Humane*, which enjoyed huge popularity nearly 400 years previously. The adaptation appears as the first section of his *The Droomme of Doomes Day*, "The View of Worldly Vanities":

> Let wyse men search narrowly, let them heedely consider the height of the heavens, the breadth of the yearth, and the depth of the Sea [...] and let them alwayes eyther learne or teach, and in so doing, what shall they fynde out of this busie toyle of our life, but traveyle and payne? That knewe he by experience, which sayed: For asmuch as in great wisedome and knowledge there is great disdayne, and he which increaseth knowledge increaseth also payne & travayle [1:18], for although whilest that he sercheth it out, he must sweat many tymes, and watch many nightes with sweat and labor, yet is there scarcely any thing so vyle, or any thing so easy, that man can fully and thorowly understand it, nor that he can clerely comprehende it, unlesse perchaunce that is perfectly knowne, that nothinge is perfectly knowne.[67]

Like Francis Bacon and Pierre du Moulin, Gascoigne, voicing Innocent's much earlier concerns, goes on to develop the thesis of the human failure to grasp the "reason of Gods workes, yea the more he laboreth to seeke it, so much the lesse shall he fynde it, therefore they faile in the searching, how narrowly so ever they search".[68] Paraphrasing chapter 7:29, Gascoigne concludes, "God first made man, and he hath wrapped him selfe in sundry and infinite questions."[69] Not long after, Pierre Charron, a close friend and disciple of Montaigne, in his *Of Wisdome: Three Bookes* (*De la sagesse*, 1601), sets out a lengthy discourse on "the knowledge of our selves and our humane condition, which is the foundation of Wisdome".[70] When discussing the responsibilities of parents to their children in undertaking the proper teaching of science, Charron is reminded of Ecclesiastes:

> One of the sufficientest men of knowledge that ever was, spake of Science, as of a thing not onely vaine, but hurtfull, painefull, and tedious. To be briefe, Science may make us more humane and courteous, but not more honest [...]. The wise man said, that he that increaseth knowledge, increaseth sorrow.[71]

For Ecclesiastes's readers in this period, it seems the only way to avoid sorrow is to avoid the "sciences" altogether—although the irony of such sentiments in books that largely drove forward the study of the humanities was entirely lost.

[1] HATTAWAY 1968, p. 512.

[2] This essay is adapted from portions of my book *Ecclesiastes through the Centuries* (Wiley-Blackwell, 2012), and I would like to thank the publishers for allowing this material to be used here.

[3] HATTAWAY 1968, p. 510.

[4] CAMERON 2001, p. XXIII–XXIV. See also Luther's comments, below.

[5] ROSIN 1997, p. 6–7, 76.

[6] See Eccles. 1:8.

[7] See PERRY 1993a, PERRY 1993b, but also FISCH 1988, and MILLS 2003.

[8] See, e.g., essays I:2, 20, 36, 39; II:12, 28; III:9 in DE MONTAIGNE 1991.

[9] Ibid., p.252 n.1. See also essays I:36, 39; II:12; III:9.

[10] Ibid., p. 552.

[11] Ibid., p. 555–556.

[12] Ibid., p. 565.

[13] FISCH 1988, p. 158.

[14] PERRY 1993a, p. 265.

[15] Ibid.

[16] Essay III:2; DE MONTAIGNE 1991, p. 907–908.

[17] ROSIN 1997, p. 28–33.

[18] INNOCENTIUS III 1978, p. 2–5.

[19] See *THE PARADISE OF DAINTY DEVICES* 1927.

[20] See DE MONTAIGNE 1991, p. XXXIII.

[21] HATTAWAY 1968, p. 511.

[22] Ibid., p. 521.

[23] The *Treatie* was published posthumously in 1633 and "written in his Youth".

[24] GREVILLE 1633, p. 48. The book includes his *Treatie of Humane Learning*. Unless otherwise noted all italics are in the original texts.

[25] BACON 1730, p. 415.

[26] Ibid.

[27] Ibid., p. 415–416.

[28] Further on the theme of knowledge in Renaissance readings, see CHRISTIANSON 2012, and particularly the commentary on 1:17–18 and 8:16–17 therein.

[29] TEMPLE 1690, p. 83–84.

[30] MURPHY 1992, p. LI.

[31] ELIASON 1989, p. 41 n.5.

[32] JEROME 2000, ad loc.

[33] Letter 49, in JEROME 1954, p. 73.

[34] ETTLINGER 1985, p. 320.

[35] See ELIASON 1989, p. 51–53.

[36] Ibid., p. 53 footnotes 30 and 31.

[37] LUTHER 1972, p. 4; see also his comments on Eccles. 2:1–3, p. 31–33.

[38] Ibid., p. 10 et passim.

[39] CAMERON 2001, p. 88.

[40] ROSIN 1997, p. 25.

[41] DE MONTAIGNE 1991, p. 1070.

[42] Ibid., p. 1070–1071.

[43] See PERRY 1993a.

[44] JERMIN 1639, p. 2; see also GRANGER 1621 and MAYER 1653.

[45] Essay 59 in BACON 1730.

[46] Ibid., p. 380 and 382.

[47] See the Dedication in COLLOP 1667.

[48] The translator of the 1652 edition informs us that it is "40 years since I translated this piece out of French, and laid it by in loose papers," but there is also a 1609 translation.

[49] DU MOULIN 1652, p. 1–3.

[50] Ibid., p. 4.

[51] Ibid., p. 26–31.

[52] We might note that later Puritan commentators begin to resume Jerome's reading in the mid-seventeenth century.

[53] For a range of examples, see CHRISTIANSON 2012.

[54] GILMAN 1980, p. 387.

[55] HÖLTGEN 2004.

[56] See Book I, Emblem VI, in QUARLES 1635, p. 24–26.

[57] VAN MIEGROET 1998, p. 880.

[58] Both still-lifes and portraits; see HAAK 1984, p. 125; DE GIROLAMI CHENEY 1992, p. 120; PUYVELDE AND PUYVELDE 1971, p. 235.

[59] SCHAMA 1991, p. 20.

[60] TRAGICOMEDIA 2004.

[61] See ibid.

[62] See HAAK 1984.

[63] CAVALLI-BJÖRKMAN 1998, p. 501–508.

[64] *VANITAS: MEDITATIONS ON LIFE* 2000, p. 13–14.

[65] At the time of writing, Collier's painting may be viewed at the Tate Britain, Display Room 1650. See also the gallery website, http://www.tate.org.uk/art/artworks/collier-still-life-with-a-volume-of-withers-emblemes-n05916.

[66] See CHRISTIANSON 1998, p. 242–245.

[67] GASCOIGNE 1910, p. 223; Gascoigne's translation is very much in agreement with Lewis's critical edition of *De Contemptu*, in INNOCENTIUS III 1978, p. 108 and 110.

[68] GASCOIGNE 1910, p. 223.

[69] Ibid., p. 22.

[70] CHARRON 1640, unnumbered Preface.

[71] See ibid., p. 502.

"Omnia Vanitas": Art, Illusion, and Truth

Timothy Verdon

The biblical idea of *vanitas*—of the futility of illusory values such as beauty, pleasure, wealth, and learning—was frequently invoked in European art of the sixteenth, seventeenth, and eighteenth centuries, becoming the theme, or at least a subtext, of various genres of images then in demand: still-life depictions, "merry company" scenes, and views of ancient ruins.[1] Acknowledging both the appeal and the impermanence of earthly realities, such works conveyed the self-awareness expressed in a text of the period, William Shakespeare's *King Lear*, when the aged monarch admits: "The art of our necessities is strange, that can make vile things precious."[2] Normally created for domestic settings, images of this kind enriched family life with a wisdom rooted in the Bible and in lived experience, which each generation passed on to the next.

A standard component of *vanitas* images was a reference to time and its passage, whether through allegorical personifications of Chronos or by allusive means such as representations of hourglasses, half-eaten food, wilting flowers, or the crumbling monuments of imperial Rome. A related theme was the instability of power, whether ecclesiastical or political, through depictions of discarded tiaras, mitres, and crowns, or, after 1649, portraits of King Charles I of England, decapitated in that year by order of Parliament. Heaped books with frayed pages suggested the passing nature of academic knowledge, maps and globes the changing coordinates of geographical information, sheet music and instruments the silence that follows performance. The human skull, ultimate sign of life's transitory character, was often represented.

Yet the message of *vanitas* paintings was not, as might at first appear, negative. For if truly "*All* is vanity", as the theme's biblical source, the Old Testament book of Ecclesiastes asserts (1:1), then vain too is the claim that "all is vanity", and behind Ecclesiastes's pessimism must lie a reason for hope, a truth greater than any of its partial manifestations. At most we may say that *vanitas* images are paradoxical, since, while they proclaim the valuelessness of beauty, pleasure, wealth, and learning, they are themselves beautiful, enjoyable, costly, and learned. This calculated contradiction is part of the interest such images have for viewers even today.

Ambiguity and Realism

Vanitas images transmit their message through ambiguity, presenting as satisfying things that ultimately delude. A famous early example is the painting by Agnolo Bronzino showing a nude Venus lasciviously embraced by Cupid, her son, who kneels on a crimson cushion symbolizing the vice of lust (**figure 1**).[3] Behind them, in the upper right of the composition, Father

Figure 1:
Agnolo Bronzino, *Venus, Cupid, Folly, and Time*, ca. 1545.
Oil on panel, 146 × 116 cm (57.48 × 45.66 in.).
London (England), The National Gallery.

Figure 2:
Gerrit van Honthorst, *Merry Company with a Lute Player*, ca. 1619.
Oil on canvas, 144 × 212 cm (56.69 × 83.46 in.).
Florence (Italy), Gallerie degli Uffizi.

Figure 3:
Dirck van Baburen, *Merry Company*, ca. 1623.
Oil on canvas, 108 × 153 cm (42.51 × 60.23 in.).
Mainz (Germany), Landesmuseum.

Time draws back a blue drape to disclose a woman in the upper left, his daughter Truth, the idea being that sooner or later 'time' reveals the 'truth' about everything. Here, the truth revealed is that the pleasure given by illicit love is deceptive: two theater masks in the lower right in fact symbolize falsity, and a hag at our left, clawing at her hair, communicates that, when youth and beauty pass, all that remains of sinful pleasure is remorse. The image, indeed, is thought to allude to the new venereal disease of the period, syphilis.[4]

Executed in the 1540s at the court of Duke Cosimo de' Medici I, Bronzino's painting uses the mythological terminology and allegorical mode dear to aristocratic viewers in Renaissance Italy. This is not the approach of later *vanitas* images, however, for in northern Europe, where the theme was most popular, the middle-class patrons for whom artists worked preferred straightforward description. In German and Dutch art, for example, the futility of lust is communicated by showing revellers in a brothel, with an occasional figure of old age or death included as a concession to allegory, as in Gerrit van Honthorst's *Merry Company with a Lute Player,* ca. 1619–1620 (**figure 2**), or Dirck van Baburen's *Merry Company*, ca. 1623 (**figure 3**).

Figure 4:
Hieronymus Bosch, *The Ship of Fools*, ca. 1494.
Oil on panel, 58 × 43 cm (22.83 × 16.92 in.).
Paris (France), Musée du Louvre.

Realism of content and of style was a standard feature of northern European culture, which from the late fifteenth century onward turned an unpitying eye upon human life. The German satire *Das Narrenschiff (The Ship of Fools)*, written by Alsatian humanist Sebastian Brant (see **cat. n. III.10**) and published in 1494 with illustrations by Albrecht Dürer, became an immediate best seller north of the Alps, translated into Latin in 1497, into French in 1498, and into English in 1509.[5] In 1494, the year Brant's book appeared, life as an aimless voyage was the subject of a painting as well: a masterpiece by the Netherlandish master Hieronymus Bosch in which human beings are shown adrift on a sea of stupidity, steered only by greed and lust (**figure 4**).[6] Still harsher is Urs Graf the Elder's 1511 woodcut illustrating a young prostitute being groped by an older man, from whose open money bag she removes coins which she then passes to a dandy in a plumed hat beside her (**figure 5**). The objects on the table before these figures—a gaming board and playing cards, a plate of fruit and drinking vessel, a lute evoking music's pleasures—anticipate the kind of still-life compositions later used in *vanitas* images, as do the skull and bones in the woodcut's lower area, which, like the rhymed couplet on the accompanying scroll, remind viewers that death puts an end to human illusions.

Death, Fortune, Anguish

The first unequivocal statements of the *vanitas* theme appear in Germany, in the same period as Graf's woodcut. Hans Schwarz's medallion of circa 1520, depicting *Death and the Maiden* (**figure 6**), for example, is a wonderfully concise version of a subject treated by other artists of the period, especially Hans Baldung Grien, in which a skeleton embracing an alluringly naked girl reveals the pointlessness of physical attraction before death's inevitability. In all such works, the maiden's dream of love, cruelly disappointed, becomes a metaphor of life's many disillusionments.

The visual sources of Schwarz's medallion are various. His image evokes depictions of the 'Dance of Death', in which the living cavort with the dead as if mortality were a grim game, and recalls the macabre realism which, on some medieval tombs, reminded the living of their inevitable end by showing skeletal remains beneath effigies of the deceased. In its circular format, Schwarz's work also calls to mind medieval 'wheel of fortune' images, in which life's mutability is suggested by human figures in successive conditions of ascent and descent, success and failure.[7]

Schwarz's medallion has a new spirit, however: an aggressiveness in the skeleton different from the simple decomposition shown on old tombs, and a ruefulness in the maiden far from the calm with which 'losers' on fortune's wheel accept their lot. A possible explanation for the drama of Schwarz's reading is the medallion's place and date of creation: Germany shortly after the 1517 publication of Martin Luther's theses regarding the church and human salvation. Among other things, the *vanitas* theme is a response to the early sixteenth-century collapse of the certainties that had sustained European Christians for a thousand years, and its development coincides with the era of religious warfare and social revolution set in motion by this trauma.

Figure 6:
Hans Schwarz, *Death and the Maiden* (medallion), ca. 1520.
Boxwood, diameter 10.8 cm; depth 1.5 cm (diameter 4.25 in.; depth .59 in.).
Berlin (Germany), Bode Museum.

"There Is No Peace"

The climate of unease was not limited to Germany, and a curiously similar mood pervades the art of Schwarz's Italian contemporary Jacopo Pontormo, of Florence, in whose religious works we find expressions of moral disorientation—anguished faces, eyes void of hope—previously unknown south of the Alps.[8] The reason for these novelties, particularly evident in Pontormo's *Transport of the Dead Christ* of 1526–1528 (**figure 7**), is suggested by a Florentine intellectual of the period, Niccolò Machiavelli, in a letter written in 1513, shortly after the election of cardinal Giovanni de' Medici as pope with the name Leo X.[9] Machiavelli, under house arrest for having supported the faction that had exiled the Medici family in 1494, wrote to a friend, Francesco Vettori, and,

Figure 7:
Jacopo Pontormo, *Transport of the Dead Christ*, 1526–1528.
Oil on panel, 313 × 192 cm (123.22 × 75.59 in.).
Florence (Italy), Santa Felicita.

deploring the reign of terror that Leo X had instituted in Florence, borrowed a phrase from the prophet Ezekiel: "[...] they have misled my people by saying Peace! when there is no peace".[10] Evoking ancient Israel's suffering during the Babylonian captivity, Machiavelli alluded to the anxiety caused when an absolute religious system shows itself to be the enemy of its own adherents. In Ezekiel, those who misled the people were temple officials who had futile visions and gave false predictions, becoming "ruin-haunting jackals"; in Florence it was a Medici pope who persecuted his family's former enemies.[11]

Machiavelli's letter follows the execution of two friends who had plotted against Cardinal de' Medici prior to his election, Pier Paolo Boscoli and Agostino Capponi, and resonates with the memory of the massacre perpetrated a year earlier at Prato, a town near Florence, by Spanish troops allied with the papacy. On that occasion, Giovanni de' Medici, still a cardinal and Pope Julius II's emissary, had informed the pontiff of the incident, saying that Spanish troops had "sacked the territory, not without a certain amount of cruelty and killing, which proved to be indispensable [...]".[12] He had added that "the taking of Prato, so brutal and fraught with suffering, displeased me personally but has this advantage, that it will serve as an example to terrorize others [...]".[13] The punishment of Prato convinced Florence, barely thirty miles distant, to capitulate, even though to do so meant allowing the Medici, exiled eighteen years earlier, to return to power.

When they did, the Medici dissembled the humiliation that their 'restoration' caused Florence, presenting it as something ineluctable. Thus, for the 1513 carnival celebrations, they had Pontormo paint three parade floats showing, respectively, an allegorical figure of Childhood, one representing Manhood, and another symbolizing Old Age, and on the three floats appeared the words: *Erimus,* "We will be" (on the first float: Childhood); *Sumus,* "We are" (on the second: Manhood); and *Fuimus,* "We were" (on the third: Old Age).[14] The pageant represented the fall of the former government and the rise of a new one as inescapable phases of human life, and the song composed for the occasion invited citizens to read the political havoc that accompanied the Medici return in fatalistic terms as a natural process of alternation in which old things necessarily yield before the advance of new ones. As recorded by Giorgio Vasari, the song's opening strophe affirmed that:

> He who gives laws to Nature,
> And disposes various states and centuries,
> Is the cause of every Good,
> And Evil too, as long as he permits, lasts in this world:
> Wherefore, contemplating the present allegory, one sees
> How, with relentless tread,
> One century comes to life after another,
> Changing good into evil, and evil into good.[15]

Vasari's account of the Florentine carnival celebrations in 1513, the year of Leo X's election, furnishes another detail. The last float in the pageant allegorized "The Golden Age" ushered in by the Medici restoration. At its centre was "a large ball in the form of a terrestrial globe, on top of which appeared an exhausted man in rusty armour, prostrate in death." From this man's back, which was split wide open, emerged a nude boy, all gilded, who represented the Golden Age come back to life after the Age of Iron, from whom the emerging boy was reborn. But the gilded child, "a baker's boy [...], for the discomfort he endured to earn ten shillings, died soon after", suffocated by the thin sheets of gold leaf that had been spread on his skin.[16] It is after this grotesque communication that Vasari quotes the carnival song's opening, "He who gives laws to Nature [...]".

History as Purposeless

In the second and third decades of the sixteenth century, a dawning sense of the absurd reversed what to many had seemed a definitive conquest, the Renaissance vision of history as cultural progress. Whereas early fifteenth-century humanists had continued to use the medieval 'wheel of fortune' model—Antonio Loschi, visiting the ruins of ancient Rome with Poggio Bracciolini in the 1420s, expressed his horror at time's depredations in cyclic terms, lamenting the once grand city's reversion to a wilderness state—later thinkers rediscovered the classical notion of an *aurea etas*, a 'golden age', in which all that the past had achieved was not only restored but improved.[17] It was in this new spirit that Leon Battista Alberti, in a book *On Painting* written in 1434–1435, claimed that Filippo Brunelleschi's new dome for Florence cathedral was a greater accomplishment than any of the ancient domes that had inspired it.[18]

The concept of cultural progress took clear form in a fresco painted for the late fifteenth-century builder pope, Sixtus IV, in his new chapel in the Vatican Palace, the 'Sistina': Pietro Perugino's *Christ Giving the Keys of Heaven to Saint Peter*, where in the background two restored Roman triumphal arches frame a much larger modern building with a dome like that of Florence cathedral.[19] This vision, in which the present clearly improves upon the past, includes the fresco on the facing wall of the chapel as well, Sandro Botticelli's *Punishment of Korah, Dathan and Abiram*, in which another Roman triumphal arch appears, but in ruins, its upper cornice badly dilapidated. The full sequence was thus: antiquity in ruins, antiquity repaired, antiquity surpassed.

The same ambitious developmental pattern shaped the greatest Renaissance hymn to progress, Giorgio Vasari's multivolume account of the achievements made by artists from the Middle Ages through the sixteenth century, the *Lives of the Most Illustrious Painters, Sculptors and Architects*, first published in 1550. Indeed, this work suggests that continual improvement is part of God's plan for humanity, a component of what Christians call 'salvation history', and Vasari opens his *Life of Michelangelo Buonarroti* with the assertion that the "benign Ruler of Heaven", seeing the countless but also fruitless efforts made by artists to bring architecture, sculpture, and painting back to the splendor they had possessed in antiquity, took pity on humankind and sent Michelangelo into the world to perfect what others had tried in vain to do. In Vasari's view, God had Michelangelo born in Florence in recognition of the contribution made by artists of that city from the time of Giotto onward.[20]

I recall this highly idealized construct in order to stress the systemic shock caused by its collapse. Explaining the change in Pontormo's style in the years in which he painted the *Transport of the Dead Christ*, Vasari recalls the artist's retreat to the solitude of a Carthusian monastery in 1523–1525 while plague raged in Florence. There, Vasari says, Pontormo's "mind was ever in search of new concepts and extravagant solutions," developing the "strangeness and bizarre manner imposed by that solitude and by the fact that he remained far from normal exchange with other persons."[21] The "bizarre manner" deplored by Vasari was of course that of German art, learned from the study of Albrecht Dürer's woodcuts, which, with their different conception of pictorial space and bodily proportions, and above all with their northern hyper-expressiveness, seemed to reject all that Florence thought it had achieved, replacing the normative Renaissance language perfected by Michelangelo with a subjective, often irrational idiom, too personal and unpredictable to be considered a 'divine' project.

This seismic tremor in Florentine art was symptomatic of the pan-European earthquake following Luther's reform, which in the very years Pontormo withdrew to Carthusian solitude saw the outbreak of knights' and peasants' revolts in south and central Germany, the secularization of the Teutonic Order in Prussia, Ulrich Zwingli's anti-Catholic *Sixty-Seven Articles* defended in public in Zurich in 1523, the first burnings of heretics at the stake in Flanders, and (bringing it all back across the Alps) the 1527 sack of Rome by troops answering to the Catholic emperor Charles V, which forced another Medici pope, Clement VII, to barricade himself in the fortress of Castel Sant'Angelo, Rome. With the scandalous sack of Rome, moreover, another and far more significant ideal construct—the notion of a Christendom co-extensive with the boundaries of Europe—fell to pieces, and the Renaissance illusion of humanly attainable order was well and truly shattered.

The Plight of Christians

The sixteenth-century aftermath is well known: wars of religion, forced conversions or changes of creed for *raisons d'état*, sectarian persecutions and massacres, mass deportations, political realignments of cities and kingdoms.[22] The next century opened with the carnage of the Thirty Years War, finally resolved by the Treaty of Westphalia in 1648, in which the various actors unabashedly acknowledged their territorial aspirations and economic interests involving the resources of new lands in the Americas or Far East. The religious question, now reduced to the prince's choice (*Cuius regio eius religio*), revealed itself a mere pretext.[23]

In all this, individual believers felt abandoned—deluded by the institutions meant to sustain their faith—and exposed to temptations in a world no longer imaginable in the theological categories once invoked by churches and states. Unsurprisingly, both Catholicism and Protestantism invented devotional practices that emphasized personal sanctification rather than institutional holiness, focusing on everyday life and not on the larger historical perspective: Quietism, Jansenism, Jesuit and Salesian spirituality, the Mennonite and Anabaptist movements, Quakerism.

An English spiritual writer of the time, John Bunyan, a self-taught nonconformist preacher who in his youth had been one of Oliver Cromwell's soldiers, describes the situation of those seeking to follow Christ in this new age, in a way that brings us abruptly back to the subject of our essay. In his grand baroque allegory, *The Pilgrim's Progress*, published in 1676, Bunyan recounts the arduous journey of a believer, called Christian, toward mankind's heavenly destination. As Christian and his friend Faithful advance from trial to trial, they presently see "a town before them, and the name of that town is Vanity", a very ancient place, founded five thousand years earlier by Beelzebub, Apollyon, and Legion. "And at the town there is a fair kept, called Vanity-fair", because the town where "'tis kept is lighter than vanity; and also because all that is there sold, or that cometh thither, is vanity." Acknowledging his biblical source—Ecclesiastes 1:1—Bunyan recalls "the saying of the wise, 'All that cometh is vanity.'"[24]

Then, as if composing a *vanitas* painting, Bunyan sets before his reader an array of desirable objects, saying, "At this fair are all such merchandise sold: as houses, lands, trades, places, honours, preferments, titles, countries, kingdoms, lusts, pleasures and delights of all sorts—as whores, bauds, wives, husbands, children, masters, servants, lives, blood, bodies, souls, silver, gold, pearls, precious stones, and what not [...]", adding that the road to heaven obliges every man and woman to pass this way. Indeed, Bunyan says, even Christ passed, "but he had no mind to the merchandise, and therefore left the town, without laying out so much as one farthing upon these vanities."[25] *Even Christ.* Among the Protestant Bunyan's sources for this catalog of vanities was an enormously popular Catholic text, Thomas à Kempis's *The Imitation of Christ*, written in the 1420s, and, after the invention of printing, reissued hundreds of times in every part of Europe. In its opening chapter, *The Imitation of Christ* too cites Ecclesiastes's phrase, "Vanity of vanities! All is vanity," spelling out in detail the various forms that vanity takes.

> It is therefore vanity to look for the perishing riches and to trust in them; it is also vanity to look for honours and to attempt to climb to a high position. It is vanity to follow the desires of the flesh and to yearn for that which must bring with it grievous punishment. It is vanity to desire to live long and not to care to live well. It is vanity to be concerned only with this present life, and to make no provision for the life that is to come. It is vanity to love that which so speedily perishes and decays, and not to hurry on to where everlasting joy awaits you.[26]

The Following of Christ

In Thomas à Kempis's *The Imitation of Christ*, Ecclesiastes's phrase and explanatory list are introduced, however, by another scriptural quotation—Jesus's promise in John 8:12: "Whoever follows me will never walk in darkness but will have the light of life." This in fact is the theme of the entire book, which presents Christian life as a *following* of Christ that illuminates the mind and gives life to the soul. The vanity of all else, to which the Ecclesiastes phrase alludes, is thus not so absolute as the Old Testament writer appears to say, but contingent upon the failure to follow Christ—part of the "darkness" in which those who do not follow him walk. What Thomas à Kempis is really saying is that for those who do not have the light of life, which is Christ, everything is futile.

Let us add that, for Thomas à Kempis, the following of Christ goes beyond conventional religiosity, requiring believers to always choose what is truly essential. Between Jesus's words at the beginning of his book, and those of Ecclesiastes a few lines further on, Thomas in fact poses questions and makes observations designed to show that all lesser goals are "vanity," even if objectively praiseworthy:

> What will you gain if you dispute learnedly on the doctrine of the Trinity, but lack humility and are thus displeasing to the Trinity? Surely great words do not make us holy and righteous; but a virtuous life makes us dear to God. I would rather feel contrition than know its definition. If you know the whole Bible by heart, and the sayings of all the philosophers, what would this profit you without the love and grace of God?[27]

This is the point at which Thomas quotes Ecclesiastes's exclamation "Vanity of vanities! All is vanity", but he mitigates the severity of those words with a phrase inspired by Deuteronomy: "Except to love God and serve him alone."[28] To "follow Christ" and to "love God" are equivalent in Thomas à Kempis's text.

This spirituality, which revived the *docta ignorantia* of early Christian monasticism—the *learned ignorance* of those who, renouncing scholarly knowledge, strove for existential intimacy with God—was practiced by the innovative religious community of which Thomas à Kempis was a member, the Brethren of the Common Life, giving rise to a new style of Christian practice known as *devotio moderna*, (modern devotion),.[29] Of Dutch foundation, the Brethren of the Common Life had houses in Germany also (Thomas himself, as his name suggests, hailed from Kempen, near Düsseldorf), and their influence would be felt by all the northern Reformers of the sixteenth and seventeenth centuries. It is thus useful, as we look at *vanitas* images produced especially in the Protestant Netherlands, to recall two of Thomas à Kempis's admonitions to readers of *The Imitation of Christ*, the first of which cites another verse of Ecclesiastes: "Call often to mind that proverb, 'The eye is not satisfied with seeing, or the ear filled with hearing.'"[30] The second admonition draws the obvious conclusion: "Endeavour, then, to withdraw your heart from the love of things that are seen, and to turn yourselves to the things that are unseen".[31]

Things Unseen

Bringing together these several threads, it is possible to attempt a first conclusion regarding the popularity of the *vanitas* theme, which, I believe, reflects a mystical dimension in sixteenth- and seventeenth-century Protestant culture today often forgotten. In its own time, however, what appears to us as negative subject matter actually had positive meaning, proposing an unseen truth greater than the "things that are seen." That positive meaning was Christ who, never depicted in *vanitas* images, is their unspoken content: the Christ who did *not* linger at Vanity Fair, the Christ whose followers do *not* walk in darkness. While the biblical sources of *vanitas* iconography are the Old Testament, in the Dutch or German reformed homes for which the images were destined, the Old Testament sources were read from the perspective of the Christian gospel as illustrating the refusal of this world's allurements made possible by Christ's illumination. The ultimate logic of *vanitas* images is in fact that of the *learned ignorance* proposed by the apostle Paul when he asked: "Where is the one who is wise? Where is the scribe? Where is the debater of this age? Has not God made foolish the wisdom of the world?"[32] For Paul, divine wisdom, by contrast, is the gospel focused on a crucified savior, Christ, whom the apostle paradoxically calls "the power of God and the wisdom of God."[33] Underlining the gap between the world's values and the truth of Christ, Paul insists that what to unbelievers seems folly and weakness, is really the opposite, since "God's foolishness is wiser than human wisdom, and God's weakness is stronger than human strength".[34]

One may ask whether it is legitimate to read *vanitas* images, which normally take the unassuming form of still-life or genre paintings, in such a theological way. Today, the impression such works produce is simply that of literal visualizations of physical objects or of characteristic scenes. Their original public probably saw them differently, however, since from the early fifteenth century onward, Flemish and Dutch artists had used still-life and genre details in religious works to allude to deeper truths, relying on the informed viewer's capacity to relate what was seen to something unseen.[35] In the *Annunciation* scene of the *Mérode Altarpiece*, for example (**figure 8**), the candle on the table next to Mary, which (judging from the wisp of smoke) has just been extinguished, alludes to the entry into the world of Christ, "The true light, which enlightens everyone" and who thus makes candlelight unnecessary.[36] Christ, whom Mary conceived at the annunciation, is physically represented in the panel's upper left area as a minuscule baby descending toward Mary's womb, but the operative sign of his presence is the freshly extinguished candle positioned at the geometric centre of the composition. The artist gave pride of place to a symbol, which, since it presents itself as a simple candle, is sometimes called *hidden*, a non-obvious sign which viewers must decode.

The process of decoding was part of the pleasure that such works gave, and Campin's painting abounds in hidden symbols, some conventional—the lilies in the pitcher on the table, alluding to Mary's purity—others highly original: the small baby figure in the upper left enters the room on a beam of light that passes through the glass of the window, for example. This was one of the medieval demonstrations that it had been possible for Mary to conceive Jesus without losing her virginity: just as light passes through glass without shattering it, so Jesus could enter Mary's womb leaving her intact.[37] What legitimated hidden symbolism was the belief that the natural world, created by the God who later inhabited and saved it, has the potential to reveal him. That is, all created things are symbols of the creator.

Campin's image thus involved viewers in distinct but related ways: as a literal description of reality and as a mystical experience of reality's layered capacity to symbolize. Penetrating the visible surface of things accurately described, Campin discloses their unseen *logic*, which is Christ himself, God's Λόγος (i.e., *Logos*, "Word"), as the Gospel of John calls him, through whom all things were made.[38] "All things came into being through him, and without him not one thing came into being", and "he was in the world, and the world came into being through him".[39] A Pauline text adds that "for in him all things in heaven and on earth were created, things visible and invisible, [...] all things have been created through him and for him. He himself is before all things, and in him all things hold together".[40]

A twentieth-century thinker, the Jesuit theologian Karl Rahner, related these New Testament affirmations to the event depicted in Campin's *Annunciation*, saying that in the mystery of the incarnation (God's "Word" made flesh in Mary's womb):

> [...] the natural depth of the symbolic reality of all things—which of itself is restricted to the world or has a merely natural transcendence towards God—has now in ontological reality received an infinite extension, by the fact that this reality has become also a determination of the Logos himself or of his milieu. Every God-given reality, where it has not been degraded to a purely human tool and to merely utilitarian purposes, states much more than itself: each in its own way is an echo and indication of all reality. And if the individual reality, by making the all present, also speaks of God—ultimately by its transcendent reference to him as the efficient, exemplary and final cause—this transcendence is made radical, even though only in a way accessible to faith, by the fact that in Christ this reality no longer refers to God merely as its cause: it points to God as him to whom this reality belongs as his substantial determination or as his own proper environment. All things are held together by the Incarnate Word in whom they exist, and hence all things possess, even in their quality of symbol, an unfathomable depth, which faith alone can sound.[41]

Figure 8:
Workshop of Robert Campin, *Annunciation* (*Mérode Altarpiece*), ca. 1427.
Oil on panel, 64.14 × 63.18 cm (25.25 × 24.87 in.).
New York, NY (US), Metropolitan Museum of Art.

Sacramental Presence

In the Catholic world, the symbolic valence of the real transpires in the church's liturgy, where ordinary objects—bread, wine, water, oil—are invested with sacramental power. The pictorial device of hidden symbolism, in fact, could reveal the spiritual content of material signs employed in the liturgy, as in Hugo van der Goes's *Adoration of the Shepherds* panel, where the body of the newborn Jesus appears above a conspicuously displayed sheaf of wheat (**figure 9**). The sheaf is positioned in the lower center of the painting, right above the altar where the priest saying Mass consecrated the bread, which, in Catholic belief, becomes Christ's body. Some forms of Protestantism, on the other hand, repudiating aspects of traditional sacramental theology and suppressing the liturgical forms which had communicated its meaning, lacked a way of visualizing the mystical depth of things. The heritage of earlier imagery offered a solution, suggesting the symbolic potential of ordinary objects, and a new kind of image was thus born, which transferred to domestic contexts a contemplative gaze hitherto reserved to ecclesiastical surroundings.

The parallel with Catholic liturgical experience invites a further reflection. In the Mass, things that are visible—bread and wine—yield before the power of something that remains invisible: Christ's body and blood. Looking at the consecrated bread and chalice of wine, believers adore the Savior, even though they cannot see him. In my reading, a similar leap of perception was operative in *vanitas* images, which show attractive objects insufficient to satisfy human spiritual hunger, but do not show the one who does satisfy, Christ, whose very absence made him *present*.

This perceptual tension is something we all occasionally experience, namely, the intuitive feeling that "there is more here [in a person or situation] than meets the eye". This is particularly important in the Christian's life of faith, and the New Testament repeatedly makes clear that, when his contemporaries looked at Jesus, they intuited he was more than the babe in swaddling clothes or the itinerant preacher that he appeared to be (and really was, but not only). They sensed he was more than what they saw, but could not yet see the fullness of his being. Jesus himself, at times, raised the level of tension, as when he told Martha, whose brother Lazarus had just died, "I am the resurrection and the life. Those who believe in me, even though they die, will live, and everyone who lives and believes in me will never die", and then asked, "Do you believe this?"[42]

Seeking faith, Jesus often asked his disciples to believe what they did not see. At the Last Supper, for example, he solemnly affirmed that bread and wine were his body and blood, although his listeners continued to see only bread and wine. Even his culminating gesture, physical resurrection from the dead, was invisible: no one actually saw him emerge from the tomb, and the New Testament proclaims his rising without ever describing it. What is more, in the Gospel accounts of his meetings with disciples in his risen condition, they have initial difficulties in recognizing him.

The problematic, intermittent or ambiguous visibility of the risen Jesus, and the physical absences that confirmed his spiritual presence, fascinated seventeenth-century Dutch artists, Rembrandt van Rijn in particular, who returned again and again to the subject of the *Supper at*

Figure 9:
Hugo van der Goes, *Adoration of the Shepherds* (*Portinari Altarpiece*), 1477–1478 (detail).
Oil on panel, 253 × 304 cm (99.6 × 119.68 in.).
Florence (Italy), Gallerie degli Uffizi.

Emmaus, in which, on Easter evening, the risen Jesus accompanied two disciples who did not yet know of his resurrection and did not recognize him.[43] Discoursing with them as the three left Jerusalem, but never revealing his identity, the man accepted the disciples' invitation to take supper with them in a village along the way, Emmaus, where they finally grasped that their companion was Jesus when they saw him bless and break the bread.[44] At the moment they understood, however, he vanished from their sight! An extraordinary drawing attributed to Rembrandt, in the Fitzwilliam Museum at Cambridge, inv. n.2139 (**figure 10**), captures the moment, showing the two amazed disciples staring at an empty chair on the far side of the table, where Jesus's disappearance in that instant confirms that indeed it was he, and no other, who just broke bread with them. The only signs of his presence are a residual efflorescence and a disturbance of the atmosphere that Rembrandt indicated with rapid pen strokes and chalk heightening above the empty chair.

Figure 10:
Rembrandt van Rijn (attributed), *Supper at Emmaus*, ca. 1640.
Pen, brown ink, brown wash, heightened with white, on paper, 19.8 × 18.3 cm (7.79 × 7.2 in.).
Cambridge (England), The Fitzwilliam Museum, inv. n.2139.

This is an extreme example, of course: dramatic, practically theatrical, akin to Italian prototypes Rembrandt could have known. More significant, for the point I am trying to make, is the *invisibility* implicit in the artist's numerous half figures of Jesus, where Rembrandt's choice of a young Jewish model made the hieratic *Christ* of earlier iconography effectively disappear.[45] With typical Protestant attention to the Scriptures, which, again, insist that Jesus's contemporaries did not clearly perceive him as the Messiah, Rembrandt shows Jesus as a handsome Jew in his early thirties, vibrant with a humanity that, in its very freedom from traditional formulae, communicates more than mere human status (**figure 11**). For his contemporaries, Rembrandt's option for evangelical *silence* in depicting Christ was probably more eloquent than the rhetoric used by theologians, whether Catholic or Protestant. In these extraordinary images, life itself, pulsing with intelligence and feeling, becomes the hidden symbol—or, rather, sacrament—of God's presence.

Significant Understatement

Another Dutch master of the seventeenth century, Johannes Vermeer, allows us to bring these observations back to our theme, for Vermeer's scenes of ordinary people often have the character of genre paintings and employ still-life elements similar to those we see in *vanitas* images.[46] With this difference however: where *vanitas* iconography stresses the superficiality of relational situations and the caducity of material things, Vermeer invites viewers to discover a quiet dignity in the women and men he depicts, imbuing the objects they possess with mystery. A servant girl pouring milk from a jug (**figure 12**),

Figure 11:
Rembrandt van Rijn, *Head of Christ*, ca. 1648–1656.
Oil on oak panel, 35.8 × 31.2 cm (14.09 × 12.28 in.).
Philadelphia, PA (US), Philadelphia Museum of Art.

a lady reading a letter, an astronomer at his desk before a globe of the world: in Vermeer, these subjects have a poetry rooted in the artist's inner life that touches the things as well as the people he saw every day. Of all his mature works, the only one lacking these qualities is Vermeer's Italianate *Allegory of Faith*, in which Dutch Protestant understatement is swallowed up by the grandiloquence of the Catholic baroque (**figure 13**).

Lest it seem factious to underscore these stereotypes, we should note that Vermeer's life was shaped by both religious cultures. His father was Protestant, his mother, from Antwerp, Catholic, and he, in turn, married a Catholic woman, residing with her in his mother-in-law's house in the Catholic quarter of Delft. Thus, although he wields them awkwardly, the traditional liturgical objects in his *Allegory of the Catholic Faith*—the crucifix, the chalice, the large altarpiece—must have been familiar to him. Yet, it was everyday things that stirred his poetic vein—the jug, the globe, the letter—not the paraphernalia of ritual, and, in that respect, Vermeer helps us grasp the way in which *vanitas* images were received. His women and men are contemplatives, and the way they use objects has something prayerful about it. The paintings on the walls of the rooms they occupy are never *vanitas* images, but Christian or mythological subjects. Yet, if we imagine Vermeer's personages contemplating the kind of works our essay treats, we feel they would have gone far beyond the obvious.

Figure 12:
Johannes Vermeer, *The Milkmaid*, ca. 1660.
Oil on canvas, 45.5 × 41 cm (17.91 × 16.14 in.).
Amsterdam (the Netherlands), Rijksmuseum.

Vanity of Vanities

Vanitas images were not pretexts for celebrating a luxury that viewers formally condemned, nor was their magnificence an index of hypocrisy. Rather, the illusory joy conveyed by things shown reminded believers of a beatitude, which "no eye has seen, nor ear heard", but which "God has prepared for those who love him."[47] Indeed, if artists showed the "vanities" they represented as alluring, they did so to exalt the spiritual victory of those who, perceiving the fallacy, chose truth instead. Ecclesiastes's affirmation that "*all* is vanity" includes that affirmation itself, since beyond the futility of material things is spiritual truth.

In any case, terms like *futility*, *vanity*, and *fallacy* are misleading, for the beauty of the things shown in *vanitas* images is real and their allure legitimate. Ecclesiastes himself admits that "moreover, it is God's gift that all should eat and drink and take pleasure in all their toil", and further insists that "whatever God does endures forever" and we should therefore neither add to, nor subtract from, what he has given.[48] *Vain* and *false* is only our assumption that the good we see today is all the good there is, the joy we experience today is all there is of joy. For, although God "has put a sense of past and future into their minds, yet they cannot find out what God has done from the beginning to the end" and as a result must continue searching.[49]

To "find out what God has done from the beginning to the end", mortals must turn to him who says: "I am the Alpha and the Omega [...] the first and the last, and the living one, I was dead, and see, I am alive forever and ever; and I have the keys of Death and of Hades".[50] Emphasizing the futility of mere earthly pleasures, *vanitas* images in fact transmit an eschatological message, implying—in what they do *not* show—belief in eternal life and in joys that last.

Figure 13:
Johannes Vermeer, *Allegory of the Catholic Faith*, ca. 1670.
Oil on canvas, 114.3 × 88.9 cm (45 × 35 in.).
New York, NY (US), Metropolitan Museum of Art.

Vanitas images do not claim that the attractive things they show are bad, but only that, for those who seek to comprehend God's project "from the beginning to the end", they are inadequate. In the fine homes of church-going burghers, such images echoed the apostle Paul's warning that "time has grown short" and that, in consequence, "let even those who have wives be as though they had none, and those who mourn as though they were not mourning, and those who rejoice as though they were not rejoicing, and those who buy as though they had no possessions, and those who deal with the world as though they had no dealings with it. For the present form of this world is passing away."[51]

A final artwork can help make the point: Vermeer's *Woman Holding a Balance* (ca. 1664) in the National Gallery of Art, Washington, DC, with its *vanitas*-style still-life of gold and pearls (**figure 14**). On the wall of this woman's handsome room is a painting illustrating the *Last Judgment*, showing the risen Christ who, as history's final arbiter, will weigh the value of human actions in the balance. Perhaps aware of the image behind her, the woman, deeply pensive, calculates her riches with detachment, as if remembering Paul's admonition to use wealth as if it were not one's own. The National Gallery website suggests that the scene may indeed echo Ignatius of Loyola's advice, in his *Spiritual Exercises*, that the faithful, prior to meditating, first examine their conscience and weigh their sins as if facing judgment day. The online comment adds: "Only such introspection could lead to virtuous choices along the path of life", and concludes, "*Woman Holding a Balance* thus allegorically urges us to conduct our lives with temperance and moderation. The woman is poised between the earthly treasures of gold and pearls and a visual reminder of the eternal consequences of her actions".[52]

Vanitas images, too, urge viewers to live with temperance and moderation, mindful that the world as we know it is passing away.

Figure 14:
Johannes Vermeer, *Woman Holding a Balance*, ca. 1664.
Oil on canvas, 39.7 × 35.5 cm (15.62 × 13.97 in.).
Washington, DC (US), National Gallery of Art.

[1] For an overview of the *vanitas* genre painting, see BERGSTRÖM 1956; STERLING 1959; ROSENBERG, *et al.* 1966; HAAK 1984; SKIRA 1989; WESTERMANN 1996; FRANITS 2004; EKSERDJIAN 2007; and PESCIO 2015.

[2] William Shakespeare, *King Lear*, London, 1608, Act 3, Scene 2.

[3] For further reading see ZERI AND DOLCETTA 1998, but also LANGMUIR 2006, ad vocem, and *GOVIER 2009*, ad loc.

[4] See COOK 2010, p. 458–460.

[5] See RUPP 2002.

[6] BOSING 1994, p. 29–30.

[7] The normal 'Wheel of Fortune' iconography has a figure on the upper rim of the wheel, shown as 'king' and expressing success; one on the wheel's right side, shown 'descending'; another at the wheel's lowest point, signifying failure; and a final figure at the right, shown 'ascending'. The most monumental example of the theme is that shown in figure 5, the *Wheel of Fortune* in the pavement of the nave of Siena Cathedral, a work of 1864 that reproduces the *fortunae rota cum hominibus* ('wheel of fortune with men') originally laid on November 10, 1372. See CACIORGNA 2004, p. 82–87.

[8] VERDON 1996, p. 47–51.

[9] There is much discussion on how to name this painting. A *Deposition* or *Taking Down from the Cross* normally shows the cross and people lowering Christ's body. Neither of these is visible in Pontormo's painting, nor is it a *Burial of Christ*, as it is sometimes called, since the 'burial' iconography shows the tomb. Hence, the choice to use this more descriptive and accurate title.

[10] See MACHIAVELLI 1961, p. 292, in which he quotes Ezek. 13:10. Author's translation.

[11] See Ezek. 13:4–9.

[12] "Hanno messo la terra ad sacco, non senza qualche crudeltà di occisione, de la quale non si è possuto far meno [...] La presa di Prato così subita e cruda, quantunque io ne abbia preso dispiacere, harà portato questo bene, che sarà esempio di terrore alli altri [...]". See VILLARI 1895, p. 176. The English translation was made by Marino Sanudo.

[13] Ibid.

[14] See the *Vita di Pontormo* in VASARI 1906, vol. VI, p. 245–295, but especially p. 251–255.

[15] "Colui che dà le leggi alla natura, / e i vari stati e i secoli dispone, / d'ogni bene è cagione, / e il male, quanto permette, al mondo dura:/ onde, questa figura contemplando, si vede/ come con certo piede/ l'un secol dopo l'altro al mondo viene, / e muta il bene in male, e 'l male in bene." Author's translation. Ibid., p. 255.

[16] "Per lo disagio che patì per guadagnare dieci scudi poco appresso si morì." Author's translation. Ibid., p. 254.

[17] "How far today's Capitoline hill is from that described by Vergil, when he sang, 'This space, once covered with horrid vegetation, is now golden'", and suggested that the same verse should now be translated: "Once golden, the Capitoline has become squalid again, covered with thorn bushes and undergrowth". See. D'ONOFRIO 1989, p. 67, see also *Aeneid* VIII, 348.

[18] "It must be admitted that it was less difficult for the Ancients—because they had models to imitate and from which they could learn—to come to a knowledge of those supreme arts which today are most difficult for us. Our fame ought to be much greater, then, if we discover unheard-of and never-before-seen arts and sciences without any model whatsoever. Who could ever be hard or envious enough to fail to praise [Filippo Brunelleschi] the architect on seeing here such a large structure [the dome of Florence Cathedral], rising above the skies, able to cover with its shadow all the Tuscan people, and constructed without the aid of centering or great quantities of wood. Since this work seems impossible of execution in our time, if I judge rightly it was probably unknown and unthought-of among the Ancients." ALBERTI 1966, p. 39–40.

[19] VERDON 2005a, p. 73–74.

[20] See the *Vita di Michelangelo* in VASARI 1906, vol. VII, p. 135–317, but see p. 135–136 in particular.

[21] "Gli piaceva quella solitudine della Certosa [...] si vede apertamente che quel cervello andava sempre investigando nuovi concetti e stravaganti modi di fare". In this way, Vasari explains "la stranezza e nuova ghiri bizzosa maniera che gli pose addosso quella solitudine, e lo star lontano dal commercio degli uomini". Author's translation. Ibid., vol. VI, p. 269.

[22] For an excellent overview of the period, see CHADWICK 1964.

[23] For the period following the Treaty of Westphalia, see CRAGG 1960, as well as TREVOR-ROPER 1967.

[24] BUNYAN 1967, p. 84.

[25] Ibid., p. 85

[26] À KEMPIS 2008, p. 28–29.

[27] Ibid.

[28] Ibid. Thomas à Kempis's conclusion is similar to the summation appended to Ecclesiastes's book: "Fear God and keep his commandments; for that is the whole duty of everyone. For God will bring every deed into judgment, including every secret thing, whether good or evil." Eccles. 12:13–14. As for Deuteronomy, see Deut. 6:13.

[29] The concept, introduced by Gregory the Great in chapter one of his account of the life of Saint Benedict in the second book of Gregory's *Dialogues* (see GREGORIUS 1924), is present as early as Augustine's *Letter to Proba*. It was revived in the fifteenth century by the German Cardinal Nicholas of Cusa, who wrote *De Docta Ignorantia* (*On Learned Ignorance*) in 1440. See GRÜNDLER 1989, p. 178.

[30] Eccles. 1:8. À KEMPIS 2008, p. 28–29.

[31] Ibid.

[32] 1 Cor. 1:20.

[33] *THE NEW TESTAMENT* 1972. 1 Cor. 1:18–31.

[34] 1 Cor. 1:26.

[35] For further reading, see SMITS 1933; but also TIMMERS 1947, PANOFSKY 1953, and FRIEDLÄNDER 1956, as well as WHINNEY 1968.

[36] John 1:9. For further reading on Campin's artwork, see DE TOLNAY 1939, CAMPBELL 1974, and THÜRLEMANN 2002.

[37] MEISS 1976, p. 3–18. See also VERDON 2005b, p. 9.

[38] See John 1:1.

[39] See John 1:3, 10.

[40] See Col. 1:16–17.

[41] RAHNER 1966, p. 221–252, especially p. 224. See also TILLICH 1960, p. 2, as well as DULLES 1980, p. 51–73; RICOEUR 1962, p. 191–218; WHEELWRIGHT 1962, p. 94 et seq.; POLANYI AND PROSCH 1975, p. 66–71; FAWCETT 1971, p. 21–25; and BARBOUR 1974, p. 58 et seq.

[42] John 11:25–26.

[43] KEYES 2011, p. 1–29. See also SILVER AND PERLOVE 2011, p. 75–107.

[44] Luke 24:13–35.

[45] See DEWITT 2011, p. 109–145, and DUCOS 2011, p. 161–177.

[46] For further reading on Vermeer, see GOLDSCHEIDER 1958; but also BLANKERT 1978, MONTIAS 1989, RENZI 1999, and ARASSE 2006.

[47] 1 Cor. 2:9.

[48] Eccles. 3:13–14.

[49] Eccles. 3:11.

[50] Rev. 1:8, 17–18.

[51] 1 Cor. 7:29–31.

[52] WHEELOCK JR., http://purl.org/nga/collection/artobject/1236.

Entries

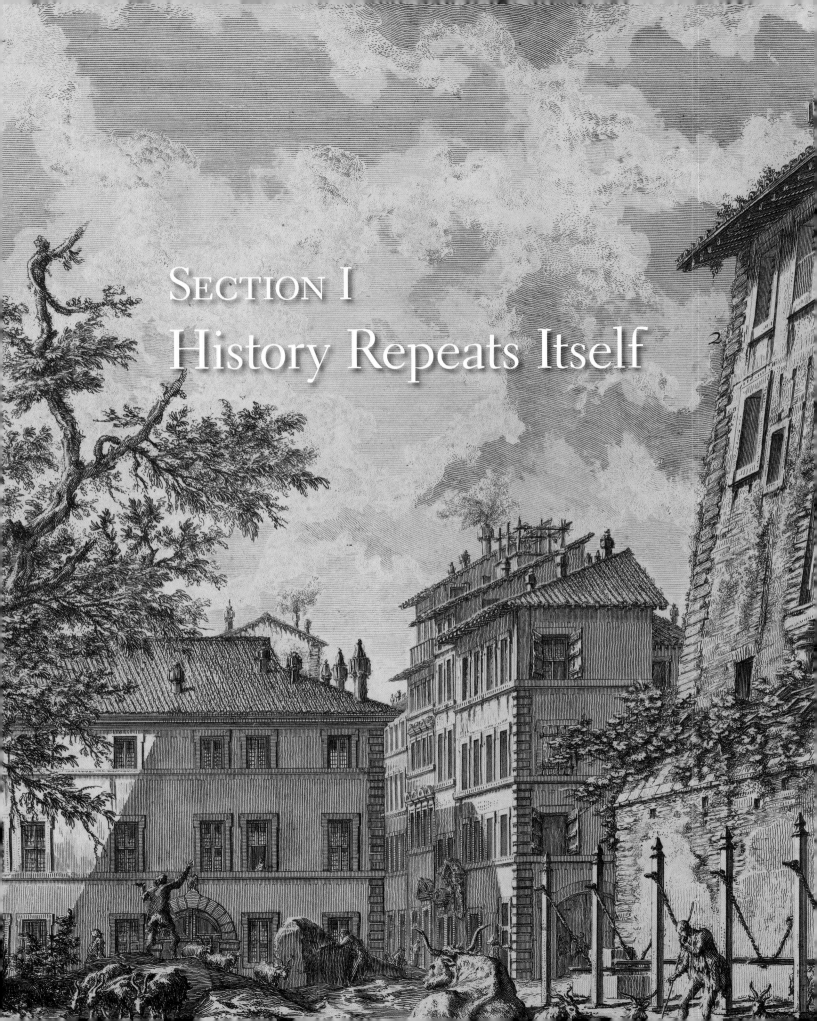

Section I
History Repeats Itself

As soone, as wee to bee, begunne;
We did beginne, to be Vndone.

FINIS AB ORIGINE PEDET

ILLVSTR. XLV.

Book. I.

The Cyclical Nature of Time and
The Worthlessness and Transience of Human Endeavors

The works of art presented here reflect important and recurring themes found in the book of Ecclesiastes: the cyclical nature of time and the worthlessness and transience of human endeavors. Nowhere is this better represented than in the ruins of the Eternal City—Rome.

The images capture our enduring fascination with the impressive achievements of an ancient empire, whose ambitious monuments, now in ruins, maintain a link to a bygone era. They also carry an important message, that nothing and no one, no matter how wealthy or powerful, escapes the inevitability of death.

A generation goes, and a generation comes, but the earth remains forever.

The people of long ago are not remembered, nor will there be any remembrance of people yet to come by those who come after them.

(Ecclesiastes 1:4, 11)

Cat. n. I.1

Bernardo Bellotto

Capriccio with the Capitoline Hill

ca. 1742.

Oil on canvas, 116 × 131 cm (45.66 × 51.57 in.).

Parma (Italy), Galleria Nazionale di Parma, inv. 237.

The Venetian artist Bernardo Bellotto often signed his works *Bernardo Canaletto*, and at times referred to himself only as Canaletto, a move designed to reinforce his connections with his master and uncle, the famous Antonio Canaletto, renowned for his city views and *capricci* (paintings that combine real and imaginary elements—see also **cat. n. I.9**). Bellotto was famous for his *vedute* (views) of European cities.[1] A valuable resource in Canaletto's workshop was a series of twenty-three drawings that provided a repertory of Roman subjects used by Canaletto, and also by Bellotto. In 1742, on the advice of his uncle, he traveled to Rome to undertake his own studies, resulting in paintings such as this *capriccio* of the Capitoline Hill in Rome.[2] Bellotto left Italy permanently and went to Dresden, Germany, in 1747, where he became court painter to Frederick Augustus II, king of Poland and elector of Saxony under the name of Augustus III. He lived mostly in Dresden from 1747 to 1766, and in 1767 settled in Warsaw (Poland). The quality and accuracy of his views of the city were such that they were used to rebuild the historic quarters of the capital after its near destruction during World War II.

Bellotto framed this composition with a fictitious architectural archway—a means to enable the artist to create deep shadow in the foreground, which serves to emphasize the sunlit architectural details of the *veduta* beyond. The low vantage point enhances the viewer's sense of the monumentality of the scene. The activity of people and animals in the foreground introduces a liveliness that offsets the austerity of the buildings. The medieval church of Santa Maria in Aracoeli can be seen on the left-hand side with the Palazzo Nuovo and the Palazzo Senatorio, set further back. At the top of the monumental stairway known as the Cordonata, is the antique statue of Castor with his horse marking the entrance to the Piazza del Campidoglio.

The *palazzi* and the piazza were designed by Michelangelo, and Bellotto's keen interest in architecture is apparent in the attention that he gives to the reproduction of detailed features of the façade of the Palazzo Nuovo, which was completed during the seventeenth century, and which replicated the Palazzo dei Conservatori opposite it, begun in 1563.[3] The buildings house the Capitoline Museums, which were opened by Pope Clement XII in 1734 to exhibit his large and exceptional collection of antiquities. The Capitoline was the center of ancient Rome and had been the seat of political power into the modern era. Because of this, objects from antiquity and buildings designed during the Renaissance held a special attraction for Grand Tourists.[4] Bellotto's romanticized painting would have been of great appeal to those seeking a quality souvenir that embodied not just an exceptional display of artistic skill but also hinted at the intellectual and cultural benefits of their own experience. In addition, the figure of the beggar, in the right-hand foreground, echoes the pose of the celebrated ancient Roman statue, *The Dying Gaul,* which had been rediscovered in the seventeenth century and was (and still is) part of the Capitoline Museums collection, where it was greatly admired and copied by artists. Bellotto's reference to the statue served to announce his own artistic skill and knowledge.

The somewhat precarious stone blocks balanced on the arch, home to the encroaching vegetation, introduce a slight tension to the work, and shift it beyond the realm of mere *vedute*. Bellotto deliberately creates a contrast between the slightly crumbling stone work of the ancient arch, the unfinished façade of the medieval Santa Maria in Aracoeli, and the bright, crisp lines of the newly constructed Palazzo Nuovo. By juxtaposing the old with the new, it acts as a reminder to the viewer that these architectural structures, symbols of civilization and the sophistication of mankind, are an attempt at creation, and are designed to outlive us. However, even the thickest of stone will eventually crumble to dust. Although they provide a link to the past and potentially the future, they paradoxically act as a reminder that we, too, like all who came before us, are destined to die and to crumble into dust.

Audrey Nicholls

[1] GAUK-ROGER 1998.

[2] *BERNARDO BELLOTTO* 2001.

[3] HARTT AND WILKINS 2006, p. 664–666.

[4] PAUL 2012, p. 21.

Cat. n. I.2
Niccolò Codazzi

The Campo Vaccino Looking toward the Capitoline Hill

ca. 1682–1684.
Oil on canvas, 72 × 95.5 cm (28.34 × 37.59 in.).
Rome (Italy), Galleria dell'Accademia Nazionale di San Luca, inv. 167.

Niccolò Codazzi was born in Naples. He was the son of the Bergamasque artist Viviano Codazzi, and it can be difficult to tell their works apart. Indeed, it was thought that *The Campo Vaccino Looking toward the Capitoline Hill* was a work by Viviano. However, since 1993 the Galleria dell'Accademia di San Luca has attributed it to Niccolò on the basis of differences in lighting effects between the two artists. Henceforth, the painting has been dated to between 1682 and 1684, which coincides with a stay in Rome around that time by Niccolò. Viviano specialized as a painter of *vedute*, painting topographical views of Rome and Naples in particular. Niccolò joined his father in Rome at an early age, and later he worked in Paris, where he became a member of the Académie Royale in 1681, and produced two paintings for the Queen's Staircase in Versailles. He then returned to Italy, eventually settling in Genoa where he died in 1693.[1] It is likely that Viviano—one of the pioneers of accurate architectural painting—trained in Rome, and may have been influenced by the fictive architectural paintings, known as *quadratura*, of Agostino Tassi, as well as the urban views of Claude Lorrain and Herman van Swanevelt, passing these interests on to Niccolò.[2]

The popularity of *vedute* paintings came about in the seventeenth century due to the transfer of the *quadratura* painting techniques, which concentrated on the rendering of perspective in architecture and the inclusion of antique elements, in particular the architectural orders, onto easel painting. Many *quadraturisti* (painters specializing in *quadratura*) based their art on architectural treatises such as Andrea Palladio's *I quattro libri dell'architettura*, published in Venice in 1570. However, Viviano Codazzi appears to have based his work on Giacomo Barozzi's *Regole delli cinque ordini d'architettura*, first published in 1562 and considered the canonical presentation of the architectural orders until the twentieth century. Indeed, this style of working, where the use of architectural treatises prevailed over observational drawing, lasted well into the eighteenth century.[3]

Vedute paintings provided visual balance to art collections, which frequently covered entire walls, as the vertical and horizontal structures of the compositions offered a contrast to less structured subject matter.[4] However, as David R. Marshall points out, in order for these paintings to be more than mere "record of fact", they required animation, and this was achieved through the inclusion of people and animals for which a specialized painter was usually employed, and, in addition to this staffage, dramatic lighting techniques.[5] In the painting in question, it is evident that Codazzi studied Lorraine and Van Swanevelt's use of *repoussoir*,

namely, an object placed in the foreground to direct the eye into the painting. The inclusion of the figures also introduced a *vanitas* element to the works, as the contrast between the living, blithely going about their daily lives, and the ancient ruins and their echoes of lives long forgotten is unavoidable. As pointed out in Ecclesiastes 1:11: "The people of long ago are not remembered, nor will there be any remembrance of people yet to come by those who come after them."

During the seventeenth century, the Roman Forum was known as the *Campo Vaccino* (see **cat. nos. I.3–I.7**). The church of Santa Maria Liberatrice, demolished at the beginning of the twentieth century (see also **cat. n. I.4**), dominates the left-hand foreground, obscuring and narrowing the view, creating a greater focus on the Capitoline Hill in the background. The tower of the Palazzo Senatorio can be seen in the distance, framed between the surviving columns of the ancient Temple of Castor and Pollux (again, see **cat. n. I.4**). The attraction of these works lay in their architectural precision and detail, highlighting the aesthetic, technical, and monumental achievements of the ancient Romans as well as remarkable sixteenth- and seventeenth-century additions to the city. They also served to showcase the abilities of the Codazzi, father and son, and those that followed them, of which there were a notable number of exceptional eighteenth-century artists, including Giovanni Battista Piranesi and Antonio Canaletto, as well as artists such as Giovanni Paolo Pannini, Hubert Robert, and Bernardo Bellotto, who expanded the genre through their development of *capricci* paintings. (see **cat. nos. I.1, I.9**).[6]

Audrey Nicholls

[1] Marica Marzinotto, *Niccolò Codazzi, Campo Vaccino*, Accademia Di San Luca, www.accademiasanluca.eu/it/galleria_accademica/opere/archive/cat_id/1840/id/1637/campo-vaccino (accessed August 2017).

[2] TREZZANI 1998, p. 509–510.

[3] MARSHALL 2014, p. 140–161.

[4] MARSHALL 1991, p. 129–131.

[5] Ibid., p. 131.

[6] ANDERS 2014, p. 53. Cat. n. I.3

Cat. n. I.3
Giovanni Battista Piranesi
Veduta di Campo Vaccino

ca. 1775.[1]
Etching, 411 × 552 mm (16.18 × 21.73 in.).
Vatican City, Biblioteca Apostolica Vaticana, *Ashby* Stampe Cartella Piranesi 14, tav. 22.

This view of the Roman Forum from the Capitoline Hill is part of the album *Vedute di Roma* (i.e., *Views of Rome*), which collates 135 prints that Giovanni Battista Piranesi carried out throughout his career, namely between the 1740s and his death in 1778.[2] This print, together with others illustrating various views of ancient and modern Rome (see **cat. nos. I.4–I.8**), became extremely popular especially among Grand Tourists, namely northern European educated noblemen who, to complete their education, undertook a journey through several European countries that had as its main goal the visit to the antique treasures of Italy.[3]

As mentioned above, this print illustrates the Roman Forum, which was also called *Campo Vaccino* (i.e., Cow Field) until the mid-nineteenth century, as it was an area of the city used as a cattle pasture. Its role as the beating heart of ancient Rome's political and economic center declined significantly during the early Middle Ages (i.e., seventh–eighth centuries) when a lack of maintenance of the sewage system serving that area, and the subsequent clogging, caused sediment deposits of mud and soil (further exacerbated following the frequent floods of the Tiber), which led to the gradual landfill of the Forum. So much so, that, by the fourteenth century, this landfill had become no less than six meters (i.e., 19.68 feet) high.[4] In the Middle Ages, and then in the early modern era (sixteenth and seventeenth centuries in particular), the area underwent further substantial changes, in that many churches and houses developed around the ancient Roman ruins, and the areas not built upon became a cattle pasture. By the seventeenth century, very little of the original Roman buildings, monuments, and squares were clearly visible. An extraordinary illustration of the condition of this area of the city during the eighteenth century is provided by Piranesi in this celebrated print.

In the foreground, on the left, we see the half-buried Arch of Septimius Severus (third century CE) with various shrubs flourishing on its surface. On the right are the three remaining columns of the Temple of Titus and Vespasian (first century CE), and on the far left, the remains of the Temple of Saturn (fifth century CE). Among the other significant landmarks that can still be seen today, there is the Curia Iulia (44 BCE) (on the right, behind the Arch of Septimius Severus) which—back then—was the Church of Sant'Adriano al Foro.[5] Opposite the Curia (and behind the Temple of Titus and Vespasian), the three surviving columns of the Temple of Castor and Pollux, and behind it, the Horti Farnesiani, or Farnese Gardens, which were celebrated gardens on the Palatine Hill belonging to the Farnese papal family.[6] Opposite the gardens, on the left-hand side of the print, is the Temple of Antoninus and Faustina (second century CE), which was turned into a church (the Church of San Lorenzo in Miranda) between the seventh century and the eleventh century CE.[7] In the far background, from left to right, are the Basilica of Maxentius, the Colosseum, the Church of Santa Francesca Romana, and the Arch of Titus.

Born in Venice (1720), where he was trained as a landscape artist, Piranesi arrived in Rome in 1740, and lived there until his death. In the Eternal City, he developed a fascination for antiquity, poetically evoked in his prints, in which the archaeological remains are looked back on with regret and nostalgia. The *vedute* of Rome that Piranesi presents to us fall within the genre of the eighteenth-century *veduta* (*vedutismo*, in Italian)—a detailed and accurate landscape, which could be either painted or drawn or etched. While 'aligned' with the trend of the *veduta*, Piranesi's views stand out because of a distinct and—in scholar Randolph Langenbach's words—"greater scenographic creativity, producing an extraordinarily large body of work that is more evocative than any of his contemporaries."[8] Indeed, Piranesi's etchings reveal his utmost admiration for ancient Roman art and architecture, the majestic decadence of which he wanted to immortalize through his prints to preserve them from the unstoppable "injuries of time" and from those who were "clandestinely destroying [the remains] to sell the rubble for [the construction] of modern buildings."[9]

Despite his "preservation activism", the result of his prints are views replete with melancholy originating in a nostalgic vision of a grandiose past, tragically lost and visible only through mostly ignored and repurposed ruins, often turned into shops, or surrounded by hovels, a part of the everyday life of the Roman citizens that passed them by, or lived or worked among them, unaware of the magnificent past right next to them.[10] It was, in fact, the very juxtaposition of modern and ancient city that deeply struck the imagination of Piranesi and the Grand Tourists. Indeed, Rome presented itself as a unique city where what was left of ancient monuments, buried in the ground and covered in shrubs, coexisted with medieval and modern buildings erected throughout the centuries by the pontiffs and their noble families, or with cultivated fields and pastures, or both. Therefore, the contrast between modernity and antiquity created a 'sublime conflict', in which the ancient ruins were seen as both a symbol of the overpowering assaults of time, nature, and man, but also as 'heroic' bulwarks surviving these same destructive forces.[11] In the eyes of the viewer, this had an overwhelming emotional impact, and was cause for incommensurable awe.

Corinna Ricasoli

1. Vestigie del Tempio di Giove Tonante
2. Vestigi del Tempio della Concordia
3. Arco di Settimio Severo
4. Antico Erario oggi S. Adriano
5. Tempio d'Antonino, e Faustina
6. Tempio di Romolo e Remo ora S. Cosimo e Dam.º
7. S. Francesca Romana
8. Arco di Tito
9. Vestigie del Palazzo de' Cesari nel Palatino
10. Colonne del Tempio di Giove Statore
11. Micragfioni dei Rostri
12. Avanzi del Tablino della Casa aurea di Nerone
13. Colosseo
14. Avanzo di due Triclinj della detta Casa aurea
15. Vestigie delle Terme di Tito

Veduta di Campo Vaccino

Presso l'Autore a Strada Felice nel palazzo Tomati vicino alla Trinità de' monti

Piranesi del Scolp.

[1] Giovanni Battista Piranesi hardly ever dated his etchings. Hence, the date of each view is still a matter of debate among scholars. See BATTAGLIA 2006, p. 93. However, the date appearing here is the one suggested by Arthur Mayger Hind. See HIND 1922, p. 36.

[2] WILTON-ELY 1994, p. 176.

[3] The term Grand Tour seems to have made its first appearance in the book *The Voyage of Italy* by Richard Lassels, published in 1670, in which the author says: "[...] and no man understands Livy and Caesar [...] like him, who hath made exactly the Grand Tour of France, and the Giro of Italy." See LASSELS 1670, no page number but de facto p. 22.

[4] MAETZKE 1986, p. 373.

[5] The Curia Iulia had been turned into a church already since 630 CE.

[6] For further reading on this and other Roman gardens, see FAGIOLO AND SCHEZEN 2001.

[7] For more on this church, see AIT 2002.

[8] LANGENBACH 2014, p. 95.

[9] "[...] vedendo io, che gli avanzi delle antiche costruzioni di Roma, sparse in gran parte per gli orti ed altri luoghi coltivati, vengono a diminuirsi di giorno in giorno o per l'ingiuria de' tempi, o per l'avarizia de' possessori, che con barbara licenza gli vanno clandestinamente atterrando, per venderne i frantumi all'uso degli edifizj moderni; mi sono avvisato di conservarli col mezzo delle stampe [...]." PIRANESI 1756, p. 1 of the Prefazione. The translation from Italian into English is by the present writer. For more on the approach to history and antiquity in the eighteenth century see ARGAN AND CONTARDI 1983, p. 351–352.

[10] This fitting definition of Piranesi as a "preservation activist" is by Randolph Langenbach. See LANGENBACH 2014, p. 97.

[11] See, in this respect, Goethe's comment, written in 1786, on the damages ancient monuments suffered from man's actions in VON GOETHE 1885, p. 123: "Yesterday I visited the nymph Egeria, and then the Hippodrome of Caracalla, the ruined tombs along the Via Appia, and the tomb of Metella, which is the first to give one a true idea of what solid masonry really is. These men worked for eternity—all causes of decay were calculated, except the rage of the spoiler, which nothing can resist."

Cat. n. I.4
Giovanni Battista Piranesi

Veduta di Campo Vaccino

ca. 1750–1778.
Etching, 467 × 700 mm (18.38 × 27.55 in.).
Vatican City, Biblioteca Apostolica Vaticana, *Ashby* Stampe Cartella Piranesi 16, tav. 1.

As with all the prints displayed in this exhibition, this alternative view of the *Campo Vaccino* is also part of the album *Vedute di Roma*. Contrary to the previous view, this does not illustrate the Roman Forum from the Capitoline Hill, but from within the Forum itself. In the foreground, we see cattle and cowherds with their carriage close to a large fountain "made of granite"—as Piranesi himself writes in the legend of the print. Our attention, however, is immediately caught by the three majestic columns belonging to the Temple of Castor and Pollux (484 BCE), the remaining structure of which was excavated in 1899.[1] Behind the columns is the former Church of Santa Maria Liberatrice al Foro Romano (1300s, but refurbished in the seventeenth century); further back (and counterclockwise) are the Horti Farnesiani, the Arch of Titus, the Church of Santa Francesca Romana and the Colosseum (see also **cat. n. I.3**). Opposite Santa Maria Liberatrice, on the left-hand side of the print, we see the colonnade of the Temple of Antonino and Faustina, which houses the Church of San Lorenzo in Miranda (see **cat. n. I.7**).[2] Next to it and further in the distance, the Temple of Romolus (75 CE), which later became the vestibule of the adjacent Basilica of Santi Cosma e Damiano.[3] Further behind, there is the Basilica of Maxentius (312 CE) (see also **cat. n. I.8**).

By looking at this print, it is evident that the true protagonist is space. The vastness of the 'cattle field'—enclosed by former temples, now churches, and by medieval and Renaissance buildings and ruins—only finds its equivalent in the broad sky, which the *Campo Vaccino* almost seems to mirror. In contrast with this almost bare archaeological area buried like a corpse under meters of landfill, is the row of trees on the left, and the herdsmen, artisans, and passersby that seem to live their everyday life completely unaware of the majestic ruins that stand above and below them. The row of trees highlights the vanishing point of the composition, which coincides with the Arch of Titus, whereas the three surviving, solitary columns of the Temple of Castor and Pollux almost function as a theater wing.

Such a theatrical and, in some instances, dramatic treatment of space in Piranesi's prints is not surprising, as it is consistent with his artistic education. Indeed, Piranesi studied with the celebrated *vedutista* Giuseppe Vasi, who in turn studied with the well-known architect Filippo Juvarra, whose set designs arguably surpassed those by the renowned scenographer Ferdinando Galli Bibbiena.[4] Their approach to space was of enormous influence on Piranesi.

This theatrical element certainly helps convey a sense of 'majestic decay' of the grandiose monuments of the past emphasized by the indifference of people as they pass by. As Patrice J. Marander convincingly points out:

> Whereas the previous Roman *vedutisti* had created convincing images of the city—or fanciful imaginary views of it in which the antique ruins always played a picturesque part—Piranesi added a decidedly theatrical dimension to his composition. [...] Through the manipulation of shades of black, the bold balancing of voids and volumes, and the creation of originally sited perspectives, his etchings attain a heroic level that sets them above the perfunctory repertoire of places pictured by other artists. It was often with these compelling images in mind that some of the most enlightened travelers to Rome approached the city, only to be sadly let down.[5]

Some travelers were indeed disappointed upon their arrival in the Eternal City. On their way to Rome most of their expectations had been met, borne out by the numerous Italianate landscapes that illustrated a solitary countryside, colorful skies, animal flocks, scattered inhabitants, and lonely ruins.[6] Then, finally, the longed-for arrival in Rome. The city, however, did not appear as majestic as they had anticipated. Piranesi's extremely popular *Vedute* created an image of Rome that led some—such as German writer Johann Wolfgang von Goethe—to speak of Piranesi's Rome as a beautiful and sensational lie.[7] However, even if not 'authentic', Piranesi's Rome was nevertheless "true to its legend."[8]

Despite the initial disillusionment, Grand Tourists were still fascinated by ancient Roman monuments, and particularly by those in the Roman Forum, made famous by Piranesi. As with tourists today, it was their wish to return home with a souvenir of their Italian journey. The ruins of the temples of the Roman Forum—particularly those of Castor and Pollux, and Vespasian and Titus (see **cat. n. I.5**)—were considered to be outstanding examples of classical architecture, and a source of great admiration and interest. The great interest in these ruins created a market for high quality souvenirs that were much sought-after, in particular small-scale marble models of the remains of these two temples, which the Grand Tourists could take back home to decorate and furnish their elegant homes (see **figure 1**, p. 75).[9]

Corinna Ricasoli

Veduta di Campo Vaccino

[1] Coarelli and Usai 1975, p. 82–83.

[2] The Church of Santa Maria Liberatrice was demolished in 1900 to bring to light the early-Christian Church of Santa Maria Antiqua (6th century CE). For Santa Maria Antiqua, see *Santa Maria Antiqua* 2016; for Santa Maria Liberatrice al Foro Romano, see Barsanti and Beccaloni 2013, p. 253–269.

[3] For further reading on this Basilica, which incorporated several Roman buildings, see Chioccioni 1963.

[4] See Garms 1982, p. 117–122, and Gavuzzo-Stewart 1999 (especially Chapter IV).

[5] Marandel 1987, p. 7–8.

[6] Praz 1964, p. 54.

[7] Ibid.

[8] Marandel 1987, p. 8.

[9] As it still is today, all landmarks (including those in other Italian cities such as Naples) were reproduced as expensive souvenirs. These two temples are but an example of these items. For further reading on this very interesting subject, see Pinelli 2010.

Figure 1:
Anonymous, *Model of The Temple of Castor and Pollux*, Rome, early 1800s.
Marble, height 71 cm (27.95 in.).
Dunham Massey, Cheshire (England), National Trust, NT 932609.1.

Cat. n. I.5
Giovanni Battista Piranesi

Veduta del Tempio di Giove Tonante

ca. 1756.
Etching, 565 × 793 mm (22.24 × 31.22 in.).
Vatican City, Biblioteca Apostolica Vaticana, Ashby Stampe Cartella Piranesi 15, tav. 4.

As with the other prints by Piranesi on display in this exhibition, this too belongs to the celebrated album *Vedute di Roma*. Contrary to Piranesi's inscription on the etching, this view shows the Temple of Vespasian and Titus (81 CE), the three columns of which are still standing in the Roman Forum today, at its western end. When Piranesi carried out this print, however, those remains were believed to belong to the Temple of Jupiter Tonans (literally, "Thundering Jove"), which was in the Roman Forum, but in another location. The Temple of Vespasian and Titus was built by emperor Titus to honor his father, Vespasian, who had been deified after his death, hence the construction of the temple. The building, however, was completed only after Titus's death at the hands of his own brother Domitian.[1] As was the case with the Temple of Castor and Pollux (see **cat. n. I.4**) this temple was also reproduced as a marble model to be sold as a souvenir to the Grand Tourists (see **figure 1** below).

As is evident in Piranesi's print, the temple was almost entirely buried by meters of landfill and surrounded by vegetation and cattle (hence the name of the area, *Campo Vaccino*).[2] On the left-hand side of the print, we see the remains of the Tabularium (78 BCE)—namely the state archives and records office of ancient Rome, built on the front slope of the Campidoglio (Capitoline Hill). This building was later incorporated into the medieval Palazzo Senatorio (i.e., Senatorial Palace) which stood atop, and in the sixteenth century, into the Palazzo Senatorio we still see today, designed by Michelangelo Buonarroti.[3] In the background, there are Renaissance buildings typical of early modern Rome.

These buildings, combined with the disinterested passersby and cattle that surround the temple, alongside the huge trees next to the majestic ruins, provide the viewer with a very strong sense of the passage of time and the inevitable oblivion we and our endeavors will face. In Ecclesiastes 1:11 we read that the "[...] people of long ago are not remembered, nor will there be any remembrance of people yet to come by those who come after them." These words perfectly describe the scene in this outstanding print, which also inevitably brings to memory the verses by the celebrated Italian poet Giacomo Leopardi (heavily influenced by Ecclesiastes).[4] In one of his most moving poems, titled *La sera del dì di festa* (i.e., *The evening of the holiday*) of ca. 1820—in a bitter meditation on how "all things in the world must pass, / and scarce leave trace behind them"—he writes:

> [...] Where is now
> The noise of those old nations? Where is now
> The fame of our great ancestors, the might
> Of that imperial Rome, the arms, the clash
> Wherewith the round earth and the ocean rang?
> All is repose and silence, and all hushed
> The world is; and of them we speak no more.[5]

Much has been said on Piranesi and whether he should be seen as a late-baroque, neoclassical, pre-romantic, or even romantic artist. Understandably, this is no place to address these lengthy academic discussions, but it is true that in his love for ruins, and in the way he illustrates them—as if, to put it in Mario Praz's words, they were "nature added to nature"—we can find the roots of a somewhat pre-romantic sensitivity.[6] Indeed, nineteenth-century writer Gustave Flaubert, upon his arrival in Rome in 1846, wrote: "I love above all the sight of vegetation resting upon old ruins. This embrace of nature, coming swiftly to bury the work of man the moment his hand is no longer there to defend it, fills me with deep and ample joy."[7]

Corinna Ricasoli

Figure 1:
Anonymous, *Model of The Temple of Vespasian and Titus*,
Rome, early 1800s.
Marble, height 71 cm (27.95 in.).
Dunham Massey, Cheshire (England),
National Trust, NT 932609.2.

[1] COARELLI AND USAI 1975, p. 75.

[2] The columns are 15.20 meters (49.86 ft.) high.

[3] COARELLI AND USAI 1975, p. 47.

[4] For further reading on Leopardi and Ecclesiastes, see MARCON AND CASOLI 2007.

[5] [...] *A pensar come tutto al mondo passa, / e quasi orma non lascia.* [...] *Or dov'è il suono / di que' popoli antichi? Or dov'è il grido / de' nostri avi famosi, e il grande impero / di quella Roma, e l'armi, e il fragorio / che n'andò per la terra e l'oceano? / Tutto è pace e silenzio, e tutto posa / il mondo, e più di lor non si ragiona.* For the English translation cited here, see LEOPARDI 1923, p. 211–213.

[6] PRAZ 1964, p. 37.

[7] VERSTEGEN AND CEEN 2013, p. 182.

Veduta del Tempio di Giove Tonante

Cat. n. I.6
Giovanni Battista Piranesi
Arco di Settimio Severo
ca. 1759.[1]
Etching, 378 × 593 mm (14.88 × 23.34 in.).
Vatican City, Biblioteca Apostolica Vaticana, *Ashby* Stampe Cartella Piranesi 14, tav. 45.

As with the previous prints, this view of the Arch of Septimius Severus is also part of the album *Vedute di Roma* which, as mentioned earlier (see **cat. n. I.3**), gathers together a series of views of Roman landmarks as they appeared in the eighteenth century.

This print provides a view of the Roman Forum, not from the Capitoline Hill, but from the Forum itself. As already mentioned in **cat. nos. I.3–I.5**, this area was also called *Campo Vaccino* (i.e. Cow Field) until the mid-nineteenth century, as it was an area of the city used as a cattle pasture. In the foreground, on the left, we see one of the few surviving monumental columns of the Forum, the Column of Phocas (608 CE) who was the Eastern Roman Emperor who donated the Pantheon to Pope Bonifacius IV in order for it to be used for Christian worship.[2] On the far right, we see part of the Curia Iulia (44 BCE).[3] In the mid-ground, at the center of the image, is the half-buried Arch of Septimius Severus (3rd century CE).[4] Further to the right is the seventeenth-century church of Santi Luca e Martina, and next to it, the Curia Iulia (44 BCE), known at that time as the Church of Sant'Adriano al Foro (see **cat. n. I.3**). In the background, on the left, we can see part of the Campidoglio—the center of civic government on the Capitoline Hill.

Surrounding these half-buried monuments, we see people engaged in their daily activities—a shepherd watching his flock, wheelwrights, passersby. None of them seem to notice the gran-diosity of the monuments that stand beside them. In addition, the altered proportions between people and monuments contributes to the sense of majesty of the ruins, which, in all their ancient grandiosity, 'stoically' and almost 'proudly' stand and resist the passing of time.

Piranesi's extremely complex treatment of the copperplate, and the dramatic use of light and dark tones imitating light and shadow, known as *chiaroscuro*, make his views particularly engaging, and the buildings, ruins, and prosaic scenes therein very powerful. As Professor John Wilton-Ely points out, "through [the *Vedute di Roma*], which were spread all over the Continent by means of the Grand Tour, Piranesi was not only to revolutionize the conventional form of the *veduta* but was to transform the European vision of classical antiquity."[5]

Corinna Ricasoli

[1] HIND 1914, p. 263.

[2] DE VORAGINE 2012, p. 756.

[3] For further reading on this monumental column, see CLARIDGE, *et al.* 2010, p. 87–88.

[4] For more information on this arch and its reliefs, again see ibid., p. 78–79.

[5] WILTON-ELY 1994, p. 176.

Arco di Settimio Severo.
Nel mezzo di questo passava l'antica Via sacra che portava i Trionfi in Campid.º

1. Erario antico, o come altri Tempio di Saturno, oggi S. Adriano. 2. S. Martina architettata da Pietro da Cortona Chiesa dell'Academia del Disegno detta di S. Luca. 3. L'antico Carcere mamertino, nel quale sono state posti i SS. Pietro e Paolo. Sopra questo si vede eretta la Chiesa di S. Giuseppe. 4. Salitta che porta al Campidoglio. 5. Abitazione del Senatore Romano. 6. Chiesa dell'Araceli fabricata sopra i fondamenti del Tempio di Giove Capitolino. 7. Colonna rimasta in piedi creduta del Ponte, che fece fare l'Imperatore Caligola per passare dal Palatino al Campidoglio.

Piranesi Architetto fec.
Presso l'Autore a Strada Felice nel palazzo Tomati vicino alla Trinità de' monti

Cat. n. I.7
Giovanni Battista Piranesi

Veduta del Tempio di Antonino e Faustina in Campo Vaccino

ca. 1758.
Etching, 406 × 546 mm (15.98 × 21.49 in.).
Vatican City, Biblioteca Apostolica Vaticana, inv. *Ashby* Stampe Cartella Piranesi 14, tav. 42.

This *View of the Temple of Antonino and Faustina in Campo Vaccino*, also part of the album *Vedute di Roma*, illustrates one of the most interesting examples of 'superimposition' of Christian churches and, more generally, of medieval and Renaissance buildings onto pre-existing ancient Roman constructions. The temple was built in 141 CE by Emperor Antoninus Pius and dedicated to his wife, Faustina, who had been deified after her death. When the emperor himself died in 161 CE, his name was added to the dedication, hence the nomenclature. Sometime between the seventh century and the eleventh century CE, the temple was turned into a Christian church—San Lorenzo in Miranda.[1] On the occasion of Emperor Charles V's visit to Rome, in 1536, many renovations were carried out throughout the city in anticipation of his visit. The medieval church of San Lorenzo in Miranda also underwent such renovations, which involved the demolition of part of the medieval church to make the colonnade—formerly included within the early-Christian building—visible again. This entailed the construction of a new façade, which is the one we see in this print, built between 1601 and 1614.[2] This *veduta* is an extraordinary example of the development of Rome—an early modern city built on top of medieval and ancient Roman constructions. We can truly say that "a generation goes, and a generation comes, but the earth remains forever."[3] The city has remained, the generations who inhabited it throughout the centuries have not.

Interestingly, in this print, we see a man admiring the ruins before him (in the foreground, on the left). He is probably looking at some of the details from the architrave of the temple with the aid of a spyglass. But aside from this one enthusiast, the other tiny figures are busy with their daily errands, such as the wheelwrights on the right, and pay no attention to the grandiosity of this ancient building. Here too, Piranesi distorts the proportions by making the temple look bigger, and the passersby smaller, thus enhancing the sense of grandeur of the remains. The appeal Piranesi's views hold also derives from the harsh but fascinating contrast between grandiose monuments, princely palaces, and hovels standing right next to them. This contrast of magnificence and squalor, of wealth and poverty, is evident in this print, where the inquisitive nobleman inspecting the architecture shows little interest in the panhandler on the steps of the church. As Mario Praz points out, Piranesi's Rome is a city without a middle class, a city of magnificence but also a *cour des miracles*,

> "inhabited by noble revelers and abject plebeians [...] Piranesi's Rome is a city where everything is alive, everything is aggressive: the vegetation moves to the assault of the walls, the walls move [as if] to the assault of the sky, and men—tiny worms that are in the shadow of those massive [buildings]—populate them precisely like worms feeding upon a carcass."[4]

Corinna Ricasoli

[1] For more on this church, see AIT 2002.

[2] *ROMA* 1999, p. 276.

[3] Eccles. 1:4.

[4] PRAZ 1964, p. 46–49.

Piranesi Architetto fec.

Veduta del Tempio di Antonino e Faustina in Campo Vaccino.   1. *S. Lorenzo in Miranda de' Speziali*

Cat. n. I.8
Giovanni Battista Piranesi
Veduta degli avanzi del Tempio della Pace
ca. 1757–1774.
Etching, 416 × 552 mm (16.37 × 21.73 in.).
Vatican City, Biblioteca Apostolica Vaticana, *Ashby* Stampe Cartella Piranesi 14, tav. 38.

This *View of the Remains of the Temple of Peace* (later reissued under the title *View of the Remains of the Dining Room of the Golden House of Nero, Commonly Called the Temple of Peace*), is an interesting example of misattributions and errors made at the dawn of modern archaeology. The ancient Roman monument illustrated in this print is in fact the Basilica of Maxentius and Constantine (312 CE), and not Nero's *Domus Aurea*, nor the Temple of Peace (although they are both close by).

The monumental ruins of the basilica are surrounded by blocks of marble and the remains of ancient walls, as well as a modern building—a house. An imposing site where justice was administered and business conducted has been transformed into a simple, wide courtyard amidst grazing land. As with previous prints, the scene is populated with tiny figures, mostly common-ers and shepherds looking after their flock. They carry on with their daily activities, regardless of the enduring yet fragile ruins standing before them. The visible cracks on the walls and arches of the Roman basilica—akin to deep wrinkles on a face—along-side the shrubs that have taken up residence there are perhaps the most touching detail of this print. The ruins have survived the centuries, but nevertheless they are slowly surrendering to the passage of time. While celebrating the grandiosity of this now distant past, of this lost civilization that built such majestic mon-uments, and by illustrating them with incommensurable awe,

Piranesi is also writing the "monumental epitaph" of Rome's for-mer glory.[1] As Mario Praz points out, Piranesi was mainly a 'me-morializer'—the past he illustrates is irretrievably lost and can only be reminisced through imagination.[2] In other words, Pira-nesi is the 'bard' of what Praz fittingly defines as "monumental death."[3]

"Then I considered all that my hands had done and the toil I had spent in doing it, and again, all was vanity and a chasing after wind", says Ecclesiastes.[4] Piranesi's prints clearly illustrate that time passes, and all human endeavors with it. With a very well-chosen and vivid metaphor, Praz says that, in Piranesi's *ve-dute*, the shrubs growing on such majestic ruins are like grave vermin feeding upon a corpse, and that Piranesi's vision of Rome is "both a dramatic elegy of the ancient city and the first wail of the modern city".[5]

Corinna Ricasoli

[1] PRAZ 1964, p. 40.

[2] Ibid., p. 45. See also *PIRANESI E LA VEDUTA* 1989.

[3] PRAZ 1964, p. 45.

[4] Eccles. 2:11.

[5] PRAZ 1964, p. 45.

Questo fù cominciato da Claudio e terminato da Vespasiano Imperatori.   *Ricchezze dell'Imperio Romano.*   1. *Da qui fù trasportata*
Conservavansi in esso il Candellabro, le Tavole della Legge, l'Arca, la Manna,   *da Paolo V. la gran Colonna, che si vede innalzata nella Piazza di S. Maria M.re*
le Trombe, colle quali pubblicavasi il Giubileo, Vasi Sacri, e tutte le migliori   2. *Muri e Piloni, che reggevano la parte opposta del Tempio.*   3. *Muro di Por-*
Spoglie del Tempio di Gierusalemme, distrutta da Tito; e finalm.te le maggiori   *tico contiguo ad altro moderno.*

VEDUTA DEGLI AVANZI DEL TEMPIO DELLA PACE.

Cat. n. I.9
Hubert Robert

Capriccio of Ancient Ruins

after 1756–1757.
Oil on canvas, 98 × 135 cm (38.58 × 53.14 in.).
Parma (Italy), Galleria Nazionale di Parma, inv. 1148.

Hubert Robert was a highly successful and prolific French artist who is renowned for his romanticized architectural landscapes, known as *capricci*, which are paintings that combine real and imaginary archaeological elements.

Initially educated in Paris, he travelled to Rome as part of the French Ambassador's entourage in 1754, where he spent the following eleven years, and it was there that he developed his lifelong interest in the depiction of the city's ancient ruins. In Rome, he was taught at the French Academy by Giovanni Paolo Pannini and also came into contact with the works of Giovanni Battista Piranesi (see **cat. nos. I.3–I.8**).[1] In addition to his Italian inspired works, Robert also painted images of France and he mixed easily in the most elite and influential Parisian circles. During the French Revolution, he was arrested and narrowly avoided the guillotine, and throughout his incarceration he continued to paint. He also went on to design interiors and gardens for the aristocracy and wealthy bourgeoisie. From the 1770s until the time of his death, Robert was involved in the development of the Louvre as 'Keeper of the King's collection', and then as curator of the National Museum of the Arts. He died in 1808, and according to his friend Élisabeth-Louise Vigée Le Brun, he died "brush in hand" as he prepared to go out to dinner.[2]

According to the Galleria Nazionale di Parma, it has not been possible to confirm the date of *Capriccio of Ancient Ruins*, but it is considered to date to after 1756–1757, about two years after Robert's arrival in Rome.[3] Robert returned to Paris in 1765, where he achieved great success drawing upon his Roman studies to create paintings that tapped into a popular demand for works that depicted the ancient world.[4] This was a fashion that had been triggered by the archaeological discoveries at Pompeii and Herculaneum in the first half of the eighteenth century.

The charm of Robert's paintings resides in a conjured nostalgic monumentality that celebrates the romance of ancient landscapes alongside the simplicity of pastoral pleasures. In the foreground of *Capriccio of Ancient Ruins*, a large statue reminiscent of the celebrated *Silenus and Dionysus* after Lysippus, is the dominant feature of an ornamental fountain, its prestige lost in the passage of time, a message conveyed by its transformation into prosaic washbasin.[5] On the right-hand side, a horse with rider and companions amiably ramble beneath the ruined remnants of a bygone era. They contrast with the carved stone fragment depicting charioteers and jubilant horses, a vision of pomp and vigor long obsolete, it acts as a reminder of ancient Rome's vain attempt to immortalize its existence. Composite capitals, fallen from great heights, serve as makeshift furniture against a background of precariously tilted triumphant arches, coffered vaults, and a crumbling pyramid. Nature has encroached upon the scene, an unrestrained invader of mortar and stone; it is nature that endures, it is the natural world that stretches its empire as far as the eye can see, its sun rising and setting with each passing day. Robert's contemporary, Denis Diderot, the famous philosopher, writer, and art critic, gave the artist the nickname "Robert of the Ruins" and wrote that "these ruins inspire in me grand ideas. Everything comes to nothing. Everything passes. Nothing in the world endures. Only Time remains".[6]

Audrey Nicholls

[1] DE CAYEUX 1998, p. 448. Robert was likely influenced by Piranesi's *Antichità Romane*, published in 1756. The two must have certainly been acquainted, as Robert stayed in the Palazzo Mancini on the Via del Corso, then seat of the *Académie de France à Rome*, and Piranesi's engraving studio was then opposite the same Palazzo, and many of his pupils were indeed French. See MYERS 1991, p. 172, and ROWELL 2012, p. 12.

[2] DE CAYEUX 1998, p. 449.

[3] See GALLERIA NAZIONALE DI PARMA 2000, p. 117.

[4] TARABRA 2008, p. 75.

[5] The statue in the painting, however, differs from Lysippus's in that instead of a grapevine there is a serpent coiled around the trunk.

[6] D'ARCY WOOD 2001, p. 128. See also DUBIN 2010, p. 2, and ERIKSEN 2014, p. 70.

Cat. n. I.10
Hendrik Frans van Lint

The Colosseum at Rome

1740s.
Oil on canvas, 46 × 66 cm (18.11 × 25.98 in.).
Bradford (England), Bradford Museums and Galleries, inv. 1942-015.

Hendrik Frans van Lint was born in Antwerp, the son of the Flemish painter, Peter van Lint and his wife, Anna Marren. Unlike his father, his style does not reflect an interest in the work of Rubens. This is probably due to the fact that his father was seventy-five years old by the time Hendrick was born in 1684, and subsequently died in 1690.[1] Around 1696–1697 he entered the workshop of Pierre van Bredael and shortly after 1700 he traveled to Rome, where he remained for the rest of his life, apart from a brief return to Antwerp in 1710. He painted numerous images of famous Roman landmarks, both realistic and imaginary, an example of which is this painting of the Colosseum.

Van Lint also liked to paint the countryside surrounding Rome, including Tivoli, with its picturesque landscape and ancient ruins. During these trips, he made preparatory studies for his paintings using pencil and pen or wash drawings. He would then combine these images with imaginary elements creating *capricci* that included buildings, hillsides, foliage, and, frequently, archaeological monuments that he relocated and replicated in great detail. He often signed his paintings as "monsù Studio"— a pseudonym awarded to him by his colleagues in the *Schildersbent*, namely the fraternity of Dutch and Flemish artists in Rome. Edgar Peters Bowran suggests that this pseudonym may relate to his meticulous approach to his work and his fascination with the paintings of Claude Lorrain. Van Lint often copied the works of Lorrain, occasionally signing them with his own name.[2] He was also strongly influenced by Gaspar van Wittel, who was the first artist to introduce the Colosseum as the sole subject of a painting, and the first to make views of the city the primary source of his entire production.[3] Van Lint may have been an associate of Van Wittel's between 1700 and 1710. His paintings were sought after by Grand Tourists and also featured in the prestigious collections of many eminent Roman families. Don Lorenzo Onofrio II Colonna had over seventy of his works in his collection, which were listed in the 1783 inventory of the Galleria Colonna in Rome. Van Lint was accepted as a member of the Congregazione dei Virtuosi al Pantheon in 1744, and elected rector in 1752. He died in Rome in 1763.[4]

The Colosseum provides the dramatic background to this romantic and theatrically staged painting. The massive scale of the Colosseum is over-emphasized through an exaggeration of the inner circumference of the stadium. People and a variety of domestic animals add color and interest to the scene, and also provide a bucolic visual contrast with the original entertainment purpose of the venue, which included witnessing wild animals, gladiators, and prisoners fight for their lives. The associated roar and spectacle of those pastimes has been replaced with a gentle domesticity, reflecting the development of a more civilized society, but one that nonetheless harps back to its ancient visceral roots. An awareness of this additional dimension of the work heightens its appeal, with its bittersweet acknowledgement that everything and everyone has its allotted time and space, all of which swiftly pass. As one of Ecclesiastes's most well-known verses proclaims, "For everything there is a season, and a time for every matter under heaven" (3:1).

Audrey Nicholls

[1] Busiri Vici 1987, p. 27.

[2] Bowron 2000, p. 388. See also Tiberia 2010, p. 372.

[3] Laureati 2005, p. 83–87.

[4] Bowron 2000, p. 388. Other Roman patrician families that collected works by Van Lint include the Altoviti, Capponi, Pamphili, Sacchetti, and Soderini.

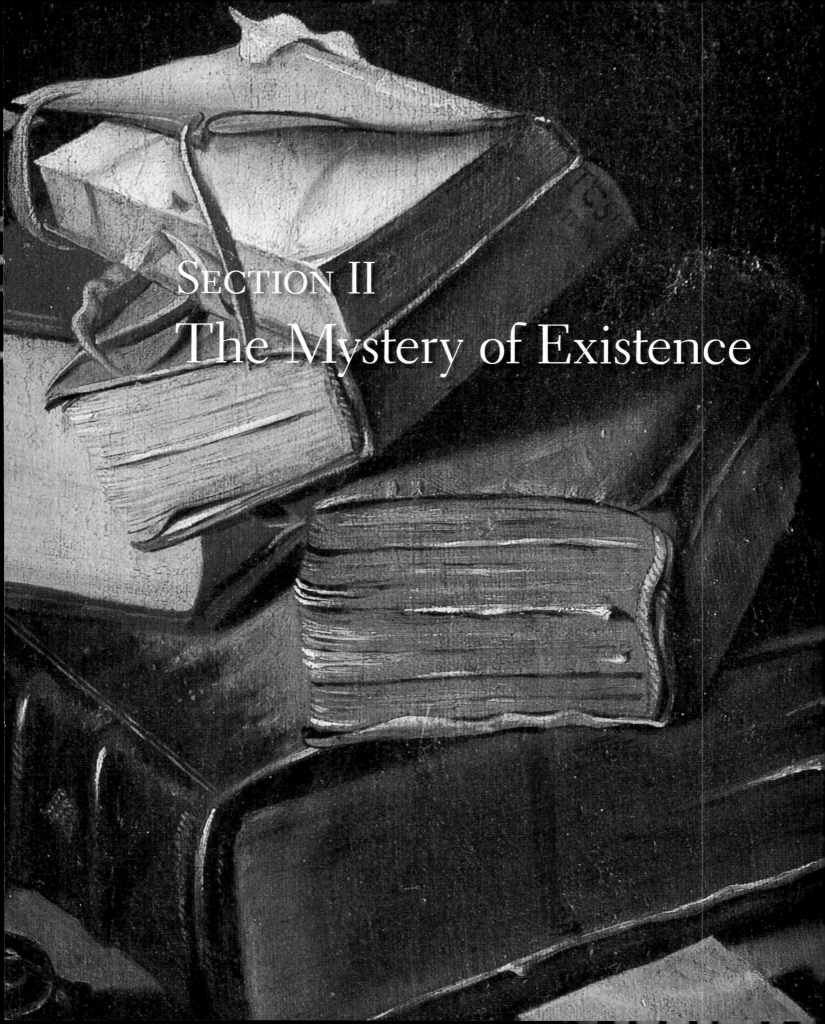

SECTION II
The Mystery of Existence

Above thy Knowledge, *doe not rise,*
But, with Sobrietie, be wise,

PERENOLIASTUMSAPE

ILLVSTR. XIII.

Book.3

The Limitations of Knowledge

Ecclesiastes questions the purpose of knowledge. What, it asks, is to be gained from a lifetime of accumulated learning? Death will come for the wise man as well as the fool.

These paintings from the early modern era glory in the intellectual achievements of humanity—philosophy, science, anatomy, literature, and theology—symbolized by objects such as books, drawings, globes, and artworks. These objects, carelessly piled up and devoid of life, beg the question of how much value should be placed on the pursuit of knowledge. The presence of *memento mori* objects (reminders of the inevitability of death), such as the skull, invited meditation on mortality and the afterlife.

Then I said to myself, "What happens to the fool will happen to me also; why then have I been so very wise?" And I said to myself that this also is vanity. For there is no enduring remembrance of the wise or of fools, seeing that in the days to come all will have been long forgotten. How can the wise die just like fools?

When I applied my mind to know wisdom, and to see the business that is done on earth [...] then I saw all the work of God, that no one can find out what is happening under the sun. [...] even though those who are wise claim to know, they cannot find it out.

(Ecclesiastes 2:15–16, 8:16–17)

Cat. n. II.1
Anonymous (Jacques Bizet?)
Still-Life with Old Books
mid-17th century.
Oil on canvas (possibly originally on panel), 52 × 60.5 cm (20.47 × 23.81 in.).
Inscription: (on a letter at the bottom left) *A Monsieur / Monsieur, C[?] Bizet / annonay.*
Bourg-en-Bresse (France), Musée du Monastère royal de Brou, inv. 853.143.

Books have always been a favorite subject for painters, for formal reasons as much as symbolic, evoking the book, namely the Bible. This *Still-Life with Old Books* represents a pile of old books of the sixteenth and seventeenth centuries, with an inkwell, a pencil-box, and a quill, which seems to have just been used to write a letter.[1] The bird's-eye view could indicate a former function of fireplace-front, intended to plug the unused fireplace during the summertime.[2] If this is the case, these flammable used books assembled in an unbalanced pile, may allude to the books being burnt in the fireplace and reflect the vanity of knowledge. But the effect of this accumulation may just as easily represent a simple descriptive still-life with no moral connotation.[3]

Folded in the foreground on the left, a letter to "Mr. Bizet (at) Annonay", has long been read as the signature of the Flemish painter Charles-Emmanuel Bizet (1633–1691). But his style is obviously different and more related to a French painter. Later, he was supposed to be a painter settled in Annonay, in Ardèche, France. But no record is to be found of a 'Bizet' in the archives in Annonay.

On the other hand, the painting had been acquired by a couple of Bressan collectors, the Lorins, who gave it to the museum of Bourg-en-Bresse in 1853. Moreover, a family of Protestant printers and notaries called Bizet is traceable in Bourg-en-Bresse during all the seventeenth century.[4] We know as well that one of the girls Bizet, Antoinette, married a bookseller from Grenoble, François Chaix (so-called Laplace). In particular, a master painter and glazier, Jacques Bizet, is quoted at Bourg in 1652–1654.[5] Annonay (in Ardèche) was also a Protestant territory, which could explain the links with the family. Except for portraits, inscriptions are generally a signature of the painter and do not indicate the patron.

Magali Briat-Philippe

[1] For further reading on this painting, see the following exhibition catalogs in which it was featured: LES PEINTRES DE LA RÉALITÉ 1934, TROIS SIÈCLES DE PEINTURE FRANÇAISE 1949, NATURES MORTES FRANÇAISES 1951, NATURES MORTES 1954, NATURES MORTES 1956, LE XVIIE SIÈCLE FRANÇAIS 1958, THE SPLENDID CENTURY 1960, LE LIVRE 1972, LES VANITÉS 1990, L'ÂGE D'OR 1991, PEINTURES FRANÇAISES ET ITALIENNES 1999, p. 41, *1853 UN MUSÉE EST NÉ* 2003, p. 67, LE TROMPE-L'OEIL 2005, p. 96–97, ORANGERIE 2006, p. 116–117. But see also DE LASTIC SAINT-JAL 1955, p. 26–31, VERGNET-RUIZ AND LACLOTTE 1962, p. 226, FARÉ 1962, vol. I, p. 48, 108, 109; vol. II, fig. 137, BATTERSBY 1974, p. 118, FARÉ AND FARÉ 1976, p. 149–151, BERGEZ 2004.

[2] FARÉ AND FARÉ 1976.

[3] FOUCART 1990, p. 61.

[4] CHAIX 1977, p. 42. AD01, B277, 270, 271, 274.

[5] See *PEINTURE RELIGIEUSE EN BRESSE* 1984, p. 16 and the archival references therein.

Cat. n. II.2
Jan Davidsz de Heem

Still-Life with Books and a Globe

1628.
Panel, 28.1 × 33.3 cm (11.06 × 13.11 in.).
Inscription: *Johannes / de Heem / Fecit Anno / 1628.*
Amsterdam (the Netherlands), The Kremer Collection, GK-25.

Born in Utrecht in 1606, the earliest work of Jan Davidsz de Heem was influenced by Balthasar van der Ast (1593/1594–1657), although nothing is known about his formative years.[1] In 1625 de Heem moved to Leiden, where he would marry a year later. The painter moved around quite often for work while based in Antwerp from 1636 onward. In 1672, after residing in Utrecht for a number of years, Jan Davidsz returned to Antwerp where he died in 1684.[2] He is generally regarded as one of the most important and multifaceted still-life painters of the Dutch Golden Age. Among his many children were Cornelis de Heem and Jan Jansz de Heem, who also would become painters.

Still-lifes with books were extremely popular in the second quarter of the seventeenth century, particularly among painters in Leiden.[3] It is not entirely clear who brought the genre to the northern Netherlands initially. Its earliest practitioner appears to have been Jacques de Gheyn II, who is thought to have painted a still-life with this motif as early as 1621, although the date on the painting is uncertain. An important role should be assigned to De Heem himself, whose dated still-lifes with books must be counted among the first of their kind. In any case, the subject was tackled by the pick of Leiden painters, among them two of De Heem's contemporaries, who in 1628 had yet to make a name for themselves: Jan Lievens and Rembrandt. De Heem, who was nothing if not chameleon-like in his style, was clearly inspired by the painters active in his new place of residence.[4] It seems likely that there was a large market in Leiden for still-lifes with books: the local university, the country's oldest, drew many students, scholars, and writers who would have appreciated the motif. In this context, it is interesting to note that Johan Coornhert, De Heem's stepfather, was a bookbinder and bookseller, and he may have been helpful in finding buyers for the painter's work.

This signed *Still-Life with Books and a Globe* of 1628 dates from the Leiden period of Jan Davidsz de Heem.[5] The panel is an early work in the artist's oeuvre, whose dated pictures begin to appear from 1625. The table is piled with a total of eleven volumes, arranged haphazardly on top of and next to one another, as well as on the lectern. Next to the inkstand we even find one that has been rolled up. The painter added both his signature and the date in the very center, on a book with bent and curling pages that has apparently lost its binding. De Heem painted six further still-lifes with books while in Leiden, where he had settled by 1625.[6] In addition, we know of a genre scene, also dating to 1628, which includes not only a self-portrait but also a table laden with books (Oxford, Ashmolean Museum).[7] The style and technique, as well as the visible window and wooden partition, indicate that the Kremer painting was the first in the series.[8]

The subtle light falling on the rear wall is depicted with exceptional beauty in all of De Heem's still-lifes with books. The (natural) source of this light, however, is revealed only in this earliest example, where we find a window at the upper left. The rendering of the light in rectangular patches is also unique, as in the other still-lifes a single diagonal serves to divide the lambent and shadowed areas.[9] To the left of the table set against the wall in a comparable work of 1629 (Liberec, Oblastní Galerie), we see the wooden partition the artist apparently used to vary the luminosity.[10] A similar partition can be found in our version as well, as was revealed during restoration in 2002. This makes the sharp delineation of the bright areas entirely plausible. The restoration also revealed the picture's original delicate tonality. The extremely soft colors used for some of the book covers—characteristic of the still-lifes of the Leiden masters in this period—demonstrate the young painter's talent.

Symbols of mortality were often incorporated into this sort of picture: in De Heem's other still-lifes with books we find such explicit references as a skull, the word *finis* (end), or the phrase *vanitas vanitatum* (vanity of vanities), which actually appears twice.[11] In this case, however, the symbolism is subtler. Books played an important role in seventeenth-century moral thought, being regarded as a source of wisdom and knowledge. In an emblem book of 1611 by Gabriel Rollenhagen, for example, the reader is encouraged to renounce worldly goods and devote himself to study.[12] In this picture, both the books and the globe may be understood as sources of—transient—knowledge. As we see here, though, even books themselves—which were to make the ideas of mortal authors immortal—are subject to decay: they have clearly been well used—their pages are creased and torn and some have even lost their bindings—and can thus be interpreted as a literal reference to the limitations of knowledge and the ephemerality of all earthly things. In two other similar De Heem still-lifes, both also of 1628—one in the Mauritshuis in The Hague (**figure 1**, p. 97), the other in the Frits Lugt Collection in Paris—this symbolic dimension is enriched by the inclusion of publications dealing with the vicissitudes of fate.[13] It is even thought that the two aforementioned still-lifes in The Hague and Paris were painted on commission.[14] The monochrome, finely tuned coloration and loose brushwork make the Kremer version a particularly attractive painting, one whose earliest provenance could be traced no further back than the twentieth century.[15] In

the painting in question, however, not a single edition can be identified, as no titles or authors' names, even if fragmentary, have been reproduced.

Quentin Buvelot

[1] Segal 1998.

[2] Ibid.

[3] See Buvelot and Buijs 2002, p. 205 (footnote 214 and bibliography therein).

[4] Like his contemporaries, Lievens and Rembrandt, he, too, used the handle of his brush or other sharp tool to scratch into the wet paint, in order, for example, to indicate the pages of several of the tomes. De Heem used this technique in his other still-lifes as well.

[5] For further reading on this painting, see Schreuder 1997, p. 13–18, Buvelot 2002, p. 99, 100, 205 (footnote 111), Buvelot 2008a, p. 84–87.

[6] For a discussion of the other still-lifes, see Buvelot 2002, p. 96, 98, 205–206 (footnotes 7–12).

[7] Segal 1991, p. 127–128, Meijer 2003, p. 216–219.

[8] The date on one of the works in this group (formerly Aachen, Suermondt-Ludwig Museum, lost since World War II) is not, as previously thought, 1625 but rather 1629.

[9] Broos 1987, p. 185–189, Segal 1991, p. 128–131.

[10] Wieseman 1999, p. 168.

[11] Segal 1991, p. 130.

[12] Ibid.

[13] Buvelot 2002, p. 99, 101.

[14] Ibid., p. 101.

[15] The monogram 'DG' on the wax seal on the reverse of the panel—probably belonging to the former owner—has yet to be identified.

Figure 1:
Jan Davidsz de Heem, *Still-Life with Books and a Violin*, 1628.
Oil on panel, 36.1 × 48.5 cm (14.21 × 19.09 in.).
The Hague (the Netherlands), Mauritshuis, inv. 613, acquired with the support of the Rembrandt Association, 1912.

Cat. n. II.3
Simon Luttichuijs

Still-Life with a Skull

ca. 1645.
Oil on panel, 47 × 36 cm (18.50 × 14.17 in.).
Gdańsk (Poland), Muzeum Narodowe w Gdańsku, MNG/SD/96/ME (MNG SD/330/M).

Simon Luttichuijs often painted still-lifes and was influenced by Jan Davidsz de Heem. The Leiden-style still-lifes by the extraordinarily talented Luttichuijs are full of artistry and most of them are *vanitas* paintings.[1]

The objects depicted in the Gdańsk painting were not imagined. The skull rests on an open book of alchemy by Andreas Libavius titled *Syntagma Selectorum*, published in Frankfurt in 1611. Next to it, propped up against a globe, is the anatomical treatise *Historia Anatomica Humani Corporis et Singularium eius partium multis* by Andreas Laurentius, published in Frankfurt in 1600. One can even make out the page numbers: 190 and 191. The anatomical figures in the textbook duplicate the famous *De humani corpori fabrica Libri Septem* by Vesalius, published in Basel in 1543. The painting contains interesting images, including a study of an old woman, Rembrandt's mother, known from a copperplate print by Jan Lievens and a copy of his painting *Bust of an Old Woman* (Los Angeles, Getty Center Archive) from ca. 1630–1631. By the wall, we can see a frame with a *Bust of a Man in Oriental Dress*, known from a copy of a painting by Lievens (Paris, Musée du Petit Palais) and a copperplate print by Lievens with the same title; perhaps a portrait of Rembrandt's father. There are two prints lying on the table: Rembrandt's *Old Man with Flowing Beard* from 1631 and a *Bust of a Bearded Old Man* by Jan Lievens. All these *tronies* (physiognomic studies depicting different human types) were made in Rembrandt's studio in close collaboration with Jan Lievens (1630–1631). On the left side on the wall is a small still-life. High above the table, precisely along the axis of the globe and the skull that lies in front of it, hangs a glass ball on a string which reflects part of the still-life placed in the foreground, a painter at his easel with another man behind him inside a studio with a large window.

Luttichuijs's painting is an example of so-called scholarly types of still-lifes in the Leiden tradition. They usually depicted tables covered with books, old documents, celestial and terrestrial globes, and literary texts, objects which carried an underlying meaning that would have been clear to the viewer. Their iconography can be explained within the context of the Calvinist creed as well as an elaborate agenda concerning art theory, the artist's status and his appearance on the surface of polished objects.[2] The artworks depicted in the painting, in this case prints from Rembrandt's studio (mainly by Lievens), paintings and actual books, not only represent the idea of transience according to the maxim of *homo bulla*—man is a bubble (as ex-pressed by the skull and the spherical, reflective mirror suspended on a string)—but also give an affirmative assessment of the value of work and artistic effort.[3] The painter, who is reflected in his work, plays the role of a moral mediator between the viewer and the painting, and underscores Christian virtues. His image in the spherical mirror alludes to the *topos* of pictorial perfection related to the idea of the mirror of nature, perceived in the context of mortality and revealed by the allusion to emblem 55 *Quae itali vulgo impresas vocant* from the *Nucleus Emblematum Selectissimorum*.[4] The emblem depicts Jesus delivering a sermon against a landscape background, with a sphere suspended above the crowd with one hand coming out from the clouds holding a string, while another cuts this string with scissors. The image is accompanied by a caption in Latin saying: "All human things are suspended by a thin thread, God will cut it when He likes, be pious."[5] The same emblem appeared in Wither's English edition from 1635, and urged man to be contrite and repent.[6] Only God's grace can lead to eternal life. This was an admonition to artists and their viewers to recognize the true value of a spiritual life and their fate.

The glass sphere in the Gdańsk painting, in the form of a convex mirror that reflects distorted images, was a reminder of the sham of things temporal, and also underscored the importance of painting (as in the image as a mirror of nature) and its effect on the viewer by creating an illusion of reality. In addition to the faithful mirror image there was deceit: the deception that the image engendered in the viewer. This ambiguity was related to how man perceives the world and to pictorial illusion.[7] Such a concept was a sign of artistic virtuosity. Playful irony and craftiness invited the cultured viewer to a game. The aim was not to obscure any trace of falsifying reality, but to draw attention to the image: a painterly artifact with a high market value, an advertisement for art. The image of the artist reflected in the sphere is the work's signature and an expression of opinions on the role of the artist's studio. The Gdańsk painting by Luttichuijs is one of the earliest allegorical still-lifes to underscore the artist's status, as it was painted before David Bailly's *Self-Portrait with Vanitas Symbols* (Leiden, Stedelijk Museum De Lakenhal) from 1651, and before the paintings by Cornelis Brize, Samuel van Hoogstraten, Cornelius Norbertus Gijsbrechts, and Abraham van Beyeren that took up the same subject.

Beata Purc-Stępniak

[1] There are four known versions of this still-life by Luttichuijs, which are mainly identical, except for minor details, in that each painting has different books that are placed in the same way. The making of four similar paintings suggests that they had a special meaning. Perhaps it was Luttichuijs himself that decided to paint them, or Jan Lievens (whom he knew) and Rembrandt ordered the paintings as a "memento" of their collaboration with Luttichuijs in Leiden, ca. 1631–1632. This symbolic message in Luttichuijs's four paintings is indicated in that they can be grouped into pairs. With similar props, the Gdańsk painting can be matched with the one from Amsterdam. The painting comes from the collection of Gdańsk merchant Jacob Kabrun, donated to the Gdańsk Town Council in 1814, and then to the Stadtmuseum Danzig. See SECKER 1913, p. 30–31; *VERZEICHNISS EINES THIELES* 1856, no. 64; *STADTMUSEUM ZU DANZIG* 1902, p. 12; MARTIN 1913, p. XXI; VAN STRATEN 1992, p. 121–142; GÓRECKA-PETRAJTIS AND SZWED 1993, p. 24; PURC-STĘPNIAK 2002, p. 80; PURC-STĘPNIAK 2003, p. 279–300; PURC-STĘPNIAK 2004b, p. 136; PURC-STĘPNIAK 2005, p. 140–142; EBERT 2009, p. 91–112, 355–356, HOLLÄNDER 1923, SUMOWSKI 1983, p. 2938, PURC-STĘPNIAK 2004a, p. 123–124. *OLD MASTER PAINTINGS* 2004, p. 96, cat. 31.

[2] TÜMPEL 1983, p. 314, SCHAAR 1983, p. 348.

[3] See copperplate prints analogous to the prints depicted in the painting in BERNHARD 1976, p. 198, 212, 267, 268 and VAN STRATEN 1992, p. 121–142, BRUSATI 1990/1991, p. 168–182.

[4] See BRUSATI 1990/1991, p. 168–182, BRUSATI 1999, p. 59–71. See also ROLLENHAGEN 1611, and ROLLENHAGEN 1983.

[5] A thread as a symbol of all things and of life subject to death appears on the emblem *Toutes choses sont perissables* by Gilles Corrozet from 1543, see HENKEL AND SCHÖNE 1967, p. 954.

[6] WITHER 1635, p. 213.

[7] Paul (1 Cor. 13:12) was often quoted to express an opinion that the temporal world is a reflection of a delusion and a hindrance on the road to know God. Reaching for the world's riches and gifts leads not only to self-delusion, but also to the damnation of the soul, if it does not recognize its dependence on God in time and succumbs to the illusion of the reflection in the mirror. SCHILLING 1979, p. 65–66; BIAŁOSTOCKI 1982; *LEXIKON DER CHRISTLICHEN IKONOGRAPHIE* 1994, p. 188–190; HARTLAUB 1951, p. 110–111. The same idea was expressed in Otto van Veen's emblematic self-portrait from 1584 (Brussels, Bibliothèque Royale) where the painter depicted himself half turned and looking at the viewer, reflected in a mirror suspended on a string. In a moment, the string will be cut with scissors by Atropos, one of the Fates (for more on Atropos cutting the thread of life, see **cat. n. III.2**—Pietro Bellotti, *The Fate Atropos*). The mirror serves to get to know oneself, so the artist can use it to recognize his mortal nature and the nature of the world. See RAUPP 1984, p. 302, and ASEMISSEN AND SCHWEIKHART 1994, p. 141–142. The artist is a sign of *virtus*. For a painter, time means using his creative capabilities to the fullest, to improve his skills. Just like a mirror, a sphere plays the role of a *vanitas* motif; it is a symbol of how life elapses. Van Veen's self-portrait was inspired by a letter by Horace (Epist. I. 4,13) that recommends to live each day as if it were one's last. Karel van Mander relates this to the artist and his work. See RAUPP 1984, p. 308, PURC-STĘPNIAK 2004a, p. 188–196, *ALBUM WYSTAWY GRZECH* 2015, p. 190.

My Wit *got* Wings, *and, high had flowne;*
But, Povertie *did keepe mee downe.*

INGENIO. PAVPERTATE PREMOR SVBLEVOR

Social Injustices

Concerns regarding the hoarding of wealth and abuse of power generated an interest in social injustice, while images of the suffering poor served as a reminder of social responsibility and as a realization that wealth does not travel into the next life: *As they came from their mother's womb, so they shall go again, naked as they came; they shall take nothing for their toil, which they may carry away with their hands* (Ecclesiastes 5:15).

Again I saw all the oppressions that are practiced under the sun. Look, the tears of the oppressed—with no one to comfort them!

If you see [...] the oppression of the poor and the violation of justice and right, do not be amazed at the matter; for the high official is watched by a higher, and there are yet higher ones over them.

(Ecclesiastes 4:1, 5:8)

Cat. n. II.4
Anonymous (Dirck van Baburen? Jusepe de Ribera?)

Beggar

ca. 1610s.
Oil on canvas, 106 × 76 cm (41.73 × 29.92 in.).
Rome (Italy), Galleria Borghese, inv. 325.

The authorship of this painting is still a matter of significant debate among scholars, and a unanimously accepted attribution has yet to be reached. The two artists most frequently linked with the painting are Dirck van Baburen or Jusepe de Ribera, called Lo Spagnoletto. Van Baburen—a Dutch artist born in a town near Utrecht around 1594—is considered one of the most important innovators in Dutch painting and, together with Hendrick ter Brugghen and Gerrit van Honthorst, he is one of the initiators of the so-called Utrecht Caravaggism, namely a trend set by the abovementioned group of painters from Utrecht, who traveled to Rome in the early 1600s and, after being profoundly influenced by Caravaggio's style, introduced Caravaggism in their hometown upon their return.[1]

Ribera, a Spanish painter and printmaker, is considered one of the most important artists in seventeenth-century Europe. Born in Spain (Játiva) he spent most of his life in Italy, mainly in Naples, where for over twenty years he was the most prominent artist in the city, exerting considerable influence on his Neapolitan colleagues. In his early career, Ribera was greatly influenced by Caravaggio and his northern followers, but the artworks dating from his artistic maturity show the influence of Venetian and Flemish art, especially in the use of vibrant color.[2]

As mentioned above, the attribution history of this painting, which depicts a beggar dressed in rags, holding a hat out for alms, is quite controversial. Nothing is known about the painting, nor the client who commissioned it, nor its provenance before 1693, when it is first mentioned in a Borghese household inventory of that same year, in which "a painting 4 palms big with a portrait of an old beggar holding a hat asking for alms" was improbably attributed to Caravaggio.[3] Later, in a 1790 household inventory, the same painting is described as "a bum, Spagnoletto", whereas in the Borghese fideicommissum of 1833, the same canvas is described as "portrait of a man, Flemish School".[4] Giovanni Piancastelli, first director of the Galleria Borghese, also considered it to be by a Flemish artist, whereas art historian Adolfo Venturi—in associating the canvas with the *Taking of Christ* (**figure 1**, p. 106), also in the Galleria Borghese—attributed this and the *Beggar* to Manfredi.[5] Art historian Roberto Longhi attributed it to Van Baburen's early Roman production, and noticed some similarities with the style of the young Ribera (who also worked in Rome).[6] According to Paola Della Pergola, this painting should be given to Van Baburen on rather convincing general stylistic grounds, especially if compared to the figure of Judas in the aforementioned *Taking of Christ*.[7] The attribution to Van Baburen was

also confirmed by Benedict Nicolson who, in 1979, awarded it to the artist with certainty, so much so that he included the painting among the autograph artworks by Van Baburen.[8] Later, however, he proposed the name of Wouter Crabeth II, also accepted by Nicola Spinosa who later changed his mind to Ribera (see below).[9] Van Baburen was also considered the author of this canvas by Arnaud Brejon de Lavergnée, in 1993.[10]

In recent years, however, Gianni Papi has claimed this painting should instead be given to the young Ribera.[11] His theory is mostly based on the attribution to Spagnoletto that appears in the 1790 inventory, and on the belief that the author of the *Beggar* should be identified with the hitherto-unrecognized so-called Master of the Judgment of Solomon (i.e., an anonymous Caravaggesque painter who carried out a series of canvases, the most celebrated of which is the *Judgment of Solomon*, **figure 2**, p. 107, also in the Galleria Borghese).[12] According to Papi, the author of this *Beggar* and of the abovementioned *Judgment of Solomon* is the young Jusepe de Ribera who, in the scholar's opinion, carried out these canvases during the very early stages of his career, namely, shortly after his arrival in Italy in around 1610.[13] This thesis, accepted by Nicola Spinosa following initial skepticism and disagreement regarding the attribution of certain paintings by the so-called Master of the Judgment of Solomon to the young Ribera, has also been accepted and proposed by the organizers of the exhibition *El joven Ribera* (i.e., *The Young Ribera*)—Gabriele Finaldi, the same Gianni Papi, and Nicola Spinosa.[14] The association of the *Judgment of Solomon* with Ribera's hand is, however, rejected by scholars Alessandro Zuccari and Marco Gallo on stylistic grounds.[15] Scholar Silvia Danesi Squarzina also appears to doubt Papi's attribution of the *Beggar* to Ribera, as—just like other scholars before her—she points out the stylistic analogies between the beggar and Judas and the rogues in Van Baburen's aforementioned *Taking of Christ* at the Galleria Borghese—a view which appears the most reasonable.[16]

Moreover, aside from stylistic reasons—which are obviously based on connoisseurship, and thus on subjective and often arguable perception—another issue hitherto overlooked also lies in the methodology with which Papi's attribution to Ribera was first proposed. Papi has attributed this *Beggar* to Ribera on the basis of what is written in the 1790 inventory and on stylistic analogies with the paintings of the Master of the Judgment of Solomon. However, it should be noted that noble-household inventories were generally drawn up by the family's house manager, and not by art connoisseurs. Inventories were simply meant to be records

of the movable goods kept in the palace, and had no scholarly aim, hence the many different attributions in relation to the canvas in question.

In addition, further problems arise from the fact that Papi mostly based his theory not only on an inventory, but on an inventory drafted in 1790, some two hundred years after the painting was supposedly made. It is common knowledge that Caravaggism had been out of fashion since 1630, and inventories dating back to the late seventeenth and eighteenth centuries frequently recorded inaccurate attributions where Caravaggesque paintings were concerned. Any canvas with strong *chiaroscuro* combined with naturalistic subject matter tended to be attributed either to Caravaggio himself (as is the case with this *Beggar*, attributed to Caravaggio in the 1693 inventory), or to other famous Caravaggesque artists whose names could still be recalled, regardless of who the original artist was. Therefore, inventories cannot always be considered a reliable source when it comes to attributions, especially when a painting bears different attributions in previous and later inventories, as in this instance.

In 1998, Francesca Cappelletti pointed out that the comparison between the Judas in Van Baburen's *Taking of Christ* and the beggar allows for the latter to be plausibly ascribed to Van Baburen, especially when taking certain features into consideration, such as the wrinkled and reddened face, visible in both Judas and the beggar.[17] Cappelletti also highlights that both figures recall the Nicodemus carrying the body of Jesus in Caravaggio's *Entombment* (formerly in the Church of Santa Maria in Vallicella, and now at the Vatican Museums). The entombment was a subject matter that Van Baburen had carefully studied.[18] Nevertheless, Cappelletti points out that this attribution to Van Baburen necessarily causes the *Beggar* to be dated between 1617 and 1618, as Van Baburen had returned to Utrecht by 1620. In Italy, in the late 1610s, subjects such as beggars and the poor were yet to become fashionable in painting. Beggars, however, had been quite a common subject matter in the Low Countries as early as the sixteenth century, especially as far as prints were concerned, and were quite a common subject matter for Dutch artists, such as Van Baburen.[19]

The artwork in question was certainly meant to be emotionally moving, and to rouse in the wealthy viewer an empathy and awareness of the widespread suffering induced by poverty. The beggar is not portrayed requesting alms from another, secondary figure in the painting, rather he makes a direct appeal to the viewer. The beggar is portrayed alone, in a neutral setting, his stance suggests that he is standing, reaching out in desperation to the viewer with his empty hat. The beggar's straightforward request for alms is obviously meant to make viewers feel uncomfortable with their wealth, and by contrast their easy life. The words of Ecclesiastes 4:1 come to mind:

> Again I saw all the oppressions that are practiced under the sun. Look, the tears of the oppressed—with no one to comfort them! On the side of their oppressors there was power—with no one to comfort them.

In this respect, it is truly extraordinary that such a painting became part of the collection of one of the richest and more powerful families in Rome—the Borghese. We might hypothesize that—similarly to the Brescian families who commissioned portraits of old and young beggars from Giacomo Ceruti (see **cat. n. II.5**)—this painting was meant to demonstrate the family's concern for the poverty stricken, and that it also acted as a subtle reference to their charitable activities.

The intense naturalism with which the painter portrayed this beggar, the rags in which he is dressed, his face and hands marked

Figure 1:
Dirck van Baburen, *Taking of Christ*, ca. 1618. Oil on canvas, 139 × 202 cm (54.72 × 79.52 in.). Rome (Italy), Galleria Borghese, inv. 28.

by a life lived in poverty, his direct and suffering expression, make this canvas a true masterpiece, not only for its undoubted artistic quality, but also for its emotional impact, which can still touch us after four centuries.

Corinna Ricasoli

[1] For further reading on Van Baburen, see CAPITELLI 2016, LEMOINE 2016, FRANITS 2009, HELMUS 2005, SLATKES 1998, SCIOLLA 1981, SLATKES 1966.

[2] The bibliography on Ribera is extensive, however, the reader may refer to *EL JOVEN RIBERA* 2011, SPINOSA 2008, *JOSÉ DE RIBERA* 2005, *JUSEPE DE RIBERA* 2003, *JUSEPE DE RIBERA* 1992.

[3] DELLA PERGOLA 1955, p. 144–145. Unless otherwise noted, all translations from Italian into English appearing in this entry are my own.

[4] The fideicommissum was a devise through which the testator obliged the heir or legatee to keep the bequest received together and unaltered. Upon the heir's death, said bequest automatically went to a different heir, but always with the restraints indicated by the first testator. The three inventories, in Italian, read: "un quadro di 4 palmi con un ritratto di un vecchio povero col cappello in mano in atto di chiedere elemosina dicono che sia Giminiano del n.695 di Michelangelo caravagli [sic] con cornice dorata"; "un villano, Spagnoletto"; "Ritratto d'Uomo, della Scuola Fiamminga". Ibid.

[5] VENTURI 1893, p. 161.

[6] See LONGHI 1928, p. 26.

[7] DELLA PERGOLA 1955, p. 144–145.

[8] See NICOLSON 1979, p. 19.

[9] See NICOLSON 1990, p. 103.

[10] BREJON DE LAVERGNÉE 1993.

[11] See PAPI 2014, p. 202, PAPI 2005, p. 250, and the bibliography therein.

[12] See PAPI 2014, p. 202, PAPI 2002, p. 21–43.

[13] About Ribera in Rome, see PAPI 2003, p. 63–74.

[14] See *EL JOVEN RIBERA* 2011, but also SPINOSA 2003.

[15] See ZUCCARI 2009, p. 345–363, GALLO 2010, p. 483–488.

[16] DANESI SQUARZINA 2003, p. 4.

[17] CAPPELLETTI 1998, p. 300–301.

[18] See his *Entombment* in the Roman Church of San Pietro in Montorio, and its respective preparatory drawing at the Louvre, Département des Arts Graphiques, inv. 16515.

[19] See the many engravings portraying beggars by Lucas van Leiden, or those illustrating poor cripples after Hieronymus Bosch's drawings. Poor cripples are also the focus of some of Cornelis Massijs's prints.

Figure 2:
Master of the Judgment of Solomon, *Judgment of Solomon*, ca. 1620.
Oil on canvas, 153 × 201 cm (60.23 × 79.13 in.).
Rome (Italy), Galleria Borghese, inv. 33.

Cat. n. II.5*

Giacomo Ceruti called Il Pitocchetto

Errand Boy Seated with a Basket on His Back, Eggs, and Poultry

ca. 1735.
Oil on canvas, 130 × 95 cm (51.18 × 37.40 in.).
Milan (Italy), Pinacoteca di Brera, inv. 5650.

Born in Milan to a family originally from Brescia, nothing is known about Giacomo Ceruti's training, but he is likely to have studied in Milan, where he is known to have lived until 1718.[1] After his time in Milan he probably moved to Brescia to start a career as a painter specializing in religious and portrait paintings, the former usually considered quite mediocre works.[2] However, his most significant oeuvre consists of very high-quality paintings illustrating beggars, vagabonds, and poor people in general, called the *pitocchi* (Italian for *lice*), hence his nickname—'il Pitocchetto'. Ceruti was not the only artist to deal with such subject matter (see **cat. n. II.4**). Indeed, in both Lombardy and the Veneto, between the seventeenth and eighteenth centuries, the 'pauperistic' genre was particularly successful, and may be found in the oeuvre of artists such as Pietro Bellotti (see **cat. n. III.2**), Antonio Carneo, Alessandro Magnasco, Giacomo Francesco Cipper, Antonio Cifrondi and Jacques Callot, on whose prints of beggars Ceruti based some of his works. However, unlike Ceruti, the abovementioned artists (except for Callot) illustrated poverty and the poor in a 'traditional' way, in that they highlighted the anecdotal, caricatural, and even vulgar features of the deprived and outcast.[3] By contrast, Ceruti's everyday-life scenes portraying the poor classes are very moving, and devoid of any irony, as the artist was evidently deeply sensitive to this particular subject matter. These canvases are a blunt and disillusioned depiction of reality, which Ceruti represented with great directness, and with the use of a 'poor' and earthy color palette, consistent with the theme, and much appreciated by his Brescian clients.[4]

This painting was carried out for one of Ceruti's clients in Brescia, Italy—the Barbisoni family, who owned nine paintings by Pitocchetto, including this painting's pendant (**figure 1**, p. 111), which also illustrates a porter sitting on a basket.[5] Both paintings, now hanging in the Pinacoteca di Brera, have the same dimensions and lighting, they represent boys in a neutral setting, with a neutral background, which lends these canvases a rather Caravaggesque impression.[6] In fact, the *Errand Boy Seated with a Basket on His Back, Eggs, and Poultry*, echoes features reminiscent of the Brescian and Bergamasque painting tradition, particularly of artists such as Giovanni Girolamo Savoldo and Giovanni Battista Moroni.[7] This canvas is among Ceruti's greatest achievements both in terms of quality and the way in which the artist tackled the subject matter, which results in a painting that far surpasses a mere genre scene.[8]

The painting portrays a young boy—a porter—sitting on a rock, resting from his daily toil. The basket that he carries on his shoulders—the tool of his trade—is almost as big as himself, and

in addition to that load he also carries a basket full of eggs and poultry. Dressed in old, worn-out clothes, without shoes, his penetrating glance, directed at the observer, reveals a poignant awareness of his own miserable condition and social status.

The painting is life size, and the boy and his basket almost fill the entire space of the canvas. Previously, such a setting—namely the dark/neutral background that helps the figures stand out—had been unique to aristocratic portraits. By approaching 'pauperistic' subject matter in this way, Ceruti conferred a hitherto-unknown dignity and gravitas to his *pitocchi*. Specifically, in this canvas, Ceruti managed to carry out a very moving and heartfelt image of a young boy, through which the artist bluntly described the reality and injustice of child labor.[9]

Although it might seem odd that wealthy families would commission paintings illustrating the poor and the lowest social classes, it should be noted that these important Brescian clients were quite sensitive to social problems, especially poverty. Indeed, they were close to religious orders and confraternities promoting 'social solidarity' on the basis of the Works of Mercy, which entailed being particularly responsive to the evangelical exhortation to help those in need. This great concern for the poor, and encouragement to assist them, was common in certain Catholic thinking, and a number of books were devoted to the issue.[10] The dignity with which these beggars were seen and portrayed also stemmed from a deeply rooted belief that there was a difference between 'good poverty'—namely the poor people who were assisted by religious institutions who also supervised their morals and life style—and 'dangerous poverty', which included the unsupervised and non-regulated poor. Clearly, the poor portrayed by Ceruti fell into the first category, a sentiment occasionally reinforced in other paintings by the presence of religious buildings in the background, which provided a direct reference to charitable organizations that provided aid to the impoverished.[11]

It should be noted, however, that Ceruti's *pitocchi* paintings clearly (and primarily) had a decorative purpose, so the charitable engagement these artworks referred to had to be subtle, to some degree at least.[12] Despite the 'mundane' function of these canvases, both Ceruti and his clients were obviously well aware that poverty was a very serious issue that had to be addressed with great respect—hence the application of the 'aristocratic-portrait model' in the depiction of the *pitocchi*.[13] In Ceruti's paintings, the poor become a symbol of courage, dignity, and honesty, quietly enduring a life of disadvantage and suffering.[14]

Corinna Ricasoli

[1] Carminati 2000, p. 193, Caprara 1980, p. 60.

[2] In his portraits, he is clearly influenced by artists such as Giovanni Battista Moroni and Fra Galgario. Carminati 2000, p. 193.

[3] Ibid., D'Adda 2002, p. 228.

[4] Among his most important commissions, there is a series of paintings carried out for the Avogadro family in Brescia, which consists of around fifteen canvases, all illustrating beggars, porters, deprived people. They are all portrayed full-length as if they were nobles. Carminati 2000, p. 193, D'Adda 2002, p. 228. Apart from high local aristocracy, his clients would also include governors of various cities in the Veneto region, and parish priests, whom he has portrayed. Carminati 2000, p. 193. For Ceruti's earthy palette, see also D'Adda 2002, p. 228. Only after his stay in Venice in 1736, where he worked on several portraits and still-lifes, and after his stay in Padua, a deep change in his palette may be noticed, as he was deeply influenced by the use of color by Marco and Sebastiano Ricci, of Giovanni Battista Pittoni the Younger, and Giovanni Battista Tiepolo, who used brighter, vivid colors. Carminati 2000, p. 193.

[5] Gregori 1982, p. 441–442, Frangi 1987, p. 179, Porzio 1989, p. 120, D'Adda 2002, p. 228, Bandera 2009, p. 139.

[6] Porzio 1989, p. 118, D'Adda 2002, p. 228.

[7] Porzio 1989, p. 118.

[8] Ibid.

[9] Frangi 1998, p. 47–48.

[10] See Jacques-Bénigne Bossuet's very successful sermon *De l'éminente dignité des pauvres dans l'Eglise* (i.e., *On the Eminent Dignity of the Poor in the Church*) of 1659, in which he states that, contrary to the rich, the poor were in a spiritually privileged position, as they were the real heirs of the evangelical precept of poverty. In other words, in Bossuet's opinion, the poor are not only people to be pitied and thus assisted, but they should be honored, as they are worthy of great respect, because without the poor, there would be no salvation for the rich, and only those who consider the poor as "the firstborn of the Church" really understand the mystery of charity. Bossuet's collection of sermons was clearly well-known in northern Italy, as it was published in 1736 by the celebrated Venetian publisher Giovanni Battista Albrizzi. See ibid., p. 58–59. See also Menozzi 1980, p. 38 and 134, who emphasizes Jansenist commitment to the modernization of 'social solidarity', which entailed the involvement of lay people in charity management. Other significant early modern publications on the matter of the poor are Ludovico Antonio Muratori's *Della carità cristiana*, published in 1723, but also Jesuit Daniello Bartoli's *La povertà contenta* of 1650, in which, according to the author, the poor were immune from sin and guilt, which concerned the rich instead. He too believed that thanks to the poor and their need for help and alms, the rich could mend their ways. Frangi 1998, p. 57.

[11] Frangi 1998, p. 58.

[12] Ibid., p. 59.

[13] Ibid., p. 54.

[14] Carminati 2000, p. 193.

Figure 1:
Giacomo Ceruti, *Porter Seated on a Basket*, 1735.
Oil on canvas, 130 × 95.5 cm (51.18 × 37.59 in.).
Milan (Italy), Pinacoteca di Brera, inv. 5649.

Even as the Smoke doth paſſe away;
So, ſhall all Worldly-pompe decay.

ILLVSTR. XXXVI.   Book. 2

The Futility of Wealth

The futility of wealth was also a concern, as its pursuit and hoarding guaranteed neither happiness nor longevity, nor immortality for oneself or loved ones, but rather it led to worry and sleepless nights: *Sweet is the sleep of laborers, whether they eat little or much; but the surfeit of the rich will not let them sleep* (Ecclesiastes 5:12).

The lover of money will not be satisfied with money; nor the lover of wealth, with gain. This also is vanity.

(Ecclesiastes 5:10)

Cat. n. II.6
Pieter Boel

Allegory of Worldly Vanities

1663.
Oil on canvas, 207.5 × 261 cm (81 × 102.75 in.).
Inscription: *PETRUS BOEL A. 1663.*
Lille (France), Palais des Beaux-Arts, P 78.

The son of Jan Boel, an engraver who lived in Antwerp, Pieter Boel may have been a student of Frans Snyders and quite certainly of Jan Fyt—both were painters specializing in animals and still-lifes. Boel later traveled to Italy, particularly to Rome and Genoa. After his return to Antwerp, in 1650, he was admitted as a member of the Guild of St. Luke, the corporation of painters. In 1668, he moved to Paris, where he worked at Gobelins—the celebrated craftsmen's factory—under the direction of Charles Le Brun. In 1674, the year of his death, he finally became *peintre ordinaire du roi* (painter in ordinary to the king).

Despite its size and impressiveness, this majestic still-life is nevertheless a *vanitas*. Consistent with the Flemish tradition, the detailed rendering of the objects tends to distract us from the somberness of the subject matter. Indeed, the objects on display question the purpose of human endeavors and earthly possessions to which they allude. What is the meaning of our existence on this earth? The answer to this question, given in part by the brush of this great Flemish master, seems to be at the very top of the composition—the skull.

Dated 1663, the canvas was likely carried out in Antwerp. Although we do not know where it was meant to be originally displayed, its outstanding, decorative features suggest it was to be hung in a wealthy patron's house. Its provenance history is documented, and we know it belonged to the nineteenth-century French painter, Constant Troyon, who displayed it in his dining room.[1] In all likelihood, this canvas was the only old-master painting belonging to the artist.[2]

It might seem surprising that Troyon, an artist who specialized in painting animals, kept a *vanitas* painting carried out by Boel, rather than a painting which displayed the latter artist's predilection for the portrayal of living animals and dead game (birds in particular), in the style of Fyt.[3] In this painting there are no animals to distract from the abundance of unique objects on display, and it is the quality of their depiction rather than the generous dimension of the work that sets this canvas apart.[4]

The basis of the composition—a gallery in ruins with hoarded objects placed upon a tomb—make this still-life, or rather, *absence* of life, particularly evident. The theatricality of the heavy curtain and the three balustrades in the distance accentuate the feeling of somber desolation.

Within this grandiloquent context, the manner with which these precious objects are displayed is not random. Boel followed a clever compositional format—the vertical and horizontal lines of the architecture and of the sarcophagus give a rhythm to the background; similarly, the many items arranged around a large, ornate goldsmith's plate are placed within a pyramidal structure. With their horizontality, the cushion, the crozier, or the saber allow for the hoarding of these diversely-shaped objects. The miter, the ermine bordure, and some well-oriented sculptures suggest further verticality. The viewer's gaze is therefore guided to the very top of this luxurious display, where a human skull flanks a turban.

Albert Pomme de Mirimonde has interpreted these *worldly vanities* as an allusion to three types of human activities.[5] The *vita contemplativa* (contemplative life), referring to knowledge, is represented by the books and the globe. The latter also symbolizes the *vita pratica* (practical life), namely earthly power and riches, evoked by the numerous allusions to temporal and spiritual power, such as the ermine cloak, the royal crown, the sultan's turban, the saber of the emir, the quiver, the cuirass and helmet of the warrior, the miter and the crozier of the bishop. Lastly, there are many references to earthly pleasures and beauty, which are connected to the *vita voluptuaria* (voluptuary life). Thus, precious things and artworks are close to objects used for artmaking, such as a palette, brushes, and musical instruments.[6]

But the encyclopedic character of these refined objects, the abundance of which makes them escape all classification, and their aesthetic appeal, can lead to a somewhat different interpretation. Perhaps they refer to the distinctions of a lavish and accomplished life that inevitably lead to death?[7] Aside from the obvious decorative aim, which these objects clearly illustrate, the iconography of certain sculptures or goldsmiths may perhaps allude to the theme of vanity. The large central plate probably represents a mythological scene that has not yet been clearly identified. It could represent Venus and Adonis preparing for the wild boar hunt where he will be killed.[8] Are these subjects alluding to vengeance, or to the love of the gods who act as a warning?

Whatever the exact meaning of this arsenal of riches, the inscription visible on the tomb—VANITATI S[ACRIFICIUM] (Sacrifice to vanity)—erases all doubts by clearly stating its allegorical purpose. Studious life, power, riches, and delights: all human ambition is a vain pursuit. And if the message were not clear enough, the laurel-crowned skull, a traditional motif within the genre, confirms this appalling *memento*: death alone triumphs over the futility of earthly activities, presented here as an offering. A detail could go almost unnoticed because of this profusion: a plain ring hanging on a nail, like a formal echo of

the rich volute of the crozier. The symbolism it bears reminds us of what is essential. Without a beginning or an end—a synonym of eternity—it comes to remind us of the inexorable course of time.

Donatienne Dujardin[9]

[1] Mantz 1872, p. 378.

[2] Foucart-Walter 2001, p. 15 (footnote 13), which mentions the catalog of the Troyon sale, occurred after his death.

[3] Ibid., p. 13. Pieter Boel was employed by Gobelins as an animal painter.

[4] There are two other vanities by Pieter Boel: *Vanitas*, Musées royaux des Beaux-Arts de Belgique (the figures, parrot and skull are by Jacob Jordaens) and *Still-Life with Globe and Cockatoos*, circa 1658, Vienna, Akademie der Bildenden Künste. In these two exemplars, the animal is shown together with dogs, a macaw, and a cockatoo.

[5] Foucart-Walter 2001, p. 15 (footnote 12). *The Vanities of The World* is the title under which the painting figured in the sales catalog, put together after the death of Constant Troyon. Pomme de Mirimonde 1964, p. 113, 119.

[6] Pomme de Mirimonde 1964, p. 107. The motif of musical instruments is common in Pieter Boel's still-lifes, whether *vanitas* or hunting trophies. Whereas musical instruments were very popular in the Netherlands for their symbolism, they are, however, poorly represented in the Flemish school. See Greindl 1956, p. 91–96, 123.

[7] Liedtke 1993, p. 79–83.

[8] Albert Pomme de Mirimonde also sees in it Artemis and Orion. See Pomme de Mirimonde 1964, p. 123, 125. H. Oursel also suggests it may be Artemis begging Neptune. See *Le siècle de Rubens* 1977.

[9] Translated from French by Corinna Ricasoli.

Cat. n. II.7

Gerrit van Honthorst

Old Woman Examining a Coin by a Lantern (*Sight* or *Avarice*)

ca. 1623.

Oil on canvas, 75 × 60 cm (29.52 × 23.62 in.).

Inscription: *G v Honthorst fc / 162[3?]* (abraded).

Amsterdam (the Netherlands), The Kremer Collection, GK-28.

Old Woman Examining a Coin by a Lantern is a superb example of the work of Gerrit van Honthorst (see also **cat nos. IV.3–IV.4**).[1] Together with Hendrick ter Brugghen and Dirck van Baburen, Van Honthorst is one of the most important and best-known of the Caravaggesques who worked in the northern Netherlands. While in Rome, the three artists had been captivated by the work of Caravaggio (hence the name Caravaggesques), who had introduced a radical realism into the art of painting, as well as strong *chiaroscuro* effects and cropped figures filling the picture plane. After his return to Utrecht in 1620, Van Honthorst started producing genre pieces such as the painting discussed here, each one depicting a single figure seen as a bust, almost without exception illuminated by an artificial light source.[2] Nocturnal scenes of this kind earned Van Honthorst the apt nickname of 'Gherardo delle Notti' ('Gerard of the night scenes').

Some years ago, *Old Woman Examining a Coin by a Lantern* underwent restoration, and its details and colors can since be properly appreciated again. Here, Van Honthorst portrays an old woman against a plain background. In one hand, she has a coin she is studying intently, while in the other she holds a bulging purse. There is a second purse, brimming with coins, before her breast, brightly illuminated by the light from the candle. The light also falls on part of her face, giving us a clear view of her eyes. With just a few strokes of blue paint the painter contrived to bring the pupils to life. Van Honthorst has made the coin in the woman's hand visible by allowing its outer edge to catch the light. The lantern hanging from a hook and the light spread by the candle are suggestively rendered with just a small number of boldly placed strokes. Despite the rapid, loose brushwork he used for the wrinkled face and flabby neck, here too Van Honthorst has superbly exploited the play of light. The painter has created a kind of halo effect around the headscarf, by leaving the light-brown ground visible in places. In the upper left corner, we discern the remains of the authentic signature that someone tried to rub out at some point, presumably in order to sell the painting under another name—that of Caravaggio himself? The date '162' is still clearly legible, except for the last figure of the year, which has been read variously in the past. Recent analysis suggests that the figure is most probably a '3'.[3] This would make the scene one of Van Honthorst's earliest genre pieces, produced in the early 1620s, shortly after his return from Italy.

Characteristically, Van Honthorst has used the light-dark contrasts that are so central to Caravaggism to suggest depth. Thus, the outstretched arm with the coin—which, aside from the fingers, is completely shrouded in darkness—enhances the scene's three-dimensionality by being sharply silhouetted against the brightly illuminated purse. Other features typical of this artist are the close cropping of the figure—the left shoulder and elbow are only partly visible—and his choice of a simple model.[4] Van Honthorst would later be followed in his depiction of an old woman as the primary figure by his own teacher, the well-known Utrecht painter Abraham Bloemaert. The latter's son, Cornelis Bloemaert, made prints of several of his father's scenes with half-figures. These prints were widely disseminated, as were those he produced after similar paintings by Van Honthorst. Thanks to one of these prints, we know that Van Honthorst painted another, similar scene of a woman with a purse. In this painting—now lost, and known only from the print and a few painted copies—the figure is not studying a coin, and has an empty purse.[5] The lit candle in the hands of the woman, who gazes directly at the viewer in this scene, has assumed the role of the lantern depicted here.

The caption of the print provides a key to understanding the scene, which proves to be a variant on a popular subject: Avarice or Greed, one of the seven deadly sins.[6] The apparently mundane scene in the painting described here can also be construed as a rendering of this theme. The pince-nez, the purse, and the coin held between the fingers are all traditional attributes of avarice. In the seventeenth century, avarice was thought to increase in old age as the other passions were gradually extinguished—an idea deriving from classical antiquity.[7] Since the scales and books of accounts often included in depictions of greed are missing here, this scene, in which the woman is scrutinizing the coin intensely, has sometimes been interpreted as a visualization of sight, one of the five senses. A contemporary of Van Honthorst, Crispijn van de Passe, produced a print in which sight is represented by an old woman studying a coin by candlelight, wearing a little pair of glasses, just as in this painting.[8]

It is highly probable that Rembrandt drew inspiration from Van Honthorst in his youth.[9] His *Old Man Counting Money* (*Avarice*) from 1627 (**figure 1**, p. 121) depicts an old man studying a coin by candlelight. Rembrandt must have derived the subject from Van Honthorst, but chose instead to depict a man to convey the theme of greed. Rembrandt also adopted a detail, almost literally, from Van Honthorst's other painting, the composition of which became well-known from the Bloemaert print. For in that work the old woman has her hand before the candlelight, just as the old man in Rembrandt's painting. That the latter's knowledge

of the work was not confined to the print can be inferred from another detail of his painting. Just as in the scene discussed here, the man painted by Rembrandt is holding a coin between his fingers, a motif absent from the print. Other artists, too, appear to have been inspired by *Old Woman Examining a Coin by a Lantern*.[10] Both Rembrandt and Van Honthorst present their figures in a fairly negative light: they portray counting money as a reprehensible way of spending one's time. While greed and miserliness are sinful at any stage of life, this applies with particular force to the aged, whose final days are slipping away.

Quentin Buvelot

[1] The bibliography on Gerrit van Honthorst is very broad, but for further reading on the artist, please refer to JUDSON 1959, and JUDSON AND EKKART 1999.

[2] See JUDSON AND EKKART 1999, p. 182.

[3] See BUVELOT 2008b, p. 98. I wish to thank Petria Noble for the information provided.

[4] Similar old women appear in other works by Van Honthorst. JUDSON AND EKKART 1999, nos. 281, 283.

[5] Ibid., no. 228 and pl. 130.

[6] Ibid., p. 181, and JANSSEN 2005, p. 61.

[7] TÜMPEL 1971, p. 27–30, KOREVAAR 2005, p. 150–151.

[8] SELLINK 2000, p. 77, JUDSON AND EKKART 1999, p. 182.

[9] NISSEN 1914, p. 73–80, BRUYN AND PEESE BINKHORST 1982, p. 140–141, JUDSON AND EKKART 1999, p. 182.

[10] BUVELOT 1995, p. 63.

Figure 1:
Rembrandt Harmensz van Rijn,
Old Man Counting Money (*Avarice*), 1627.
Panel, 31.7 × 42.5 cm (12.48 × 16.73 in.).
Berlin (Germany), Staatliche Museen zu Berlin, Gemäldegalerie.

SECTION III
Nothing Lasts

This Day, my Houre-glasse, forth is runne,
Thy Torch, to Morrow, may bee done.

The Unpredictability of One's Fate

Life is always followed by death. These artworks reflect upon the inevitability of death and the inability to predict its arrival. A number of the works overtly refer to the unpredictable arrival of death in the form of winged skulls and skeletons.

Youth Surprised by Death depicts a wonderful example of the personification of Death: a skeleton holding an hourglass grips a young man's shoulder to remind him that his hour has come. The hourglass, however, is still quite full, which is what the youth's gesture seems to be alluding to, in what appears to be his naive attempt to reason with Death.

But death surprises us in the midst of our earthly existence, and we are powerless when it happens.

For no one can anticipate the time of disaster. Like fish taken in a cruel net, and like birds caught in a snare, so mortals are snared at a time of calamity, when it suddenly falls upon them.

(Ecclesiastes 9:12)

Cat. n. III.1
Anonymous Italian
Model of a Winged Skull
ca. 1650s.
Terracotta, 26 × 42 × 15 cm (10.23 × 16.53 × 5.9 in.).
Leeds (England), Tomasso Brothers Fine Art.

Very little is known about the provenance and maker of this terracotta representing a winged skull. On general stylistic grounds, it is likely that it was made in Italy—possibly in Rome—around the mid-seventeenth century. In all probability, it was meant to serve as a model for a marble winged skull to be placed on a monumental tomb.

The winged skull was a very popular feature in seventeenth-century art, and baroque tombs in particular. Indeed, after the Council of Trent (1545–1563), the serene representations of death, proper to Renaissance funerary monuments, disappeared in favor of a more terrifying image of death, at first in the form of a skull and then of a skeleton.[1] Skulls and skeletons were represented with great naturalism, both in terms of choice of the marble used for these sculptures (which sometimes had an ivory tone to recall the color of a real human skull), and in terms of the actual features of the skull itself, the imitation of which often went as far as to represent it with some missing teeth (as is the case with this terracotta model) making the whole image very realistic. A variation of this motif is the winged skull, such as the one taken into consideration here. This is probably a less realistic representation of death, but the presence of wings makes it a very emblematic example of an extremely popular seventeenth-century theme: the suddenness of death, which may 'fly' and reach us unexpectedly.[2]

The popularity of skull imagery was related to Jesuit religious instruction, and the way in which they encouraged the faithful to use an actual skull (or a surrogate) to better concentrate the mind on death and physical decay during the meditations suggested by Ignatius of Loyola in his *Exercitia Spiritualia* (i.e., *Spiritual Exercises*) of 1548.[3] The sight of a (rotting) corpse, or a skeleton, or a 'simple' skull—an extremely common occurrence throughout the seventeenth century—became the perfect means to proselytize, because it impressed and activated "the most sensitive chords" of either the listeners in church or—in the case of burials—of the passersby.[4] The skull is therefore almost omnipresent in seventeenth-century funerary art as it is connected to meditation, and particularly to meditation on death and human transience.

Such meditations on death—especially when associated with the powerful presence of a tomb, which was the manifest evidence of one's finite existence—were indeed seen as the best means to encourage the abandonment of worldly pleasures, which was the first step toward the path of salvation.[5] On funerary monuments, the winged skull, often a symbol of Death personified, reminded the living of the inevitability of death, thus serving as a *memento mori*. It referenced the idea of the 'nothingness' and fragility of our existence, and ultimately of our *vanitas*.[6]

Indeed, in baroque tombs, the *vanitas* elements—such as this winged skull—were displayed in direct and proportional response according to the grandiloquence of the tomb, of which they are a part. This was obviously a way to avoid the dreaded sin of vanity. In fact, the (winged) skull as a funerary decorative element, which may be seen in monumental tombs dating back to the late sixteenth century, and up until the first half of the eighteenth century, was a pointed message addressed to passersby to remind them of the elusiveness of life, and the uncertainty of our fate.

However, it should be noted that in the second half of the seventeenth century, in addition to being the symbol for meditations on death, the skull also became an emblem of the afterlife, of the departed and their soul, and thus—in Catholic countries at least—a reference to Purgatory. As scholar Pierroberto Scaramella correctly points out, "this connection between the skull and the soul in Purgatory, which was certainly symbolic in preaching, was understood as real, and not as a metaphor, by the lower social classes."[7] In other words, the skull was also used as "a reminder of the explicit obligations of suffrage" and that such meditation and prayer could lead to the release of loved ones from Purgatory.[8] The tomb was a significant 'presence' in other ways as well: without doubt, it acted both as a 'silent' prayer on behalf of the tomb's occupant and as an exhortation to prayer as far as passersby were concerned.[9] According to Catholic doctrine, prayers for the souls of the departed are essential for their salvation and rapid passage through Purgatory, the existence of which was emphatically reiterated by the Council of Trent in the face of Protestant dissent.[10] Therefore, in baroque burials, the skull and its winged variant, such as that analyzed here, had a significant role in the salvation of the soul of both the living and the dead.

Corinna Ricasoli

[1] See SCARAMELLA 2002, p. 64, and the bibliography therein. See also RICASOLI 2015, as well as RICASOLI 2014 and respective bibliography.
[2] MÂLE 1984, p. 185.
[3] See LOYOLA 1687, p. 73, and PAUCCI 1751, p. 291–293, but also RICASOLI 2014, p. 59–60, SCARAMELLA 2002, p. 64. It should be noted that the skull is also a common element in the *studiolo* (i.e., a private room used as a study or library and, later, as a cabinet of curiosities), because reading and studying were also seen as connected to meditation and prayer. See ARIÈS 1980, p. 381.
[4] SCARAMELLA 2002, p. 65–66.
[5] Ibid., p. 65.
[6] COHEN 1973, p. 117.
[7] SCARAMELLA 2002, p. 73.
[8] Ibid.
[9] RICASOLI 2014, p. 233.
[10] Ibid.

Cat. n. III.2

Pietro Bellotti

The Fate Atropos

after 1659.

Oil on canvas, 62 × 49.2 cm (24.40 × 19.37 in.).

Budapest (Hungary), Szépművészeti Múzeum, inv. 984.

This painting arrived in Hungary as part of the collection of János Lászó Pyrker, who was not only the Archbishop of Eger (Northern Hungary), but also an erudite art collector, patron, and famed writer.[1] He purchased the bulk of his gallery during his patriarchate in Venice (1820–1827) and during the time of his trips to Italy. Stirred by the patriotic spirit of the Reform Era, Pyrker, at the 1836 parliamentary session, donated one hundred and ninety-two, mostly sixteenth- to eighteenth-century Italian paintings of his collection, including Bellotti's *Atropos,* to the Hungarian National Museum. In 1877, his collection entered into the National Picture Gallery, predecessor of the Museum of Fine Arts, and was exhibited at the Hungarian Academy of Sciences, Budapest. In the 1846 catalog of the Pyrker collection, the painting was already included under the name of Bellotti, and apart from some circumspect attributions his authorship has never been queried.[2]

Pietro Bellotti was esteemed as "exquisite painter, especially for portraits and *capriccio* half-figures, and a faithful copyist of nature".[3] He was connected to both the Lombard and Venetian schools. He developed his style under numerous, divergent cultural and artistic impulses. In Venice, he was apprenticed to Girolamo Forabosco but was also impressed by the *tenebrosi* and the art of the Genoese Bernardo Strozzi, who worked in the city of lagoons from 1632/1633 onward. The astonishing verisimilitude of his portraits, whether real likenesses or character heads, was inspired by Northern realism and the art of such followers of Michelangelo Merisi da Caravaggio as Jusepe de Ribera. As a protégée of Cardinal Giulio Mazzarino, he worked in France in 1661–1662, where he probably got acquainted with the works of Georges de la Tour and Nicolas Lagneau. After a second Venetian period, he worked in Munich at the court of Ferdinand Maria, Elector of Bavaria and, between 1670 and 1674, for the Duke of Uceda in Milan. In 1681, he became the superintendent of the art gallery of Ferdinando Carlo Gonzaga, Duke of Mantua. From 1685 until his death he re-settled in his native land, in the vicinity of Lake Garda. His art served as a source of inspiration for numerous artists, including the Venetian Niccolò Cassana, the Lombard painters of reality, such as Giacomo Ceruti (**cat. n. II.5**) and Giacomo Francesco Cipper as well as the German Balthasar Denner and Christian Seybold.

Whether owing to his own excessive concern, or because of the success of the subject matter, Bellotti produced several renditions of the *Parcae*, or the 'Fates', the Roman equivalents of the *Moirai*, goddesses of destiny in Greek mythology. Luciano Anelli, author of the catalogue raisonné on Bellotti, enumerates two renderings of Nona (Clotho), the one who spins the thread of life, nine depictions of Decima (Lachesis), she who measures the thread of life, and three versions of Morta (Atropos), the inevitable, who cuts the thread of life.

In the painting, of a size much favored by the artist, Atropos appears as a crone; "her face, neck and hands resemble creased paper".[4] As the craquelure webs the surface of the painting, so do the wrinkles cover her sagged face. The suggestivity of the depiction, created by the naturalistic details and high degree of psychological sensitivity, is further enhanced by the close-up depiction of the model. The accuracy of perception and the soberness of the expression is counterbalanced by the warmth and soft modelling of the fuchsia-colored robe.

As in most of Bellotti's paintings, a particular focus is put on the hands. In her left hand, Atropos holds three spindles, while with the huge shears in her right she cuts the three threads uncoiling from them. Over her bald forehead she wears a withered wreath, which adds to her grotesque appearance. The plant, having been identified by Debaisieux as a bough of yew, was correctly described by Annelli as a branch of cypress.[5] In antiquity, the cypress (*cupressus sempervirens*) was regarded as an emblem of mourning and was sacred to the three Fates and the Furies as well as the rulers of the underworld. The motif rarely, if ever, appears in the artworks of the Renaissance and the baroque, which commonly represent Atropos as a bareheaded young maiden or an old woman wearing a headscarf.[6] If Atropos's identity were not revealed by her attributes, the representation could also be regarded as an allegory of old age, transience, and physical decay.

According to Anelli, Bellotti's representations of the three Fates constituted a series, even if they were not produced at the same date.[7] The scholar dates the Budapest *Atropos* to post 1659, a few years after the representations of Lachesis, the most sumptuous of which, signed and dated to 1654, is held at the Staatsgalerie, Stuttgart (inv. 284).[8] The preparatory drawing of the painting, which was connected to the Budapest painting by Francesco Frangi, is held in a Munich private collection.[9] The sketch shows the same composition as the painting, though in a somewhat smaller size. But whereas in the drawing the Fate's countenance is softened by a faint, slightly malformed smile, in the painted version her features are controlled by an all-pervading bitterness. The third, slightly smaller and tighter version of the rendition in the Musée des Beaux-Arts, Caen, is attributed to an unknown French follower of the artist.[10]

Zsuzsanna Dobos

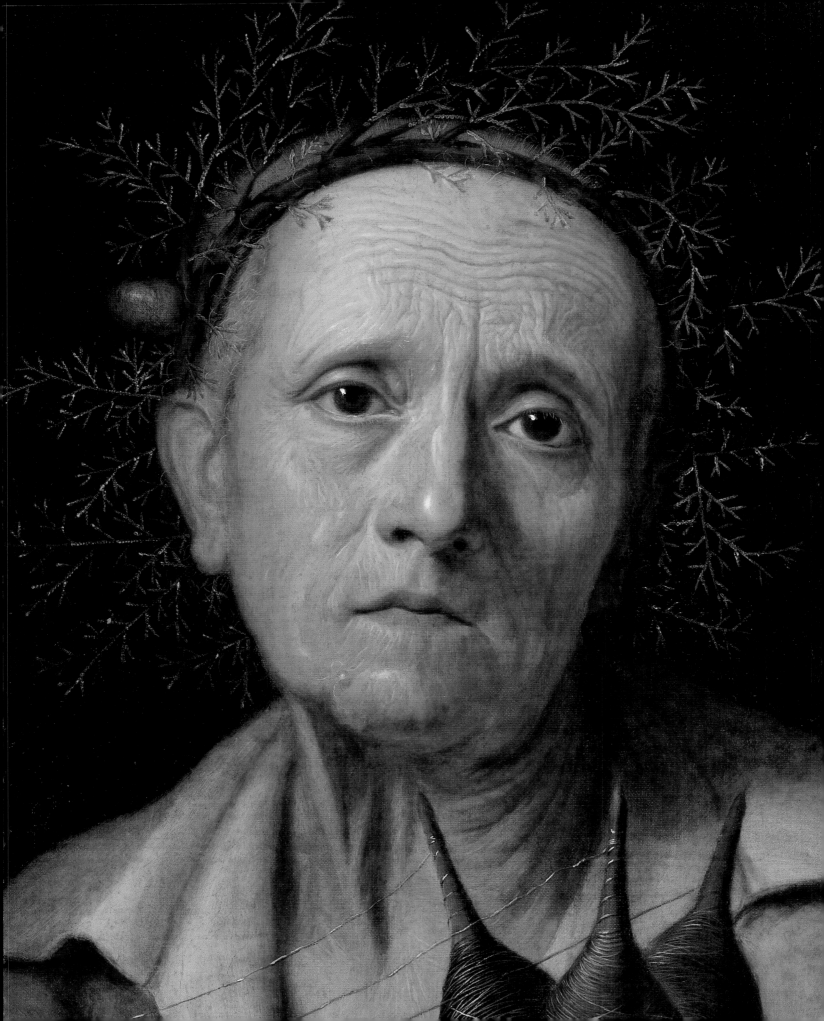

[1] On Pyrker see *PYRKER EMLÉKKÖNYV* 1987 and *PYRKER ÉRSEK KÉPTÁRA* 2002.

[2] See MÁTRAY 1846, p. 50 (no. 76). The painting is indicated as a work "of an unknown North-Italian painter" in the museum inventory and in PIGLER 1954, p. 184. Published as by Bellotti: PIGLER 1967, p. 55, SAFARIK 1973, p. 354–355, *MEISTERZEICHNUNGEN* 1987, no. 27; *A SUMMARY CATALOG* 1991, p. 8; ANELLI 1996, p. 6, 14 (no. 15), ANELLI AND BONOMI 1996, p. 99, 166, 168, 171 (no. 128), 259, *PYRKER ÉRSEK KÉPTÁRA* 2002, cat. no. 1.

[3] "Squisitissimo pittore, singolarmente nei ritratti e nelle mezze figure di capriccio, e fedelissimo copiatore della natura". See BRUNATI 1837, p. 26.

[4] PALLUCCHINI 1981, p. 284. With these words, Pallucchini described the *Lachesis* in the Staatsgalerie, Stuttgart (inv. 284).

[5] DEBAISIEUX 1994, p. 70–71, ANELLI AND BONOMI 1996, p. 166.

[6] For a later, nineteenth-century representation of Atropos with a wreath of cypress see DUCHESNE AND RÉVEIL 1830, p. 468.

[7] ANELLI AND BONOMI 1996, p. 166–167.

[8] IBID., p. 164, 376.

[9] Black chalk, brush and brown ink, hightened with white, on blue paper, 320 × 239 mm. *MEISTERZEICHNUNGEN* 1987, cat. no 27, MASTER DRAWINGS 1987, cat. no. 27; FRANGI 1993, cat. no. 47, p. 96–97.

[10] ANELLI AND BONOMI 1996, p. 167, DEBAISIEUX 1994, p. 70–71 (as "attributed to Pietro Bellotti").

Cat. n. III.3
Giovanni Martinelli
Youth Surprised by Death

1640s?
Oil on canvas, 60 × 80 cm (23.62 × 31.49 in.).
Florence (Italy), Gallerie degli Uffizi, inv. 3185.

A native of Montevarchi, a town near Florence, very little is known about Giovanni Martinelli's life.[1] The little information we can gather can be found in the records of the Florentine Accademia del Disegno, namely the academy of artists endorsed by the Medici since 1563.[2] Martinelli was a student of Jacopo Ligozzi's, and is documented in Florence in 1621. Judging from his works from the 1630s onward, in which there is a clear influence of Caravaggio, Orazio Gentileschi, Valentin de Boulogne, Simon Vouet, and Massimo Stanzione, he is believed to have stayed in Rome during the second half of the 1620s.[3] He then returned to Florence around the mid-1630s, where he lived until his death in 1659, and where he mainly received commissions from private collectors.[4]

Despite the work carried out by art historians, it has not been possible to completely reconstruct his artistic career. Indeed, the information provided by both archival documents and his few dated paintings is insufficient to establish a definitive chronology of his artworks. In addition, the few artworks mentioned in historical sources are now lost.[5] However, it is evident that in addition to sacred art, most of Martinelli's oeuvre consists of allegorical paintings addressing philosophical and moral subject matter, such as the one taken into consideration here. These paintings, intended for private collectors, were probably inspired by the work of Angelo Caroselli (which he may have seen in Rome), and by Ligozzi's allegorical drawings representing the overpowering presence of death, carried out around 1625.[6]

Youth Surprised by Death was initially attributed to Jacopo Vignali in the Uffizi catalog of 1890, and later considered to be the work of an anonymous seventeenth-century Tuscan artist.[7] The painting was damaged by the 1993 Mafia bombing of the Uffizi (see also **cat. n. IV.1**), after which it was restored.[8]

This painting is one of Martinelli's many allegorical canvases, aimed at encouraging meditations on the unpredictability of our fate. The main characters in the painting are Death, obviously embodied by the skeleton, and Youth, represented by the young man.[9] Death appears to this clearly wealthy young gentleman—made apparent by his embroidered shirt and jacket—who, quite surprisingly, seems unperturbed by the presence of Death. In fact, although Death is showing him an hourglass and gripping his shoulder to remind him that his hour has come, he does not look frightened, rather simply puzzled. Possibly, Martinelli's aim was to illustrate how fallacious it is for youth to believe in their own sense of invincibility and immortality. Indeed, this theme was addressed by Martinelli in another canvas titled *Death Comes to the Table* or *Memento Mori* (**figure 1**, p. 135). There, however, the young man being 'called' by death is filled with terror (as are the other young dinner guests at the table) and disbelief. He points at himself, clearly questioning the untimely 'call' of Death (again represented by a skeleton with an hourglass) to make sure it is really he who must die.

In Martinelli's painting, the inevitability and unpredictability of death are perfectly exemplified by the skeleton holding an hourglass—an object associated with death as it symbolizes the inexorable passage of time. As Samuel L. Macey points out, "in a secularizing world [...] man began to visualize his existence less and less in terms of eternity. [...] The hourglass offered a very dramatic symbol of time coming to an end insofar as the individual mortal was concerned."[10] Also, the imagery of Death holding an hourglass symbolizes the fact that death surprises all people in the midst of their earthly existence. This is especially the case with the young man portrayed by Martinelli. Indeed, the hourglass held by the skeleton in the painting in question is not empty, but in fact quite full, which is what the youth's gesture seems to be alluding to, in what appears to be a naive attempt to reason with Death.[11] But "[...] no one has power [...] over the day of death", says Ecclesiastes, and everybody—except Youth—realizes that reasoning with Death is impossible, no matter how young, rich, beautiful, full of life we are, or how much more fun we still wish to have.[12] As Ecclesiastes 2:1–11 also emphasizes, we should not delude ourselves into believing that earthly pleasures really are a means to deny, forget, and ultimately avoid death. They too shall pass, as they are transient, and we will then have to deal with our common and inevitable fate.

As mentioned above, many of Martinelli's paintings address philosophical and moral subject matter. This is particularly evident in this canvas, in which the untimely death of the young man is cause for reflection on the risks of an unexpected, and therefore potentially 'bad', death. Ever since the Middle Ages, and continuing well into the early modern era, a sudden and an unexpected death was considered problematic and 'bad'. The opposite scenario was that of a 'good', that is, an anticipated, death, which allowed for the *moriens* (i.e., the dying person) to receive the last rites.[13] If one has lived 'a good life' according to Catholic ethical principles, with an awareness that with each passing day we draw closer to death, then even if it occurs unexpectedly, death need not be feared.[14] The most fearsome scenario occurred when it involved the death of a young person who may have indulged without cause for thought in earthly pleasures, in this instance it

could mean that death could occur while in a state of sin and without the crucial last rites, the consequence of which was the eternal damnation of the soul.[15]

Therefore, Martinelli's painting functions as a *memento mori* directed in particular at the younger generation, and it evidently represents the troublesome question of whether an individual ever finds him or herself truly ready to die and face God's judgment.

Corinna Ricasoli

[1] Spinelli 2011, p. 23.

[2] All artists active in the city were affiliated with the Accademia, as this would guarantee their professional standing. For further reading on the birth, role, and functioning of the Accademia del Disegno in Florence, see Waźbiński 1987, Goldstein 1975, p. 145–152, and Faietti 2011, p. 13–37. See also Carrara 2008, p. 129–162, Wittkower and Wittkower 2007, p. 254, Ruffini 2011, p. 2, De Girolami Cheney 2007, p. 128, Summers 1969, Jack Ward 1972, but also Jack Ward 1976, and Barzman 1985.

[3] D'Afflitto 2008, and Spinelli 2011, p. 27.

[4] Spinelli 2011, p. 28.

[5] D'Afflitto 2008.

[6] See, for instance, Caroselli's *Young Student Tempted by the Senses* (Berlin, Private Collection), *Music and the Vanity of Power* (Florence, Galleria Corsini). See also Ligozzi's *Allegory of Death Strangling a Warrior* (New York, Pierpont Morgan Library, I,91) and *Death Trapping the Hunters* (Paris, Louvre, Département des Arts Graphiques, inv. 5033). These subjects were very popular among the Florentine intelligentsia, and may also be found in the oeuvre of Lorenzo Lippi and Cesare Dandini.

[7] Caneva 2001, p. 96. The Uffizi owns several paintings by Martinelli, none of which are unfortunately on display.

[8] Ibid.

[9] For the early modern representations of Death as a 'clean' skeleton, also known as *morte secca* (*dry death*), see Vertova 1992, p. 103–128, but also **cat. n. III.1**, and **cat. n. III.7**.

[10] Macey 1987, p. 44.

[11] La Costa 2005, p. 331.

[12] Eccles. 8:8.

[13] Ricasoli 2014, p. 44, Di Nola 1995, p. 76.

[14] See Ricasoli 2014, p. 43–52 and the bibliography therein, but also Ricasoli 2015, p. 456–467.

[15] La Costa 2005, p. 331.

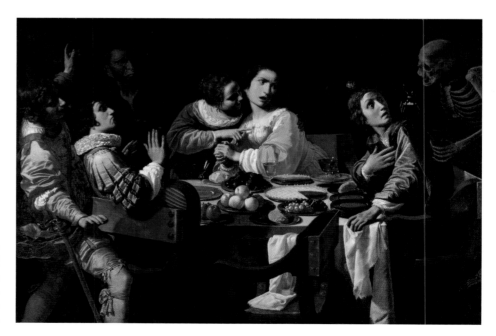

Figure 1:
Giovanni Martinelli, *Death Comes to the Banquet Table* (*Memento Mori*), ca. 1630.
Oil on canvas, 120.65 × 173.99 cm (47.5 × 68.5 in.).
New Orleans, LA (US),
New Orleans Museum of Art, inv. 56.57.

Hee, that on Earthly-things ,doth truſt,
Dependeth, upon Smoake, and Duſt.

ILLVSTR. XXIII.   Book.2

The Transience of Things

Some references to transience are more subtle: flowers that will wilt, fruit that will turn to rot, flies heralding decay.

Seventeenth-century still-life paintings, seemingly domestic artworks laden with expensive and exotic treasures, carry religious references to the passion of Jesus and the resurrection. Obvious symbols such as grapes and wine are accompanied by symbols less instantly recognizable today, but nonetheless operating as such.

Dead flies make the perfumer's ointment give off a foul odor [...].

(Ecclesiastes 10:1)

Cat. n. III.4
Edwaert Collier

Vanitas Still-Life with a Skull, Musical Instruments, a Globe, Books, and Writing Paraphernalia

1661.
Oil on canvas, 91 × 76 cm (35.82 × 29.92 in.).
Inscription: (on top edge of the book) *EC 1661*.
Amsterdam (the Netherlands), Salomon Lilian Dutch Old Master Paintings.

This *Vanitas Still-Life* belongs to Collier's early period.[1] He was born around 1640 in Breda, and moved to Haarlem in the 1650s. He probably received his training there, since his earliest works reveal the influence of Pieter Claesz. The painting is the earliest example of Claesz's impact on Collier. In 1655, Claesz painted a similar composition, particularly noticeable in the order of the objects. The young Collier, however, changed the contents of the book and added a curtain instead of a column in the back of the painting, as well as a laurel wreath on the skull.[2] Collier's early work also shows the influence of Vincent Laurensz van der Vinne. Collier's large *Vanitas Still-life* from 1656 was inscribed *V. Laurens* several times on one of the documents included in the composition.[3] He eventually moved to Leiden, where his residence is fully documented from 1667 to 1693, during which time he was admitted to the Guild of St. Luke in Leiden (1673). In 1693, Collier moved to London, and seems to have previously traveled there on several occasions, as many of his *trompe l'oeil* paintings incorporate English documents. His late works are brilliant *trompe l'oeil* assemblages of papers, combs, quill pens, scissors, watches, and other objects tucked into letter racks. Clearly legible papers, such as newspapers or dated parliamentary speeches, pin these works to a time and place. From the numerous examples, it seems likely that he returned to Leiden in 1702 and was still there in 1706. He must have moved back to London in 1707 because an extant work of his is signed with the addition 'fecit London' and dated from this year. His burial in London was registered the year after.

This vertically composed painting is Collier's earliest dated *Vanitas Still-Life*, in which all objects refer to the Old Testament book of Ecclesiastes, from which the term *vanitas* was derived, to remind the viewer of the transience of life and the vanity of worldly things. Although painted when he lived in Haarlem, Collier's detailed rendering of the objects show his affinities with the Leiden *fijnschilders*. On a table draped with a cloth, a skull, an hourglass, and a globe stand behind a book, opened to a page entitled *De Historien der Martelaren*, (*The History of Martyrs*), depicting an illustration of martyrs who are about to be executed.[4] The terrestrial globe shows the continent of America and represents the vanity of learning and earthly power. The laurel wreath on the skull served as a reminder of the fleetingness of victory. In front of the open book on our painting, an overturned *roemer* lying on top of a pearl necklace can be seen. They both symbolize fragility, while the pearl *collier*, which is both the name of the artist and the French word for necklace, was used as a self-referential symbol in several other paintings.[5] Among the musical instruments are a violin, a lute, and a shawm. Just as the hourglass unmistakably alludes to the transitory nature of human existence (the march of time), the instruments suggest the parallel between the fleeting nature of music and that of time, and refer to earthly pleasure (see also **cat. n. IV.7**, *Vanitas Still-Life* by N. Le Peschier). The snapped string of the violin symbolizes the broken threads of time and evokes the ephemerality of earthly existence. This works in tandem with the oil lamp, the consumed wick of which suggests the extinguishing of life.[6] The open almanac, coins, and glasses, shown next to a fallen inkwell and open quill-case, are also symbols referring to the transience of earthly interests.

Wendela Wagenaar-Burgemeister

[1] For further reading on the painting, see also MEIJER 1994, p. 181.

[2] BRUNNER-BULST 2004, p. 336.

[3] WURFBAIN 1998, p. 568.

[4] VAN HAEMSTEDE 1634, f. 71V, see also TUOMINEN 2014, p. 43–44, 269.

[5] WAHRMAN 2012, p. 68.

[6] WAGENAAR-BURGEMEISTER 2016, p. 12.

Cat. n. III.5
Giovanna Garzoni
Still-Life with Melon and Grapes

1640s.
Tempera and gouache on parchment, 35.5 × 49.5 cm (13.97 × 19.48 in.).
Poggio a Caiano (Florence, Italy), Museo della Natura Morta, inv. 4777.

Giovanna Garzoni was a celebrated miniaturist and still-life painter, and is considered one of the most important female painters in Italian art. Very little is known about her childhood or early training. She was born in Ascoli, in the Marche region, and archival evidence suggests that her parents were Venetian and that she may have been introduced to the making of art in Venice by her maternal grandfather, who was a goldsmith, or her uncle, who was a painter and printmaker.[1] In 1616, Garzoni traveled to Rome where she was encouraged to study the botanical engravings in what was considered to be the canonical text on the subject, the *Commentarii* by doctor and naturalist Pietro Andrea Mattioli.[2]

Garzoni went on to work for distinguished collectors in Venice, Florence, Rome, Naples, and Turin. While in Turin, from 1632–1637, her patron was Christine of France, Duchess of Savoy, and Garzoni would have had access to the court's collection of Netherlandish art.[3] Her style was also influenced by Fede Galizia, Panfilo Nuvolone, and Jacopo Ligozzi, the latter a Veronese artist at the Medici court whose works are considered to be the foundation of still-life painting in Florence (see also **cat. n. III.3**).[4] Like Ligozzi, Garzoni preferred to paint her still-life subjects in their actual dimensions and in great detail; she had a distinctive technique of stippling with the point of a brush.[5]

From 1642 until 1651, Garzoni was in Florence where she worked for the Grand Duke Ferdinando II de' Medici and his wife, the Grand Duchess Vittoria, and their court, and her best-known works are a series of twenty still-lifes of fruit and vegetables executed between 1650 and 1662 for Ferdinando II de' Medici.[6] Giovanna Garzoni never married, and she died in Rome at the age of seventy. Her highly successful career enabled her to accumulate considerable wealth, and she left her entire estate to the Accademia di San Luca, Rome, on the understanding that she was to be buried in the Accademia's church of Santi Luca e Martina. Her tomb was erected there in 1698.[7]

The still-life genre increased in popularity during the seventeenth century and this was advantageous for female artists such as Garzoni, the subject matter of flowers and still-life was, unlike history painting and fresco, deemed suitable for women, partially due to its smaller scale. It also had the advantage that its subject matter was inexpensive, available, and did not require knowledge of anatomical proportion.[8]

The painting *Still-Life with Melon and Grapes* is listed in a nineteenth-century inventory of the Medici villa of Poggio Imperiale; indeed, the same bowl, melon, fly, grapevine, and snail also appear in another more complex work by Garzoni, *The Old Man of Artimino*, which was listed in a seventeenth-century inventory of the villa. The Medici court had a particular interest in scientific categorization. However, this work is not merely an accurate and decorative reproduction of a melon and grapes, it also functions as a *vanitas* image and can be readily identified as such by the numerous allusions to death and resurrection within the painting.

The grapevine in Christian imagery represents Jesus and his sacrifice, and is based on the Gospel of John (15:1–8) where he says "I am the true vine". It is also perceived as a symbol of the Eucharist and the promise of redemption. The snail creeping on the grapevine has been interpreted as an allusion to the resurrection as it hides during times of cold or drought and re-emerges when conditions are right.[9] The purpose of the fly, which is prominently placed, is likely to be multifaceted—simultaneously representing the struggle between good and evil, it is also associated with death and decay and therefore acts as a *memento mori*. It was also thought the presence of a painted fly could ward off actual flies, who were associated with the plague. Furthermore, artists used the depiction of flies to show off their illusionistic skills.[10] The melon could be interpreted as a symbol of abundance, and was linked to luxury and the sin of gluttony; in northern European painting, it was a symbol for the need for moderation.[11]

Audrey Nicholls

[1] Baldasso 2005, p. 302–304.

[2] Tongiorgi Tomasi 2002, p. 77.

[3] Borzello 2000, p. 61.

[4] Strocchi 2003, p. 487.

[5] Borzello 2000, p. 62, 68, Tongiorgi Tomasi 2002, p. 82.

[6] Tongiorgi Tomasi 2002, p. 71, 77.

[7] Salvagni 2008, p. 51 (footnote 43).

[8] Borzello 2000, p. 62.

[9] Impelluso 2004, p. 32, 105, 112.

[10] Werness 2004, p. 183, 336–337.

[11] Barnes and Rose 2002, p. 38.

Cat. n. III.6
Johannes Hannot

Still-Life with a Lobster

second half of the 17th century.
Oil on canvas, 78.8 × 92.8 cm (31.02 × 36.53 in.).
Inscription: *I D Heem* (false signature on the lower left, covering the authentic signature revealed by X-ray)
Lille (France), Palais des Beaux-Arts, P 914.

The artwork originally entered the collections of the Palais des Beaux-Arts as a canvas by Jan Davidsz de Heem, but was later attributed to Johannes Hannot—one of his many followers. The painting is signed on the edge of the table, where there is a *trompe l'oeil*—a trick often used by De Heem and his students.[1] It was only following some diagnosis, carried out in 1979, that some traces of Hannot's original signature—later covered by a counterfeit—were found. This painting is in fact consistent with the artist's production. Other examples of lost signatures underlying that of the master are indeed known.[2]

The biography of Johannes Hannot is poorly documented. His father, Michiel, a tailor from Flanders, moved to Leiden in 1629.[3] Johannes had registered as a member of the guild of St. Luke from 1650 onward, but also had another job, like a number of painters from the northern Netherlands at that time who would often be merchants or innkeepers.[4] As a wine merchant, he met judges and wardens of the city, who were all part of his circle of customers.[5]

Was one of these notables perhaps the purchaser of this still-life? This type of production belonged indeed to the subjects sought for the decoration of the bourgeois houses, always more numerous where there was a prosperous economy.

An accumulation of food is elegantly arranged on a table covered with a green tablecloth with golden fringes. The base of a column in the background highlights the prestige and staging of the arrangement, which rests on an imaginary diagonal line.[6] Painted in a colorful palette, abundant foods and delicate objects are distributed on both sides of this axis. This composition is not unlike that of the *Still-Life with a Lobster* by Jan Davidsz de Heem (Toledo Museum of Art). Several other analogies with this table may suggest that this canvas by Hannot may have been directly inspired by it.[7]

Fruit dominates the composition, as is often the case with Hannot's still-lifes, where the notes of yellow, red, orange, and brilliant green dominate. Grapes, plums, peaches, apricots, cherries, the pomegranate, and the lemon indicate this is a luxurious banquet. The orange's central position is perhaps an allusion to the House of Orange, often represented through this fruit in portraits.[8] Fish and shellfish—here represented by a lobster and some shrimp—belong to lean foods according to the traditional codification. Fatty foods are only represented by a pie that has been partly eaten. To accompany these exceptional products, precious tableware is required: Venetian-style glasses, pewter dishes, and a silver *tazza*. These became recurring motifs of ceremonial tables, together with fringed tablecloths and napkins, or white, creased tablecloths, especially visible in the works of De Heem and Abraham van Beyeren.[9]

Because these paintings repeat a codified repertoire, in some instances directly derived from that of De Heem, these layouts are not representative of a specific situation, however natural they may look.[10] Behind the aesthetic research and the virtuosity of which these paintings testify to, a traditional symbolism persists—a moral dilemma between visual delight and religious fear.[11] Thus, cherries can symbolize the passion of Christ or paradise, and peaches recall the forbidden fruit. Grapes, like the wine nearby, refer to the Eucharist, while the lobster, the main character of the painting, evokes the resurrection because of its molt.

The insects, often present in *vanitas* paintings, are also present in this sophisticated table, where the fly in the foreground acts like a *trompe l'oeil*. Other than being evidently connected to decay, the fly is also associated with the devil. When accompanied by a butterfly, a symbol of the resurrection of the soul, they can together refer to the struggle between good and evil. And what about the knocked-down silver cup, the fragile glasses, or the damaged vine and grape seed that represent obvious evocations of the precariousness of existence?

The underlying Christian messages act as warnings. They invite reflection on both the transience of things and on temperance. This may be what the lemon symbolizes in the foreground. This fruit, associated with wine, mitigates the effect of alcohol, and could indeed be a symbol of temperance. In a context of exceptional economic growth, accumulation and dissipation of wealth was tempting.[12] Material wealth was hardly compatible with the values of austerity peculiar to Protestant society, from which came the main recipients of these ceremonial paintings.[13]

Representing a material affirmation of self through the richness and beauty that it puts on the stage, Johannes Hannot's *Still-Life with a Lobster* may be considered a condemnation of luxury and excesses that move the soul away from salvation.

Donatienne Dujardin[14]

[1] Auffret 1989, p. 141.

[2] Meijer 2003, p. 211 (footnote 211).

[3] Auffret 1989, p. 140.

[4] Thieme, *et al.* 1922, p. 596. Ebert-Schifferer 1999, p. 96.

[5] Auffret 1989, p. 140.

[6] Meijer 2003, p. 220. The base of a column appears regularly in the background of the still-lifes by De Heem from the late 1630s onward.

[7] See *Donation d'Antoine Brasseur* 1981, especially p. 75–76.

[8] See Welu 1979, p. 35.

[9] Examples include: Abraham Hendricksz van Beyeren, *Still-Life of Apparatus*, circa 1665, Amsterdam, Rijksmuseum (SK-A-3944); Jan Davidsz de Heem, *A Table of Desserts*, 1640, Paris, Musée du Louvre (inv. 1321).

[10] The vine leaf with a butterfly may be found in several compositions by De Heem, such as *Still-Life with Peeled Lemon* (Paris, Louvre Museum, inv. 1320) or *Still-Life with a Lobster* (Toledo Museum of Art, inv. 1952.25).

[11] Ebert-Schifferer 1999, p. 134.

[12] In the Netherlands lived the wealthiest bourgeoisie in Europe. See ibid., p. 132.

[13] Ibid., p. 122.

[14] Translated from French by Corinna Ricasoli.

All Flesh, is like the wither'd Hay,
And, so it springs, and fades away.

OMNIS CARO ŒNUM · ☉ ·

ILLVSTR. XLVIII.

Book. 4

The Transience of Youth and Beauty

The loss of youth and beauty either through an unexpected early death or through the aging process were also popular themes, acting as warnings against physical vanity and, in some instances, of the dangers of being spiritually unprepared for the arrival of death.

Rejoice, young man, while you are young, and let your heart cheer you in the days of your youth. [...] Banish anxiety from your mind, and put away pain from your body; for youth and the dawn of life are vanity.

(Ecclesiastes 11:9–10)

Cat. n. III.7
Agostino dei Musi?

Mortalia Facta Peribunt

16th century.
Engraving, 35.9 × 25.2 cm (14.13 × 9.92 in.).
Inscription: *Mortalia facta peribvnt.*
Washington, DC (US), The National Gallery of Art, inv. 1961.17.6.

The monogram in the lower right-hand side of this engraving bears the letter M, which has led some to attribute the engraving to the so-called Monogrammist M.[1] It has also been suggested that the work may be attributed to Agostino dei Musi, called Agostino Veneziano, or to the School of Agostino dei Musi.[2] Agostino Veneziano used the monogram 'AV'. He began his career in Venice and, after a period in Florence, he went to Rome, in 1516, where he spent the following ten years, producing prints after artists such as Raphael, Giulio Romano, Rosso Fiorentino, and Michelangelo.[3] This has led some to opine that the 'M' relates to Michelangelo and that the artist provided the design for the engraving. Certainly, from a stylistic standpoint the references to Michelangelo are unmistakable—the rather masculine features of the body, the pose, which is reflective of *The Dying Slave* (Louvre), and the pilaster, which also relates to drawings for the same tomb design for Julius II, suggest a strong connection.[4]

Another reason to suspect the intervention of Michelangelo has been suggested by Anne Freedberg, who argued that the work can be interpreted to represent, in allegorical form, Platonic or Neo-Platonic ideas that relate to the soul. She noted that in Plato's *Phaedrus*, the philosopher writes: "The immortal soul soars upward into heaven, but the mortal drops her plumes and settles upon the earth".[5] Another sentence reads: "If, however, she [the soul] drops her wings and falls to earth, then she takes the form of man [...]".[6] Freedberg links the feathered wing in the foreground with this concept, going as far as to suggest that the mortal woman is mourning the loss of her wings.[7] The idea that the print carries an underlying reference to Platonic or Neo-Platonic ideas is credible, given the intellectual and erudite court of the Medici in Florence which Michelangelo experienced early in his career, influencing his life and work thereafter.

The inscription *Mortalia facta peribunt* (All that is mortal must perish) suggests that the engraving was primarily designed as a warning against the transience of beauty. Visual representations of Death as a skeleton with a cloak or hood holding an hourglass began to appear in the first half of the fifteenth century and, from that time, appeared in numerous allegories including images of Death surprising a naked woman at her toilet. Death carries away its victims under the orders of Time, whose symbols also include the hourglass and, in addition, wings (see also **cat. n. III.12**), one of which can be seen almost tipping the woman's toe. At Death's knee is a wheel, which is the principal attribute of Fortune, and symbolizes how the Wheel of Fortune can turn and raise people to the highest levels of society but can also bring about their downfall. Death, represented as a sinewy, decomposing, skeletal, corpse sneaks up on the woman who is so vainly enamored with herself that she has yet to sense its presence.

The woman is twisted around in order to examine her image in the mirror from behind, which has the effect of displaying her naked body to the viewer. In the New Testament, the Apocalypse (Revelation 16:15) warns that the savior will come as a thief to the unprepared and woe to those who are taken unawares. The metaphor in art for being unprepared, and for sin, is nakedness. The most frequent sin represented by a nude woman was that of lust—a sin that paradoxically could be said to be provoked by the engraving.[8]

Her pose is such that it suggests dance, and perhaps this was intended to not only enhance the sense of eroticism, but also as a reference to the *danse macabre*, which was a dance representing people from all walks of life being led to their graves that was performed in religious drama. It acted, as does the engraving, as a reminder that worldly possessions were vain glories, as death could arrive at any time.

Audrey Nicholls

[1] Von Bartsch 1801–1821, p. 541.

[2] Freedberg 1960, p. 106. A copy of the print in the Royal Collection Trust, London, has been attributed to Agostino dei Musi (RCIN 830714), whereas the Minneapolis Institute of Art attributes their copy (P.68.220) to the School of Augustino dei Musi.

[3] Witcombe 1998.

[4] Freedberg 1960, p. 106.

[5] Ibid.

[6] Ibid.

[7] Ibid. See Nehames and Woodruff 1997, p. 524–526.

[8] Warner 2000, p. 295.

MORTALIA FACTA PERIBVNT

Cat. n. III.8*
Pompeo Batoni

Time Orders Old Age to Destroy Beauty

1746.
Oil on canvas,135.3 × 96.5 cm (53.26 × 37.99 in.).
Inscription: *P. B. 1746*.[1]
London (England), National Gallery, NG6316.

Pompeo Batoni, the most celebrated painter of eighteenth-century Rome, was born in Lucca (Tuscany), the son of a goldsmith. He moved to Rome in May 1727, and quickly attracted attention for his exquisite drawings after the antique. These especially appealed to wealthy foreign tourists, including the British (and particularly Irish) *milordi* of the Grand Tour, who also enabled him to develop as an ambitious portraitist; Batoni's wider reputation still rests on the glamorous 'swagger portraits' which were among the eagerly sought-after souvenirs of his sitters' time in the Eternal City. Among both his local patrons and well-to-do Lucchese sponsors, however, Batoni was prized as a painter of altarpieces, narratives, and sacred and profane allegories, of which the *Time Orders Old Age to Destroy Beauty* is a memorable example.[2]

Such allegories were a particular source of pride for Batoni. He saw them as a showcase for his abilities as an imaginative and scholarly *auteur* working in the grand tradition of Italian subject painting; they exemplified his own resourceful powers of poetic invention and skill in composition, while also referencing the great art of the past.[3] With its heroic, classically-inspired figures, and steals from Renaissance masters such as Batoni's beloved Raphael, *Time Orders Old Age to Destroy Beauty* admirably rises to the challenge, exhibiting all the trademarks of its author's highly finished, ornamental style.[4] A mastery of luminous color is supplemented by a particular skill in organizing light and shade; the forms are modeled with a surprising softness and subtlety in the shadows, giving way to a vigorous surety of touch in the highlighted areas, particularly around the head and shoulders of Time. It is here, and in the general interrelationship of the figures, that one can best appreciate Batoni's excellence as a draftsman and his skill in choreographing figures within compact compositions. The artist also affords himself a rare *trompe-l'oeil* flourish, as Time's wing brushes up and out of the picture frame at the extreme right.

It is clear from a complementary pendant, the *Allegory of Lasciviousness* now in the Hermitage, St. Petersburg (GE-3735), that *Time Orders Old Age to Destroy Beauty* was conceived with a moral imperative in mind—one sympathetic to the famous introductory maxim of the book of Ecclesiastes: "Vanity of vanities, all is vanity".[5] Batoni delivered the pair to their commissioner, the Lucchese connoisseur and collector Bartolomeo Talenti, in the early months of 1747. In accompanying letters to Talenti, the artist proudly promoted the works as the "offspring of my imagination", providing careful explanations of their iconography. This has proved particularly useful in the case of the *Allegory of Lasciviousness* which depicts, in Batoni's words, "Lasciviousness who pushes away from herself the lover left without wealth, who at the same time will be embraced by Poverty, daughter of Lasciviousness". The symbolism of *Time Orders Old Age to Destroy Beauty* was more obvious: "you will see Time seated in command of Old Age, who will be a handsome old hag who scratches the face of a young woman of singular beauty."[6] The iconography of the latter work also drew on a number of well-entrenched pictorial traditions: the swarthy, nut-brown figure of Old Age, her wisps of grey hair emergent under a peasant's headscarf, is familiar from sixteenth-century Venetian painting, particularly the *Col Tempo* (also known as *La Vecchia*) of ca.1506–1510 in the Gallerie dell'Accademia, Venice (272), by Giorgione. The juxtaposition of two representations of femininity, one young, fresh-faced, and alluring, the other old and withered, was also a common trope of narrative painting from the Renaissance onward—see, for example, Gerrit von Honthorst's *Concert* elsewhere in this exhibition (see **cat. n. IV.4**). Although Batoni is notable for introducing a personification of Old Age as his assassin, Time's antagonistic relationship with Beauty was also frequently represented, and notable treatments of the theme by two painters previously active in seventeenth-century Rome, Giovanni Domenico Cerrini and Simon Vouet exist in the Prado Museum, Madrid (P00097 and P02987). In the case of Vouet's rendering, however, it is Beauty, assisted by personifications of Love and Hope, who energetically gains the upper hand, vanquishing a prostrate Time. Furthermore, the associated theme of the conflict between Time and Love has been placed at the forefront of the numerous interpretations of the famous *Allegory of Venus, Cupid, Folly and Time* of 1545 by Agnolo di Cosimo, called Bronzino (see **figure 1**, p. 45), also in the National Gallery, London (NG651).[7] It is almost inevitable that the latter should also have influenced Batoni, and there are compositional similarities in the positioning of certain limbs and gestures within an upright, tightly packed design (particularly evident, for example, in the way Old Age violently reaches across the upper register of the composition in a manner similar to Bronzino's figure of Time). With his grandfatherly beard and hourglass, Time is, to modern eyes, still an instantly recognizable figure in both paintings.

A surviving preparatory drawing (Worcester Museum, Worcester, Massachusetts, inv. 1979.18) reveals how Batoni refined his representation of Time: instead of clutching an hourglass (the sands of which have already run out), the artist originally conceived that Time should cradle his other customary

attribute, a scythe (see also **cat. n. III.12**).[8] In the work as painted, Batoni transformed the long handle into a staff clutched by Old Age as an emblem of infirmity and lifelong toil. It now also acts as a supportive counterbalance to the shocking violence with which the old harridan, at Time's almost casual behest, shoots out a gnarled claw to disfigure the face of the statuesque, immobile figure of Beauty. The latter's unresponsive, unassuming expression may seem an emotionally stilted misstep on Batoni's part, but it is arguably essential to the painting's intended didacticism: Beauty is naively unsuspecting of its imminent vulnerability at the hands of Time, and its agent, Old Age.

Philip Cottrell

[1] The inventory number '187' at the bottom right derives from the painting's time in the Koucheleff Besborodko Collection.

[2] For recent, detailed accounts of Batoni's career, see *Pompeo Batoni* 2007 and Bowron 2016.

[3] For Batoni as a painter of allegory, with specific reference to the work under discussion, see Clark 1959, p. 236 and *Pompeo Batoni* 2007, p. 8, 29–30, 138.

[4] As first noticed by Clark 1959, p. 236, the figure of Beauty is freely adapted from François Duquesnoy's statue of *St. Susanna* (1630–1633) in the church of S. Maria di Loreto in Rome while the figure of Time is drawn (in reverse) from the figure of Paris in Marcantonio Raimondi's *Judgment of Paris* (ca. 1517–1520), after a design by Raphael.

[5] Eccles. 1:2, KJV. The *Allegory of Lasciviousness*, oil on canvas, 138 × 100 cm (54.33 × 39.37 in.), is discussed in Imbellone 2008, p. 208–209. By 1798, both *Time orders Old Age to destroy Beauty* and *Allegory of Lasciviousness* had entered the collection of the Russian prince, Alexander Andréevitch Besborodko, alongside two other Batoni allegories of uncertain origin, *Philosophy Reigning over the Arts*, dated 1747, now also Hermitage Museum, St. Petersburg (GE-3734), and *Time Revealing Truth*, ca. 1745–1746, now Museum of Art, Rhode Island School of Design, Providence (inv. 59.065). While in the Besborodko Collection, consecutive inventory numbers were inscribed on all four which confused their intended pairings. This shared provenance also raised the possibility that the four were originally of one series, and were all commissioned by Talenti. The theory was, however, convincingly dismissed in *Pompeo Batoni* 2007, p. 30. See also Levey 1971, p. 9–10.

[6] Batoni first mentions the commission in a letter to Talenti of 4 July 1744, declaring that the subjects were "dalla mia fantasia". His description of *Lasciviousness* appears in a subsequent letter of 18 July 1744: "La Lascivia che discaccia da se l'amante ridotto senza ricchezze, quale verrà nello stesso tempo abbracciato dalla Povertà figlia della Lascvia". He describes *Time orders Old Age to destroy Beauty* in another letter in August of the same year (the day is unspecified): "onde si vedrà il tempo a sedere in atto di commandare alla vecchiezza, che sarà una bella vecchia, che tocchi il volto d'una giovane d'una singolare bellezza…". These were dispatched to Talenti on 20 February 1747, and had reached their destination by 22 March. The correspondence is discussed and quoted extensively in Bowron 2016, p. 107.

[7] See Bosch 1990.

[8] Red chalk on paper, 28.1 × 21.8 cm (11.06 × 8.58 in.).

Cat. n. III.9
Attributed to Daniel Preisler

Memento Mori

ca. 1660.
Oil on panel, 45 × 35 cm (17.71 × 13.77 in.).
Inscription: (top) *Memento mori*, (bottom) *Die Schönheit ist ein flüchtig ding / Welch weiser Mann wolt den setzen sein / Zuversicht auf ein solch Gut das bald / Als wie ein Glas zubricht.*
Munich (Germany), Kunstkammer Georg Laue.

The attribution to the German painter Daniel Preisler derives from a comparison with a signed painting in the Germanisches Nationalmuseum (German National Museum) in Nuremberg, in which the artist represented himself playing the lute among his family shortly before his death in 1665.[1] This painting shows Preisler's second wife, Magdalena, whose face is strikingly similar to that of the young woman represented on the present panel. Indeed, the same facial features recur throughout Preisler's oeuvre, suggesting that Magdalena acted as a model for him. Originally from Prague, the Preisler family immigrated to Saxony for religious reasons when Daniel was young. In 1642, he was apprenticed to the Dresden court painter Christian Schiebling. However, he surpassed his master quite quickly and settled in Nuremberg in 1652, where he became a renowned artist and a member of the city council. Joachim von Sandrart praises Preisler's work in his art-historical book entitled *Teutsche Academie* (1675), noting that some German princes offered him a position at their court.[2] While Preisler seems to have specialized in portraits, he clearly had a predilection for allegories. For instance, his family portrait can be read as an allegory of the five senses, as an allegory of vanity, as well as a reference to salvation history. For this *Memento Mori* painting, he used his skill as an accomplished portraitist to create a pictorial allegory that stands out through its artistic quality as well as through its unusual iconography.

At first sight, the panel presents itself like a portrait with a Latin inscription at the top, German verses at the bottom, and an oval medallion opening at the center to reveal a female bust.[3] The bust, however, is split into two halves, showing the woman alive on one side, at the peak of her beauty, and dead on the other side, as a decaying corpse. In accordance with the Latin inscription *Memento Mori* (remember that you have to die), and with the German verses ("Beauty is an elusive thing, what wise man would trust so confidently in such a thing that breaks as easily as glass"), the painting focuses on the fleetingness of human existence and underlines the transience of youth and beauty, thus warning the beholder against excessive vanity. At the same time, this allegoric depiction gives a clue as to why mankind is mortal—while the beautiful young woman carries a pearl necklace, a snake is encircling the neck of her dead body as a visual reminder of Eve's dealing with the serpent that led directly to the fall of humanity.

Memento mori artworks were popular in the early modern era, but the representation of a woman with a split face, half dead and half living, is rarely found in paintings. Rather, it is peculiar to small-scale sculptures—mostly of rosary beads carved in ivo-

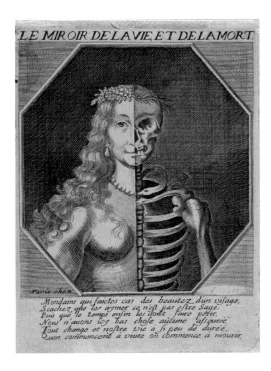

Figure 1:
French engraver, *Le miroir de la vie et de la mort*, 17th century.
Print, 15 x 11 cm (5.9 x 4.3 in.).
Hamburg (Germany), Museum für Kunst und Gewerbe, n. E1956.58.69.

ry and used for prayer since the early sixteenth century. These are commonly shaped as Janus heads with a living man or woman portrayed on one face and a decaying skull on the back of his or her head.[4] As a variation of this type, some seventeenth-century rosary beads show the head of a man split into two halves, between life and death, as in the present panel.[5] Engravings may have contributed to the popularity of this motif. Indeed, at least one French copperplate entitled *Le miroir de la vie et de la mort* (*The Mirror of Life and Death*", **figure 1**, p. 154) is obviously akin in composition to the artwork discussed here.[6] It might have been the source of Preisler's inspiration. Two paintings of the same type that were, however, executed in the eighteenth century, are also worth mentioning: a large canvas in a private collection and a miniature on copper in the Wellcome Collection in London (**figure 2**), both show a woman half dead and half living, albeit in the manner of a three-quarter portrait.[7]

Virginie Spenlé

[1] Tacke 1995, p. 180–181.

[2] Röttgen 1962, p. 48.

[3] Published in *The Kunstkammer* 2016, p. 105, 124.

[4] *Zum Sterben schön* 2006, p. 92–108, Barnet 1997, p. 277–278, cat. no. 278–279.

[5] *Masterpieces of Ivory* 1985, p. 248–249.

[6] Pieske 1964, p. 12.

[7] *Zauber der Medusa* 1987, p. 432, cat. no. 417, *For Your Eyes Only* 2014, p. 103, cat. no. 144, Arnold and Olsen 2003, p. 135.

Figure 2:
Florentine artist?, *Memento Mori*, 18th century.
Oil on copper, 9.7 × 8.8 cm (3.81 × 3.46 in.).
London (England), Wellcome Collection, n. WL.45064i.

Whil'ſt thou doſt, here, injoy thy breath,
Continue mindfull of thy Death.

The Inevitability of Death

Death inevitably comes to us all. Rather than fear its arrival, we should live life as best we can, otherwise—Ecclesiastes warns—it would be better for us not to have lived at all.

The universality of the inevitability of death and the hopes and fears surrounding the possibility of eternity in heaven, hell, or simply oblivion, resulted in a proliferation of artworks, including jewelry, that made direct reference to it.

Time, in its personified and iconographic form, also makes its appearance in a number of the works, perhaps most strikingly in the statuette of the *Allegory of Time*, complete with wings, hourglass, and scythe.

All go to one place; all are from the dust, and all turn to dust again.

No one has power over the wind to restrain the wind, or power over the day of death [...]

[Better] *the day of death, than the day of birth.*

(Ecclesiastes 3:20, 8:8, 7:1)

Cat. n. III.10
Bartholomaeus Bruyn the Elder

Portrait of a Man (recto), *Skull in a Niche* (verso)

ca. 1520s.
Oil on panel, 30.48 × 22.86 cm (12 × 9 in.).
Inscription: (on the verso) *Quid tibi mortalis cordi est homo quidve superbis / Cum rapiam iuvenes quotidie atque senes. / Esto memor quod pulvis eris, et vermibus esca, In gelida putris quando iacebis humo.*
Chicago, IL (US), Richard Harris Collection.

Bartholomaeus Bruyn the Elder was a highly successful painter working in Cologne, Germany, during the sixteenth century. His earliest documented work was for an altarpiece illustrating the *Coronation of the Virgin,* 1515–1516 (Smith College Museum of Art, Northampton, MA), painted for the Italian nobleman Peter von Clapis, law professor at the University of Cologne, and his wife, Bela Bonenberg, both of whom appear in the triptych. Many of Bruyn's altarpieces featured portraits, and he became the leading portrait painter in sixteenth-century Cologne. He opened a school for portraiture and introduced the genre to the region, where previously there had been no tradition of portraiture.

Initially he was influenced by Jan Joest, and also Joos van Cleve, whose style influenced his portraits prior to 1539, after which point the influence of Hans Holbein can be detected. Around 1529, he had begun to emulate the style of the Italian High Renaissance artists, particularly Raphael and Michelangelo. Knowledge of their works seems to have reached him via Jan van Scorel and Maarten Heemskerck, and through Marcantonio Raimondi's prints after Raphael. Bruyn did not sign his portraits, and attributions to him are mainly based on stylistic grounds. His sitters were his fellow citizens, and he himself was an active member of Cologne society—he was an elected member of Cologne's Auxiliary and City Councils.[1]

Little is known of the genesis of these paintings, which may have originally been conceived as a diptych to be viewed side by side. Alternatively, the portrait may have been designed to be viewed on the recto, and the skull on the verso, acting as a chilling reminder that ultimately this will be the fate of the sitter, and indeed our own. Nothing is known about the sitter of this portrait, although his attire suggests he may have been a wealthy man. Entwined around his fingers are a set of prayer beads which may indicate that the sitter was Catholic.

A religious confraternity devoted to the saying of the rosary numbered over 100,000 members in Cologne within seven years of its establishment by Jacob Sprenger in 1475, and it was heavily promoted in the sixteenth century by Catholic preachers in response to Protestant criticism of devotion to the Virgin Mary. For members of the rosary confraternity, the prayers offered protection from the fear of living in hell for eternity.[2]

The skull, the under-drawing of which is clearly visible, is placed in an otherwise empty stone niche and is bereft of any worldly goods, a reminder that we cannot take our wealth with

us. Corinna Ricasoli has identified the origins of the inscription written below, the first two lines of which were taken from a bilingual poem (Latin and German) by Sebastian Brant, *De periculoso scacorum ludo inter mortem et humanam conditionem* which can be translated as 'The dangerous chess game between death and the human condition'. The poet imagines Death and Man locked in perpetual contest, and as in chess, Man tries to defend himself from Death, but to no avail, as Death keeps moving forward, sometimes swiftly, sometimes slowly, but nevertheless inexorably. The outcome is always the same—no one has ever defeated Death. In the poem, the lines *Quid tibi mortalis cordi est homo* [:] *quid ve superbis! Cum rapiam iuvenes quotidie atque senes* are spoken by Death, and can be translated as "What is close to your heart, oh mortal man? What [is close to your heart], oh you proud? [The thought that] Every day I reap both the young and the old." The final two lines, *Esto memor quod pulvis eris, et vermibus esca, In gelida putris quando iacebis humo,*

which can be translated as "Remember that you are dust and food for [grave] vermin when you will lie rotting beneath the cold earth", are verses by Alain de Lille, and are a part of his *Parables*, the final parts of which address the issue of the vanity of the world and the misery of man.[3]

Audrey Nicholls

[1] CASWELL 1998.

[2] WINSTON 1993, p. 619, 629, 633.

[3] The reading of the inscription was possible thanks to the help of Renzo Iacobucci. The translation from Latin is by Serafino Lo Iacono. The translation into English is by Corinna Ricasoli. For the verses, see BRANT 1498, no page number. The verses on the painting are spoken by Death, as the lines are preceded by "Mors inferius loquitur", which means "Death says the following". The frame of the painting partially covers the last word, *superbis*. See also D'ALVERNY 1965, p. 52.

Cat. n. III.11
Egbert van Panderen
Mors ultima linea rerum
ca. 1610–1620.
Engraving, 18.71 × 11.73 cm (7.37 × 4.62 in.).
Chicago, IL (US), Richard Harris Collection, P203.

This print, which until now has been attributed to an anonymous sixteenth-century artist, should be attributed to Egbert van Panderen, a Dutch engraver born in Haarlem in around 1581, for reasons explained below.[1] Not much is known about the life of this printmaker, possibly because he never reached any particular degree of fame. In 1606, however, he was accepted as a member of the Guild of Saint Luke in Antwerp, the city in which he apparently lived most of his life.[2] Almost all of his oeuvre consists of reproductions from better-known masters from the Netherlands—such as Otto van Veen, David Teniers the Elder, Peter Paul Rubens, and Cornelis de Vos—and from Italy, such as Antonio Tempesta and the Cavalier d'Arpino.[3] He seems to have died after 1628, possibly in Amsterdam.[4] The earliest and few biographies on this artist are from the nineteenth century and mention his preference for the burin technique, as well as a degree of stiffness that can be detected in his style.[5]

This print illustrates a skeleton enclosed in an oval frame, decorated with hourglasses and skulls, some of which wear crowns. The uppermost skull wears the papal tiara, while the lowest is placed on top of swords and a book and wears a helmet—clearly a symbol of spiritual and temporal power, respectively. The frame itself is surrounded by two cartouches; the inscription above reads *Mors sceptra ligonibus aequat*—Latin for "Death makes scepters and hoes equal"; the inscription below quotes the celebrated verse from Horace's *Epistles*—*Mors ultima linea rerum*, namely "Death is the last line of things", meaning that death is the end of all earthly matters.[6] This verse also gives the title to this print. At the four corners of this macabre composition, skulls and bones reiterate the *memento mori* theme of this engraving. Further below, an inscription in Latin attributed to Augustine of Hippo—"You flourish in wealth and boast of the society of the great and powerful; you rejoice in the beauty of the body and the honours which men pay to you. Consider yourself, that you are mortal, that you are earth, and into the earth you shall go".[7]

This print is known through several exemplars in London, Amsterdam, and Berlin, which, however, differ from the present engraving in a number of details, in particular the inscriptions on the cartouches.

The British Museum in London owns two almost identical copies of this print (see inv. 1863,0509.805, and inv. 1862,0614.1562, **figure 1**, p. 166), hence the present consideration of an attribution of the Richard Harris exemplar to Van Panderen. The two prints at the British Museum are likely to be from the first and second state of the same copperplate, which means that an alteration was made to the copperplate after the first print (inv. 1863,0509.805) was made, and that the signature of Van Panderen was subsequently added underneath Augustine's Latin inscription and appears in inv. 1862,0614.1562. The Harris print lacks the artist's signature and has the addition of an outer double frame decorated with phytomorphic elements, which encloses the whole image, but overall, the similarities are notable, especially in relation to the inscriptions.

Other versions may be found at the Rijksmuseum in Amsterdam (RP-P-OB-24.416, **figure 2**, p. 167), and at the Kupferstichkabinett in Berlin (inv. 281-43, **figure 3**, p. 167). At first glance, it is evident that the Amsterdam version differs from the prints mentioned so far mainly due to the inscriptions on the cartouches (see footnote 8) and the lack of an inscription at the very bottom of the print.[8] The version in Berlin also has different cartouche inscriptions (see footnote 9), but—contrary to the one in Amsterdam—it has an inscription at the very bottom.[9] A closer examination and comparison of the Amsterdam, Berlin, London, and Harris exemplars show minor differences also in the various decorative skulls on the surrounding oval frame, as well as in the skeleton itself, especially in the details of its teeth, of the foramina on the cheekbones, of the internasal suture, and other similar anatomical details.

This suggests that Van Panderen may have carried out four versions of this print, possibly on different copperplates, of which only one is known in its two different states—namely, the one after which the London copies were made. In addition, given the Amsterdam print bears the names of the designer, the engraver, and the printer, and that the Berlin exemplar only bears the name of the printer, and given that these two printers are different, as are the inscriptions, we could hypothesize that rather than two different states of the same plate, these could be two different plates, given to the printers Johannes Eillarts and Raphael Sadeler I, respectively.[10]

Of the four variations of this print discussed so far, and on the basis of the inscriptions and subject matter, the Harris engraving should be associated with the prints in London in terms of overall composition, but maybe not in terms of 'use'. Indeed, the London exemplars are part of a series of four engravings illustrating the *Quattuor Servitutes Hominum* (*The Four Servitudes of Men*), namely Death, Purgatory, Heaven, and Hell—a concept connected to the Four Last Things which, according to Catholic eschatology, are ultimately what will be faced at the end of life—death, judgment, heaven, and hell.[11] Certainly, prints such as

Mors sceptra ligonibus æquat.

Mors vltima linea rerum.

Diuitijs flores, et maiorum nobilitate te iactas, et exul-
tas de pulchritudine corporis, et honoribus qui tibi ab
hominibus deferuntur? Respice te ipsum quia mortalis
es, et quia terra es, et in terram ibis.

these were a commercial product in the Catholic city of Antwerp, where concepts of salvation continued to include the need for the last rites and the existence of purgatory.[12] These *Quattuor Servitutes Hominum* are all consistent in their compositional structure—a central allegorical figure enclosed within a frame with thematically-relevant decorations, cartouches above and below the frame, and an inscription at the bottom consistent with the theme of the print.

As mentioned above, the slight anatomical differences and the more significant differences of the outer engraved frame in the Harris print suggest that the Harris engraving may have been carried out using a different copperplate, possibly given to a different printer. The sheets relating to this copperplate may have been sold individually as a *memento mori*, and not as part of the *Servitutes* series. This would further attest to the success of this composition, the message of which clearly is to be mindful of our death, as death is inevitable, regardless of our social rank.

Corinna Ricasoli

[1] The engraving was published as "Unknown artist" also in DEATH 2012—catalog of the exhibition held in London (Wellcome Collection). See also HOLLSTEIN 1964, p. 101.

[2] See VAN DER STIGHELEN 1998.

[3] Ibid., ZANI 1820, p. 108, GOULD 1838, p. 397.

[4] VAN DER STIGHELEN 1998.

[5] See THE CYCLOPAEDIA 1819, no page number, but de facto p. 516 from the frontispiece, MALASPINA DI SANNAZARO 1824, p. 207–208, DE BONI 1840, p. 742–743.

[6] Horace, *Epistles*, I, 16, 79.

[7] "Divitiis flores, et maiorum nobilitate te iactas; et exsultas de patria, de pulchritudine corporis, et honoribus qui tibi ab hominibus deferuntur: respice te ipsum, quia mortalis es, et quia terra es, et in terram ibis." The English translation cited here may be found in DEATH 2012, p. 14. For the Latin quote, see AUGUSTINUS 1838, p. 2620. Contrary to what has been published in DEATH 2012, p. 14, however, this caveat should not to be attributed to Prosper of Aquitaine, who was instead a collector of Augustine's quotations. See CANISIUS 1833, p. 641, and TIRO 1972, sententia CCCXCII.

[8] The inscriptions of the Amsterdam exemplar read: *Fui non sum etenim quid hucusque?* (I am not what I have been thus far?), and *Vanitas vanitatum et omnia vanitas. Eccl. 1.*

[9] The print in Berlin bears the following inscriptions: *Et in pulverem mortis deduxisti me. Psalm. 21* (And you lay me in the dust of death. Psalm 22:15 in NRSV), and *Putredini dixi, pater meus est: mater mea, et soror mea vermibus. Iob. 17* (I have said to corruption, Thou art my father: to the worm, Thou art my mother, and my sister. Job 17:14, KJV), and *Ossa patent, geminis que oculis extorribus orbes, fractaque convulsi septa molaris hiant. Oderis hanc huius quantumvis Icona Formae Archetijpus Formae tu tamen huius eris.* (The bones are visible, the orbits are emptied, the open holes of the teeth are broken. You will hate this, regardless of the image. You shall be, after all, the original [version] of this image), *Raphael Sadeler excudit Monaci* (Raphael Sadeler printed in Munich).

[10] Interestingly, in the Amsterdam engraving, Eillart—a printmaker—appears as the publisher instead, whereas the designer of the composition is Johannes Bernardinus S., possibly the well-known Sicilian paint-

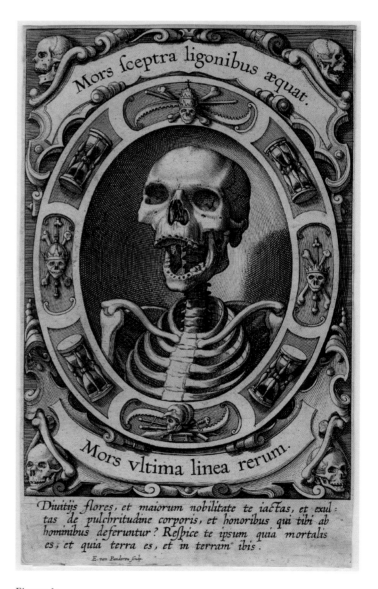

Figure 1:
Egbert van Panderen, *Mors ultima linea rerum* (*Servitus Carnis*), ca. 1610–1620.
Engraving, 18.3 × 11 cm (7.20 × 4.33 in.).
London (England), British Museum, inv. 1862,0614.1562.

er—mainly active in Naples—commonly known as Giovanni Bernardino Siciliano (hence the "S." after his name), but whose actual last name was Azzolini. Of this painter, a contemporary of Caravaggio, there appears to be very little information about a stay of his in Rome. The only source is Bernardo De Dominici's 1742 *Vite* of the Neapolitan painters, in which he mentions that "some people believe" Giovanni Bernardino Siciliano went to Rome after Domenichino's death occurred in 1641. DE DOMINICI 1742, p. 125. However, there is a 1618 record of a Giovan Bernardino Asolani among the roll call of the Roman academy of painters—the Accademia di San Luca. MINERVINI 1879, p. 31. Slight changes in last-name spellings were very common, and if this Giovan Bernardi-

no Asolani is indeed Giovanni Bernardino Siciliano, it may not be ruled out that he was in Rome sometime in the 1610s, which is when Eillarts is known to have been there too. Since we do not have enough biographical information on Van Panderen, we should not rule out a (very common) possible travel to Rome, where the three could have met and where this print, now in Amsterdam, may have been carried out.

[11] For further on the topic, see GARRIGOU-LAGRANGE 1991.

[12] See the four prints at the British Museum, inv. 1863,0509.805 (*Servitus Carnis*); inv. 1863,0509.806 (*Servitus Christi*); inv. 1863,0509.807 (*Servitus Mundi*); inv. 1863,0509.808 (*Servitus Diaboli*).

Figure 2:
Egbert van Panderen, after Joannes Bernardinus S.,
published by Johannes Eillarts, *Vanitas vanitatum et omnia vanitas* (*Bust of a Skeleton*), ca. 1590–1637.
Engraving, 15.9 × 11 cm (6.25 × 4.33 in.).
Amsterdam (the Netherlands), Rijksmuseum, RP-P-OB-24.416.

Figure 3:
Egbert van Panderen, published by Raphael Sadeler I, *Putredini dixi, Pater meus es mater mea et soror mea vermibus* (*Death*), ca. 1600.
Engraving, 17.2 × 11.5 cm (6.77 × 4.52 in.).
Berlin (Germany), Staatliche Museen, Kupferstichkabinett, inv. 281-43.

Cat. n. III.12
Johann Wolfgang von der Auwera
Allegory of Time
ca. 1730s.
Wood, 29.84 × 20.32 × 25.4 cm (11.75 × 8 × 10 in.).
Chicago, IL (US), Richard Harris Collection, S052.

Born in Würzburg, Johann Wolfgang von der Auwera initially trained under his father, who was a sculptor, and then with Claude Curé, the city's court sculptor.[1] After a period of study in Vienna, Johann Wolfgang, who was also a skilled draftsman, returned to Würzburg in 1736 and took over his father's workshop. In 1738, Johann Wolfgang was appointed court sculptor of Prince-Bishop Friedrich Karl von Schönborn, for whom he also carried out the statues for the gardens of the Veitshöchheim Castle, as well as the memorial tablets for his own and his uncle Lothar Franz von Schönborn's funerary monuments in the Bamberg Cathedral.[2] In addition to his work as court sculptor, he was also heavily involved in the decoration of several churches in Würzburg. He is considered the leading Rococo sculptor of southern Germany.

Little to nothing is known about this statuette, which was probably intended as a model for a larger sculpture. It represents the allegorical figure of Time, also known as Chronos (Χρόνος in Greek), generally identified with the Roman god Saturn. From the Renaissance onward, this was a relatively popular allegorical figure, and it was generally present either in sepulchral contexts or in large allegorical frescoes (usually in palaces), or on table/mantel clocks.

Time/Saturn is typically represented as a bearded and winged old man holding a scythe and an hourglass (see also **cat. n. III.8**). This imagery, which was quite successful in the baroque period, and mostly associated with death, can, however, hardly be found in art and literature before the sixteenth century.[3] In the rare instances in which Time is mentioned, as in Petrarch's *Trionfi* (i.e., *Triumphs*) of 1374, it makes no explicit reference to death. Time is simply described as an elderly man with a crutch (**figures 1-2**, p. 170-171). Time/Saturn was in fact either represented as an elderly deity, protector of agriculture, or as a planet, but overall, it is a figure that did not seem to interest artists or clients before the Renaissance.[4]

A shift in this approach may be noticed—in literature—from the sixteenth century onward, and particularly in a number of books, such as the *Emblemata* of 1564 by János Zsámboky—a book of emblems in which Time/Saturn is described as a naked and bearded old man, holding a scythe and threatening to sever the lives of the two people represented in the emblem (**figure 3**, p. 171).[5] This is one of the first examples in which Time/Saturn explicitly represents death.[6] Also, in Albericus Londoniensis's book *Allegoriae poeticae*, printed in 1520, the scythe was seen as a symbol of recurrence of the seasons, and therefore of the cycle of life in which birth and death alternate.[7]

From a visual standpoint, a new interest in the figure of Time/Saturn may also be found in the sixteenth century, when some artists started illustrating Petrarch's *Trionfi*. This is when Time and Saturn began to be represented as a single, unique figure.[8]

Except for these rare instances, however, until the second half of the 1500s, Saturn was not represented as a negative and destructive deity.[9] The most interesting insight as to why Time has been 'merged' with Saturn may be found in *Le imagini delli Dei de gl'Antichi* by Vincenzo Cartari. He clearly sees in Saturn the embodiment of Time.

> Time is old and badly dressed because it has always been, meaning that it began to exist together with the world when the Chaos was separated, the elements were distinct and the beginning of things started, and the sky began to turn, from the movement of which men began to measure time [...].[10]

The presence of the scythe, which replaced the crutch in early representations of Time, is a significant change in the evolution of this allegorical figure. According to Cartari, it is related to the longstanding belief that Saturn had taught people to use manure as a fertilizer which resulted in plentiful crops, hence the scythe.[11] Furthermore, Time passes inexorably, and by doing so it 'severs' and reaps all things—everything is born *with*, and eaten *by*, Time; an analogy with Saturn, who devoured his own children.[12] So, to some degree, the juxtaposition of Time/Saturn was inevitable.

Interestingly, in astrological representations, the sickle is Saturn's iconographic attribute. Saturn presides over the winter months (in fact, he rules the zodiac signs of Aquarius and Capricorn) and his scythe also symbolizes the pruning of dead branches, normally carried out at that time of year.[13] Winter and pruning are, of course, features that can be ascribed to death too: like Saturn, death reduces living beings to their basic form—to dryness.[14]

In the seventeenth and eighteenth centuries, Time's role as a pitiless and relentless winged reaper holding a scythe and an hourglass resulted in Time/Saturn sometimes replacing the skeleton in representations of Death. As mentioned above, the attribute of the scythe became a very powerful and impressive symbol, and it would have had a particularly powerful effect on those of a rural and artisanal background, all too familiar with the scythe that mows down all before it—wheat, grass, and flow-

ers; the scythe symbolizes death's leveling function from which no one can escape.[15] In some baroque iconography, the allegorical function of the skeleton in relation to Death was replaced by the allegory of Time, which was seen as less unsettling.[16] However, unlike Time, the reasons behind the iconography of Death holding a scythe were different, and can be found in the book of Revelation 14:15–19:

> And another angel came out [...] calling with a loud voice to the one who sat on the cloud, "Use your sickle and reap, for the hour to reap has come, because the harvest of the earth is fully ripe." So the one who sat on the cloud swung his sickle over the earth, and the earth was reaped. Then another angel came out of the temple in heaven, and he too had a sharp sickle. Then another angel came out from the altar [...] and he called with a loud voice to him who had the sharp sickle, "Use your sharp sickle and gather the clusters of the vine of the earth, for its grapes are ripe." So the angel swung his sickle over the earth and gathered the vintage of the earth, and he threw it into the great wine press of the wrath of God.

As far as the allegory of Time holding an hourglass is concerned, the hourglass is obviously associated with death as it is a symbol of the passing of time, and therefore of transience. This is also why skeletons representing Death often hold an hourglass (see also **cat. n. III.3**). However, if compared to the iconography of Death as a skeleton holding either an hourglass or a scythe or both, the allegory of Time is not as frequent, possibly because of its non-Christian roots in that it is linked to Chronos.

Time also finds an iconographic equivalent in the Three Fates and in their symbolization of the passing of time, particularly in the third Fate—Atropos (see also **cat. n. III.2**)—as she is the one who, similarly to Time/Saturn, cuts the thread of life.[17]

However, in some instances, especially in some eighteenth-century tombs and also in some allegorical and celebratory frescoes in palaces, Time either replaces the angels in bringing the portrait of the deceased to heaven, or simply holds the portrait of the deceased.[18] This is often a way to convey the message that, contrary to what happens to most people who are bound to be forgotten after death, the memory of the deceased will instead survive throughout the centuries, as the same agent meant to cause oblivion—Time—in this case grants a form of immortality.

Corinna Ricasoli

[1] For more on his biography and training see KRANZBÜHLER 1932, p. 182–219.

[2] For further reading on Von der Auwera as a draftsman, see TRENSCHEL 1986, p. 215–238, but also MAUÉ 1983, p. 215–238. For his sketches on garden sculpture, see RAGALLER 1979. For his garden statues, see NEUBERT 2007, and KREISEL 1953. His activity in the Würzburg palace is discussed in FRIEDRICH 2004. As for the funerary monuments, removed from the Cathedral in 1837, see LINDEMANN 1985, p. 247–259, and SEDLMAIER AND VON FREEDEN 1955.

Figure 1:
Francesco Pesellino, *The Triumphs of Fame, Time, and Eternity* (cassone panel), ca. 1450.
Tempera and gold on panel, 45.4 × 157.4 cm (17.87 × 61.96 in.).
Boston, MA (US), Isabella Stewart Gardner Museum.

[3] TENENTI 1989, p. 462. Scholar Erwin Panofski was able to identify three allegories of Time dating pre-1500—one dating back to the fourteenth century, and two from around 1400. PANOFSKY 1939, pl. no. 44 and 45.

[4] TENENTI 1989, p. 462.

[5] ZSÁMBOKY 1564, p. 23. For the medieval iconography of death with a scythe, see ARIÈS 1980, p. 127–128.

[6] TENENTI 1989, p. 462.

[7] Ibid., p. 463.

[8] Ibid., p. 462.

[9] Ibid., p. 463.

[10] "Il Tempo è vecchio, e mal vestito, perché sempre v'è stato ovvero cominciò ad essere insieme con il mondo, cioè, quando, fatta la separatione del Chaos, gli elementi furono distinti e fu dato principio alla generazione delle cose, cominciando allhora il cielo ad aggirarsici intorno, dal movimento del quale cominciarono parimente gli huomini di misurare il tempo [...]." CARTARI 1647, p. 16. The translation into English is my own.

[11] Ibid., p. 15.

[12] Ibid., p. 17.

[13] BATTISTINI 2004, p. 86.

[14] See also LIPPMANN 1895, p. 3.

[15] DI NOLA 1995, p. 39.

[16] For more on this topic, see ARIÈS 1980, p. 380, RICASOLI 2014, and RICASOLI 2015.

[17] The Fates also start to be a source of interest between the fifteenth and sixteenth centuries, but they clearly were not seen as being adequately able to strongly convey a message of death—not yet at least. See TENENTI 1989, p. 464–465.

[18] See, for example, Carlo Maratti's *Allegorical Design in Honor of Pietro da Cortona*, now at Windsor Castle, RCIN 904091.

Figure 2:
Jacopo del Sellaio, *Triumph of Time*, 1485–1490.
Tempera on panel, 75 × 90 cm (29.52 × 35.43 in.).
Fiesole (Italy), Museo Bandini.

Figure 3:
Quae sequimur fugimus, nosque fugiunt,
from *Emblemata*, 1564, p. 23, by János Zsámboky.
Glasgow (Scotland), The University of Glasgow Library.

Make use of Time, *that's* comming on;
For, *that is perish'd, which is* gone.

ILLVSTR. XLIX.

Book 4

The Fragility of Life

The precariousness of life has been the source of much anxiety through the ages. Events beyond our control—such as earthquakes, extreme weather, plague—add to our sense of insecurity, and can lead to a sense of impending doom. *Humana Fragilitas* (*Human Fragility*) is a painting in which Death dominates the composition, capturing that sense with remarkable force.

For who knows what is good for mortals while they live the few days of their vain life, which they pass like a shadow?

(Ecclesiastes 6:12)

Cat. n. III.13*
Salvator Rosa

Humana Fragilitas

ca. 1656.
Oil on canvas, 197.4 × 131.5 cm (77.71 × 51.77 in.).
Inscription: (on the scroll) *Conceptio Culpa, Nasci pena, / Labor vita, Necesse Mori*; (on the blade of the knife) *S. R.* (monogram).
Cambridge (England), Fitzwilliam Museum, PD.53-1958.

Although mainly active in Florence and Rome, Salvator Rosa was Neapolitan by birth and education (he studied with the painters Francesco Fracanzano, Jusepe de Ribera, and Aniello Falcone).[1] In addition to being a painter, he was also a talented draftsman, an excellent satirical poet, and an actor.[2] In his paintings, he combines heterogeneous formulas which reflect his disparate cultural, literary, scientific, and philosophical interests.[3] An atypical artist, Rosa posed as a stoic philosopher, and jealously guarded his own moral independence.[4] His artworks clearly show his fascination for bizarre, unusual, and often macabre content, through which he expressed an attitude of dissent toward the 'artistic establishment'. His paintings often address ethical and philosophical matters, drawn from mythology, ancient history, or the Bible.

The somber theme of *Humana Fragilitas* (Latin for *Human Fragility*) has led to the belief that the artwork was carried out in 1656, when a number of sorrowful events occurred in Rosa's personal life—his brother, son, and nephews all died of the plague.[5] The deep, depressive state into which Rosa sank prevented him from painting for a long period, so was his mind dimmed with meditations on death and the transience of human life. During this difficult period, he was able to devote himself only to etching, and laid aside painting until the end of 1656.[6] Thus, it is very likely that *Humana Fragilitas* was the first painting to be completed after this personal and artistic crisis.[7]

Humana Fragilitas, of which there exist two preparatory sketches (see footnote 8), is an allegorical painting in which death is associated with childhood in a somber nocturnal *capriccio* around a *vanitas* theme.[8] The atmosphere is ominous and somber, the sky is dark, and there is the physical and overwhelming presence of Death, represented by a huge winged skeleton. In the foreground, a woman dressed in white is seated on a glass sphere while holding a child on her lap, who, in turn, is intent on writing the motto *Conceptio culpa, nasci pena, labor vita, necesse mori* (Conception in sin, birth is pain, life is toil, death inevitable) on a cartouche held by Death itself.[9] On the left, there are two *putti*—one, on the foreground, is blowing soap bubbles, whereas the other one holds a torch. In the background, behind the seated woman, there is a herm of the Roman god Terminus, whereas a pyramid rises behind the two putti.

Although the scene takes place outdoors, no landscape is visible and all the characters are arranged within a narrow space, thus allowing the viewer to focus on the various allegorical figures that populate the canvas.[10] Despite the ominous atmosphere of this painting, it is worth noting that the palette has a wide range of pastel colors, as well as of browns and grays (as in the skeleton) that emphasize the contrast between the objects and the figures.

This canvas is particularly significant as it is replete with very interesting baroque symbolism and allegories. The first, clearly, is the main character of the painting—Death—embodied by the winged skeleton, who interferes with human events by handing the cartouche to the seated child so that he may write the above-mentioned motto.[11] Undoubtedly, this motto, which is in fact a *memento mori*, holds the painting's main message—we are born to suffer and ultimately die.[12]

In addition to the obvious allegory of Death, there are also other references to the elusiveness of life. For instance, the roses around the woman's head—a clear symbol of transience, as flowers swiftly wither; the glass sphere on which she sits not only alludes to the precariousness of our existence, but also to the classical figure of the καιρός (*kairós*), that is the passing of Fortune; Terminus, god of boundaries, references death in that it is the ultimate 'limit' of life; moreover, the wreath around Terminus's head is made of cypress—a tree related to bereavement and burial since antiquity, as is the pyramid in the background.[13] The thistle in flower, on the lower left-hand side, is traditionally associated with decadence and dying; similarly the fragile soap bubbles blown by the laurelled *putto* in the foreground.[14] The torch held by the *putto* in the background, standing on a cradle, refers to the fleetingness of our life, that ends as quickly as the torch's flame, as is written in Isaiah 43:17 ("they are extinguished, quenched like a wick"), but also in Psalm 102:3 (see **cat. n. IV.7**). In this instance, the cradle could be a reference to the grave, and interestingly, this connection between cradle and grave may also be found in a verse written by Rosa himself, in which he claims that artists and poets should only be concerned with the kind of reputation bestowed by posterity, as those who do nothing to acquire such renown "will find cradle and grave in just one day".[15] Butterflies, also present in the painting, are a very common feature in baroque art, as they are a symbol of both fragility and resurrection, whereas the knife on the ground evokes the idea of severance, such as the one caused by death. Finally, almost hidden by the woman's dress, an owl, traditionally seen as a 'funeral' bird, because it is a nocturnal animal, and because of the negative role it also covers in the Bible.[16]

The allegorical theme of human fragility is certainly unusual in painting, but it is consistent with Rosa's oeuvre, in which philosophical subject matters are quite recurrent. This canvas is an extraordinary example of Rosa's learned meditations on the

elusiveness of life, which he illustrated through the careful 'collation' of symbols and allegories that make this a masterpiece of baroque art.

Corinna Ricasoli

[1] The bibliography on Salvator Rosa is very broad, but for further insight on Rosa's life and career, the reader can refer to LANGDON 2010, p. 11–49, also *SALVATOR ROSA* 2008, and SALERNO 1963. For his Florentine and Roman period, see VOLPI 2008, p. 85–116.

[2] Salvator Rosa is the author of seven *Satire* in which he blamed—amongst other things—the morals of his times and of painting as well, especially the vulgarity in genre painting, of which, incidentally, he himself had been a painter. During his Florentine period, he held at his house the *Accademia dei Percossi*: a circle of intellectuals, literati, and scientists (among which Galileo Galilei's pupil, Evangelista Torricelli). For his poems, see ROSA AND CESAREO 1892, and ROSA AND SALVINI 1833.

[3] See ARGAN AND CONTARDI 1983, p. 336, but especially EBERT-SCHIFFERER 2010, p. 289–298. This is clearly visible in paintings such as *Philosopher in Meditation* (Piacenza, Fondazione Horak), *Democritus in Meditation* (Copenhagen, Statens Museum for Kunst), and the painter's *Self-Portrait as a Philosopher* (London, National Gallery), in which the main themes are the melancholic contemplation of both frailty of life and of human exploits.

[4] See the biographies of Rosa by Filippo Baldinucci in BALDINUCCI 1830, by Giovanni Battista Passeri in PASSERI 1772, p. 416–439, by Lione Pascoli in PASCOLI 1730, p. 63–87, and by Sydney Morgan in MORGAN 1824. Rosa's extravagance and his histrionics were only the exterior aspect of an unusual and bold attitude with which he rejected the bonds and the restrictions of traditional patronage. See LANGDON 1998, p. 149.

[5] See WASSYNG ROWORTH 1988, p. 114, and VOLPI 2010, p. 220–223. The painting was certainly carried out before 1658, which may be considered a *terminus ante quem*, as this is when it appears in the Inventory of Cardinal Flavio Chigi's paintings. The Inventory is at the Vatican Library (BAV, Arch.Chig.700, *Inventario dei beni mobili del Cardinale Flavio Chigi*, 1692, f.59).

[6] See Rosa's correspondence with his friend Giovanni Battista Ricciardi in GERRA 1937, but also WASSYNG ROWORTH 1988, p. 114–116.

[7] For his *Self-Portrait with a Skull*, also carried out in around 1656, see SPIKE 1984, p. 158–159, and WALLACE 1979, p. 11–13, 21.

[8] The drawings are in Cambridge, at the Fitzwilliam Museum (PD.5-2002), and in Leipzig, at the Museum der Bildenden Künste (NI.8493). See WALLACE 1968, p. 28, MILLER 1977, p. 272. For Rosa's draftsmanship, see MAHONEY 1977.

[9] SCARAMELLA 2002, p. 83, 85.

[10] WALLACE 1968, p. 28.

[11] For the iconography of Death in the seventeenth century, see **cat. n. III.1**, and the bibliography therein.

[12] The verse, written by a twelfth-century poet—Adam de Saint-Victor—employed by Giovanni Battista Ricciardi, Rosa's close friend, in a *canzone* dedicated to the same Rosa: "Rosa, il nascere è pena, il vivere è fatica, et il morir necessità fatale." See SCARAMELLA 2002, p. 85.

[13] See OVIDIUS NASO 1844, p. 468–469, but also RIPA AND ORLANDI 1765, p. 244.

[14] See WALLACE 1968, p. 30, who convincingly considers the laurel wreath an ironical reference to the worthlessness of human endeavors and transience of fame. Ibid.

[15] The verse ("Chi cerca di piacer solo al presente / Non creda mai d' haver a far soggiorno / In mano a i dotti, e a la futura gente. / Anzi havrà culla e tomba, in un sol giorno.") may be found in ROSA 1695, p. 34. For further reading on the issue of artists' concerns with posthumous reputation in baroque Rome, see RICASOLI 2014.

[16] See Isa. 34:11, Zeph. 2:14, Lev. 11:17–18, Deut. 14:16–17.

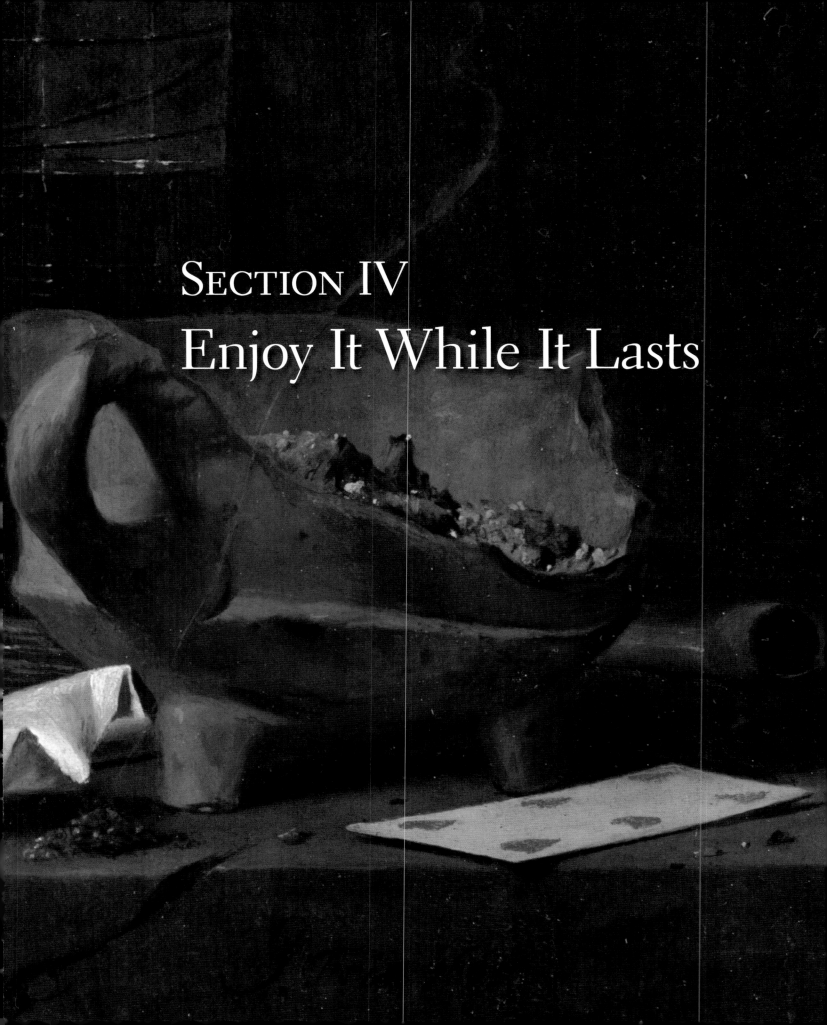

SECTION IV
Enjoy It While It Lasts

Live, *ever mindfull of thy dying;*
For, Time *is always from thee flying.*

The Earthly Pleasures of Life

Aside from concerns regarding the unpredictable advent of death and the importance of this life versus the next, Ecclesiastes ponders how we should treat 'earthly pleasures', which—it says—should be wholeheartedly embraced, as they are gifts from God. To refuse them is to turn one's back on God's wishes and risk his wrath. *Likewise all to whom God gives wealth and possessions and whom he enables to enjoy them, and to accept their lot and find enjoyment in their toil—this is the gift of God* (Ecclesiastes 5:19).

Therefore, earthly pleasures, such as food, drink, music, physical relations, and affection, are, under these circumstances, not only acceptable, but desirable.

So I commend enjoyment, for there is nothing better for people under the sun than to eat, and drink, and enjoy themselves, for this will go with them in their toil through the days of life that God gives them under the sun.

(Ecclesiastes 8:15)

Cat. n. IV.1
Anonymous painter after Bartolomeo Manfredi
The Card Players
late 17th/early 18th century.
Oil on canvas, 137 × 195.5 cm (53.93 × 76.96 in.).
Florence (Italy), Gallerie degli Uffizi, inv. 6609.

This is a copy of an important late work by the seventeenth-century painter Bartolomeo Manfredi—a leading figure among the many imitators of Michelangelo Merisi, called Caravaggio, working in early seventeenth-century Rome.[1] The original, along with its pendant, the *Musicians*, was almost completely destroyed when a Mafia bomb damaged the Uffizi in May 1993.[2] Both were commissioned on behalf of the Grand Duke of Tuscany, Cosimo II de' Medici in 1620, and this is a measure of the success Manfredi had then achieved among his fellow Caravaggesques.[3] In fact, Manfredi proved nearly as influential as Caravaggio himself, garnering numerous disciples of his own. By the 1670s, his style had even been awarded its own critical label, the "Manfrediana Methodus", by the Northern painter and art historian Joachim von Sandrart. The "Manfredi method" involved the transformation of Caravaggio's pictorial motifs into a highly saleable and much imitated pictorial formula: contemporary low-life characters, depicted knee-length around a table or some other surface, rendered with a striking anecdotal realism, and shrouded in the half-light of Caravaggio's dramatic *chiaroscuro*.[4]

The fate of the original *Card Players* has a certain grim irony. Although all sections of seventeenth-century society indulged in card playing, its appearance here, as elsewhere in the art and literature of the period, highlights its associations with the seamy, lawless underbelly of urban life. In particular, Manfredi's work typically depicts the kind of individuals who might well be considered the gangsters of early seventeenth-century Rome: the criminally-inclined soldiers of fortune, or *bravi*, who kicked around the city in rowdy packs, gambling, drinking, and generally up to no good. The pictorial trademark of these characters is their variegated, opulent costumes which are, however, frequently composed of mismatched sleeves and tunics (as Nancy Edwards has observed, this also gives the impression of attire that has been won, piece-by-piece at games of chance).[5] Among their ranks, one often encounters other ne'er-do-wells: petty thieves, fortunetellers, pickpockets, and the like. Manfredi's often poignant, thought-provoking depiction of these characters relies on how little satisfaction or delight they seem to derive from their activities. The inky shadows, which Manfredi borrowed from Caravaggio's mature religious narratives, are also expressive of the jaded, ennui-tinged reality of their rackety, catch-as-catch-can existence. The seated, vacant-eyed figure at the left of the *Card Players* adopts a head-in-hand pose typically associated with a state of melancholic world-weariness, indifferent to the routine quarrel brewing among the figures at the right. The game—almost certainly a card

craze of the period known as *Primero* (an early form of poker)—has stalled; the restless figure perched right of center has laid down his hand: a six and seven of clubs—a high score according to the rules of *Primero* where these particular cards triple their value.[6] He seems ready to quit, and is disgruntled to find himself arrested by a youth with a querulous expression to his rear who insistently draws his attention to another spread of cards. Is this actually the winning hand? Or perhaps the youth has found some suspiciously surplus cards buried in the other's belt? (such is the scam depicted in the ultimate template for such scenes—Caravaggio's *Cardsharps* of ca. 1595, now in the Kimbell Museum, Fort Worth, AP 1987.06).[7] The weather-beaten tough in the wide-brimmed hat at the right is also being drawn into the row; with money at stake, and sword hilts at the ready, things clearly have the potential to quickly turn nasty.[8]

In the spirit of the book of Ecclesiastes, card playing was used by painters such as Manfredi, and the authors of the popular moralizing tracts, *tableaux vivants*, and picaresque narratives of the period, as a means of condemning the vanity of worldly existence. The scenarios depicted advertise the moral and material pitfalls that lie in wait for unwary dupes drawn into taverns, gambling dens, and brothels (see also Honthorst's *Concert* elsewhere in this exhibition, **cat. n. IV.4**).[9] We are also reminded that life is fleeting, and one's immortal soul is immediately imperiled by such unwholesome activity; there is a lineage of motifs that connects Caravaggesque gambling scenes to a print of Death and the Devil throttling the life out of a gambler in the *Dance of Death* series by Hans Holbein the Younger (1497–1543) of the late 1520s. This plays on the dread of *mors improvisa*—a sudden, spiritually ill-prepared death in the midst of moral debauchery—hardly a remote prospect given the excessive physical indulgence, dangerous tomfoolery, and physical violence attendant on drinking and gambling.[10] One recalls that in *Hamlet* (Act III: scene 3) by William Shakespeare of ca. 1599, the title character eschews the opportunity to kill his uncle while at prayer in order that he might, instead, murder him while "At gaming, swearing, or about some act / That has no relish of salvation in't", so that the victim's "soul may be as damn'd and black / As hell, whereto it goes".[11]

The theme of transience, and a perilous misuse of time, is also echoed by what serves Manfredi's card players as a playing surface—as is often, and curiously, the case, this seems to be a chunk of ruined antique masonry, or even part of a tomb or sarcophagus; either connotes the transience of earthly things. It may also suggest the sequestered, clandestine nature of gambling in

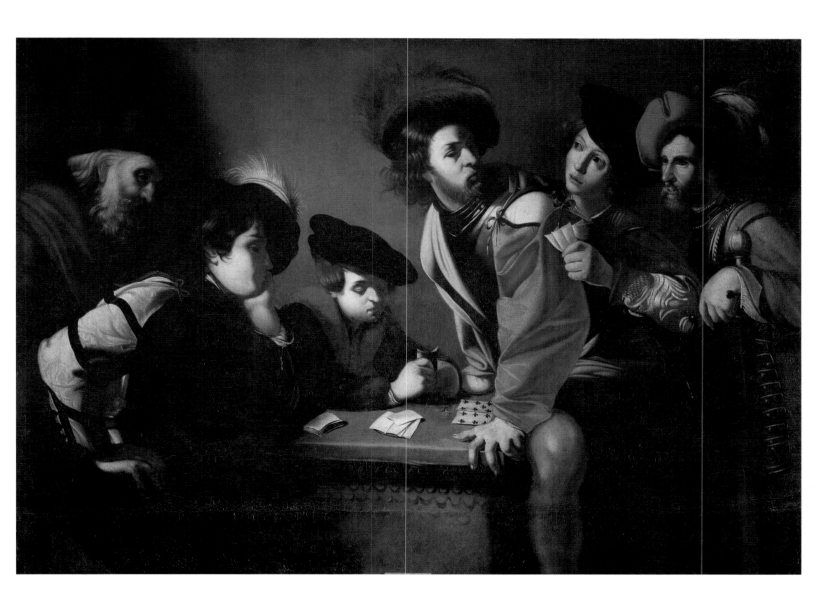

the less-frequented nooks and crannies of the city, or among its shady antique ruins. From the late sixteenth century, innumerable papal decrees forbade gambling in public places. It is almost certain that Manfredi, as with other artists of his stripe, habituated the impromptu card dens which then resulted, and were all too familiar with the city's seedy street life: Caravaggio's violent, murderous lifestyle is well documented; his rival Guido Reni was addicted to gambling; Manfredi's French follower Valentin de Boulogne died suddenly after plunging himself into a chilly fountain after a night of drunken debauchery.[12] The latter was, incidentally, a member of the *Bentvueghels* (Birds of a Feather)—a glorified drinking club largely composed of Northern artists stationed in Rome that included other followers of Manfredi. One of their initiation rites involved a drunken daybreak procession to an ancient porphyry sarcophagus dubbed the "Tomb of Bacchus" in the Roman Church of Santa Costanza.[13]

Philip Cottrell

[1] The Mantuan-born Manfredi is possibly identical with an otherwise unknown "Bartolomeo" who was recorded in Rome as Caravaggio's servant/assistant in 1602–1603. In any case, Manfredi soon emerged as one of the most faithful of Caravaggio's imitators after the latter's flight from Rome in 1606. See the recent monograph by HARTJE 2004, but also RICASOLI 2011, p. 71–72, 76.

[2] HARTJE 2004, p. 328–333. The original *Card Players* was oil on canvas, 130 × 19.15 cm (51.18 × 7.53 in.) (no inventory number was assigned). The copy presently exhibited had, from 1973, been on loan to the Florentine offices of the *Consiglio Regionale della Toscana*, but was returned to the Uffizi in 1994 as a substitute for the damaged original. Prior to this, however, both Manfredi's original *Card Players* and the *Musicians* had not survived in the best condition—this despite the restorations attendant on their appearance (alongside the present copy of the *Card Players*) in an exhibition devoted to Caravaggio and his followers at the Palazzo Pitti, Florence, in 1970. It was here that they were also properly revealed to modern scholarship as lost works by Manfredi, overturning an older attribution to Caravaggio that had persisted since 1695. See BOREA 1970a, p. 17–18, and BOREA 1970b, p. 19.

[3] The Manfredi pair were purchased for Cosimo via an agent in Rome in 1620 alongside three works by Gerrit van Honthorst. See HARTJE 2004, p. 331–332.

[4] VON SANDRART 1925, p. 170. Manfredi's disciples included the Frenchmen Nicolas Régnier, Valentin de Boulogne, and Nicolas Tournier. See CUZIN 1980, CUZIN 1988, and GREGORI 1988.

[5] EDWARDS 2011, p. 183.

[6] On *Primero* see ibid., p. 206.

[7] SPIKE 2010, p. 20–28. See also EDWARDS 2011 and LANGDON 2012.

[8] The coins on the table are not apparent in photographs of the original, nor in the two prints after it, one by Franciscus van der Steen, ca. 1660, the other by the eighteenth-century printmaker Theodore Verkruys, before 1739. See GIANFRANCESCHI 2011, p. 85–86. The original was, however, in a poorly preserved and retouched state prior to its near destruction in 1993. See also note 2 above.

[9] Of particular significance was Jesus's parable of the prodigal son (Luke 15:11–32) as dramatized and embellished in the *Rappresentazione del figliuol prodigo* by Castellano Castellani, and regularly performed from the early sixteenth century onward. Equally influential was Mateo Alemán's popular picaresque novel *La vida del picaro Guzmán de Alfarache* of 1599, which depicts the exploits of a Spanish gambler and adventurer who settles in Rome. Closer in date to Manfredi's *Card Players*, Angelo Rocca's 1617 *Trattato per la salute dell'anime* specifically targets the moral dangers of gambling. For this literary heritage see EDWARDS 2011, p. 183–184, and LANGDON 2012, p. 17; 35–43.

[10] As Von Sandrart first observed, Caravaggio's *Calling of St. Matthew* of 1599–1600 in the Church of San Luigi dei Francesi in Rome (which was another vital source of inspiration for Caravaggesque scenes of gambling) drew one of its figures from the gambling scene in Holbein's *Dance of Death*—see EDWARDS 2011, p. 184.

[11] SHAKESPEARE 2016, p. 2056.

[12] This world is also memorably represented in the exhibition BASSIFONDI DEL BAROCCO 2014.

[13] See KREN 1980, p. 69–70.

Cat. n. IV.2
Gregorius Oosterlinck

A Merry Company (*The Five Senses*)

ca. 1660.
Inscription: (on the tin jug) *GREGORIVS / OOSTERLINCK*
Oil on canvas, 100 × 151 cm (39.37 × 59.44 in.).
Amsterdam (the Netherlands), The Kremer Collection, GK-46

It is thanks to the signature, written out in full and placed prominently on a pewter jug, that we are able to identify this work by the virtually unknown Gregorius Oosterlinck, portraying a merry company of men who are smoking, drinking, and making music.[1] The manner in which Oosterlinck signed his work is suggestive of a self-assured artist who must have produced a substantial oeuvre, yet only one other painting of his is known. Little to nothing is known about this artist, not his dates of birth and death, not where he was born, nor who taught him, or if he had any pupils of his own. An engraved portrait of a man, with long wavy hair, with the name 'Gregorius Oosterlinck', may possibly be a likeness of this mysterious master (**figure 1**, p. 189), but the print's provenance and function—did it belong to a series of artists' portraits?—are unfortunately unknown.[2] At present we have only a single documented reference to his name during his lifetime, in the archives of the Guild of St. Luke's in Ghent. This suggests that Oosterlinck (there spelt 'Osterlinck') was active in this city in 1652.[3] Unfortunately, there is no information concerning how long he lived in Ghent, but this *Merry Company* may have been painted there; indeed, the figures' clothing suggests it was made in around 1660.[4]

The painting has been carried out using wide brushstrokes, and the six figures painted by Oosterlinck are set against a dark background. Our eye is immediately drawn to the man on the right, who wears a yellow costume, blue sash, and a knotted neckerchief with red and white bands of color. The rich decoration of his sword, its hilt fashioned into a seated griffon, is an attractive detail. The man smokes his pipe with an absentminded expression; the remains of his tobacco and the sticks he has used to light the pipe lie on a pewter plate on the table before him. A dog is sniffing around in search of crumbs. A man to the smoker's left, who has just drained his wine glass, is being closely watched by a waggish figure with a red cap—the way this man is wedged in between the two seated figures accentuates his pushy attitude. The youngest man at the table is playing the fiddle, and even appears to be singing along. The man on the far left, who wears a loose brown cloak, holds his wine glass elegantly by the foot, as he looks up at an old woman who is attracting his attention by placing a hand on his shoulder. The woman may be the innkeeper, but more probably she is a procuress, trying to tempt him to spend his money on a prostitute.

Oosterlinck crowded the figures into the picture plane. Yet despite this proximity, there is a striking lack of interaction between them. Possibly this is because of their separate symbolic meanings, since the painting may well be intended as an allegory of the five senses.[5] In this case, the old woman and the man stand for Touch, the fiddler for Hearing, the drinking man for Taste, the peering man for Sight, and the smoker and dog together for Smell.

Merry companies of this kind, making music, smoking, drinking, or playing cards around a table, sometimes representing the five senses, constituted a popular subject in seventeenth-century painting in the Netherlands. This motif is quite frequent in the first half of the century, with a peak in the 1620s among artists who had spent a few years in Italy where they had been introduced to the work of Caravaggio and his followers. This is particularly true for the Caravaggesque painters from Utrecht. Gerrit van Honthorst (see **cat. nos. II.7, IV.4–IV.5**) and Hendrick ter Brugghen (see **cat. n. IV.3**) are the best-known and most influential exponents of this style, which spread throughout Europe. Artists producing Caravaggesque works were also active in the southern Netherlands, in artistic centres such as Antwerp, Brussels, Ghent, and Bruges. Among them, the best-known are Abraham Janssens, Theodoor Rombouts, and Gerard Seghers, but there were many others who are lesser known and studied. In many cases, few paintings of theirs have survived, making research on these masters very difficult. This certainly applies to Gregorius Oosterlinck, a late representative of Flemish Caravaggism.

Because of the Caravaggesque nature of this *Merry Company*, reflected in the choice of subject, the warm palette, and the depiction of half-figures filling the picture plane, it is usually assumed that Oosterlinck may have worked in Italy for a time.[6] However, this is not necessarily the case. Indeed, he may have drawn sufficient inspiration from the work of other masters who had undertaken this journey. The only other known work by Oosterlinck is suggestive of the influence of Jacob van Oost the Elder (1601–1671). In fact, it was once attributed to this Bruges master, partly because the signature is damaged and poorly legible.[7] This painting, too, features a company around a table, and here too we see a woman on the left placing her hand on a man's shoulder. Two figures in this painting closely resemble a work by Van Oost, that shows a young man who is approached by procuress or a soothsayer.[8] Perhaps Oosterlinck also worked in Bruges and became acquainted with Van Oost's oeuvre in that city. The more refined technique in which this company is painted also echoes Van Oost's figures, and is indeed different from the wide brushstrokes visible in the Kremer exemplar. It is im-

possible to carry out a thorough stylistic comparison of the two works, since the other painting's whereabouts has been unknown since it was auctioned in 1985.

The scarce available information concerning Oosterlinck's life and work suggest a connection with Ghent and possibly also with Bruges. It is to be hoped that archival research in these cities may shed new light on this hitherto mysterious artist.

Lea van der Vinde

Figure 1:
Anonymous, *Portrait* (of the painter?) *Gregorius Oosterlinck*, ca. 1650–1660.
Engraving, 18.5 × 30.5 cm (7.28 × 12 in.).
Whereabouts unknown.

[1] Further bibliography on the subject may be found in POMME DE MIRIMONDE 1965, p. 168–169, DE MAERE AND WABBES 1994, p. 920, *ONE HUNDRED MASTER PAINTINGS* 2007.

[2] This portrait was on sale from a German dealer on eBay in 2013, and noticed there by the author. Unfortunately, the seller did not have information on the origin of the image.

[3] VAN DER HAEGHEN 1906, p. 50.

[4] *ONE HUNDRED MASTER PAINTINGS* 2007, p. 293.

[5] This interpretation was first done in ibid., p. 291.

[6] Ibid., p. 293. It has been suggested that he stayed in France and was acquainted with the work of the brothers Le Nain.

[7] According to the data in the Auction Catalog London (Sotheby's), July 3, 1985, no. 127, the signature reads GREGOR / OOSTERL [...]. The difficult readability may explain why it was cataloged as an anonymous French or Dutch master by the Los Angeles County Museum of Art, when it was still in their collection. See WESCHER 1954, p. 58. The LACMA auctioned the work in 1982, in an auction that took place in Los Angeles (Sotheby's), on July 21, 1982, No. 14 (proposed as Flemish School, seventeenth century). It was attributed to Jacob van Oost de Oude in the catalog at the auction New York (Sotheby's), January 20, 1983, No. 11.

[8] For more information on this painting, see MEULEMEESTER 1984, p. 266, BUIJS AND VAN BERGE-GERBAUD 1991, no. 36.

Cat. n. IV.3
Hendrick ter Brugghen
The Singing Lute Player
ca. 1624.
Oil on canvas, 100.3 × 83.5 cm (39.48 × 32.87 in.).
Amsterdam (the Netherlands), The Kremer Collection, GK-11.

It was in around 1620 that the painters Gerrit van Honthorst (see also **cat. nos. II.7, IV.4–IV.5**), Dirck van Baburen (see **cat. n. II.4**), and Hendrick ter Brugghen returned to Utrecht after a long sojourn in Italy.[1] Almost immediately, they introduced a number of important innovations that were destined to change painting in the northern Low Countries. While in Rome, the trio was heavily influenced by the art of Caravaggio, particularly in terms of an abundant use of *chiaroscuro*, as well as a naturalistic approach to the illustration of biblical narratives where figures occupy the entire picture plane. In the early work of Caravaggio and his followers, one often finds such figures in the form of single, half-length musicians. The Utrecht Caravaggesques painted both biblical and genre scenes, but their pictures of these music-makers enjoyed the greatest popularity with the buying public. Even today it is the motif most closely associated with the art of Utrecht.[2]

Ter Brugghen executed his first half-length musician in 1621. *The Singing Lute Player* described here was created several years later, probably in around 1624. It depicts a singing man, accompanying himself on the lute. He gazes out at the viewer, wearing a lively and open expression. The lighting is subtle and naturalistic, and helps underline the powerful modeling of the figure. Its rich, beautifully preserved coloration is undoubtedly one of the most attractive aspects of the painting—his attire sports vivid colors such as black, red, blue, yellow, white, and blue. Ter Brugghen separates these color accents with a neutral brown, used for the cloak and lute. The man's flamboyant costume, with its capacious puffed-sleeve shirt, cloak, and feathered beret, is certainly not something meant to be worn on a daily basis.

It has been suggested that Ter Brugghen, in imitation of his Italian predecessors, dressed his figures in this way in order to distance them—and thus the scene as a whole—from everyday life, giving the scene an exotic or fantastic tinge that enabled it to be 'read' differently and to take on new meaning.[3] However, although the lute may well be a symbolic reference to love—it had been considered the perfect wooing instrument since the Middle Ages—there is nothing else in the picture that necessarily points in this particular direction.

The painting is neither signed nor dated, although there is a more or less identical composition—bearing the mark *HTBrugghen fecit 1624*—in the National Gallery in London. It is not unusual to find several versions of the same scene in Ter Brugghen's work; undoubtedly, this was the result of the enormous popularity that his musician paintings enjoyed.[4] These copies are some-times by his own hand, but often, obvious variations in quality indicate that such copies were made by assistants in his workshop. In the instance of the painting on display here, however, there is almost no difference between this exemplar and the one in London. The execution is identical, and in both canvases the paint is applied with great self-assurance. In addition, the lack of a signature in the Kremer exemplar suggests that this singing lute player is an autograph copy of the original in the National Gallery in London which, as mentioned above, bears the artist's signature.

Another indication that the Kremer canvas is a copy by the artist is the lack of *pentimenti* (namely, corrections and changes made by the artist by painting over certain areas), which are extensive in the London exemplar, particularly along the right-hand edge of the hat and on the right sleeve, where there is clear evidence of adjustments having taken place during the painting process.[5] There are no such changes in the present exemplar. The painter had the desired final result—probably quite literally—right in front of him. Interestingly, there is one detail in the Kremer exemplar that has been preserved in a more original form than in the other version in London, namely the blue stripe on the white puffed sleeve. In the first version, the addition of smalt to the blue paint has caused it to become more transparent and to discolor over time.[6] In this singing lute player, however, this area has kept its original freshness and richness of contrast.

Peter van der Ploeg

[1] Further bibliography on the artist may be found in NICOLSON 1957, p. 200–202, NICOLSON 1958, p. 76, SLATKES AND FRANITS 2007, *DUTCH AND FLEMISH OLD MASTERS* 2002.

[2] *MASTERS OF LIGHT* 1998.

[3] In this regard, see also *NIEUW LICHT OP DE GOUDEN EEUW* 1986 and BUIJSEN 1994, p. 128–131.

[4] Both Nicolson and Slatkes suggest that there are two replicas, in addition to the first version in London; see *MASTERS OF LIGHT* 1998.

[5] MACLAREN 1991, p. 63.

[6] Ibid.

Cat. n. IV.4
Gerrit van Honthorst

Concert

ca. 1626.
Oil on canvas, 168 × 202 cm (66.14 × 79.52 in.).
Rome (Italy), Galleria Borghese, inv. 31.

Gerrit van Honthorst's *Concert* touches on the admonitory contradictions of the book of Ecclesiastes in myriad ways.[1] At first glance, the scene seems to innocently echo the reassuring exhortation "to eat, and to drink, and to be merry".[2] Indeed, such scenes are sometimes referred to as "merry companies" and were part of the stock-in-trade of this Dutch follower of the Italian painter Michelangelo Merisi, called Caravaggio.[3] But all is not as it seems: one of the revelers is actually the hapless victim of an elaborately-staged 'sting', and his situation validates the sage's warning that it is "better to go to the house of mourning than to go to the house of feasting".[4]

The dupe in question is the young *bravo* at the right, who immediately draws the eye by dint of how his flamboyant canary-yellow costume gleams in a shaft of sunlight scything its way through an otherwise dull interior. The young man's flushed cheeks complement the rose trim of his outfit, and betray the heady effects of too much wine, women, and song—literally so. His *innamorata* uses one hand to guide him through the duet laid out in a score they share between them, while her other hand sensuously strokes his ear, causing him to blush further still. The prominently positioned sword hilt affords a bawdy visual clue as to another physical reaction he experiences as a consequence of his companion's caresses. The pair's situation inevitably recalls contemporary writers on the proverbial union of love and music, from Giorgio Vasari's comment in the *Lives of the Artists* of 1568 that "love is always in the company of music", to the opening of William Shakespeare's *Twelfth Night* (Act 1, scene 1, line 1) (1601–1602), "if music be the food of love, play on".[5] But it also quickly dawns on the viewer that the girl's real intent is the palming of her victim's pearl earring, and that the other two characters are in on the scam: the musician at the left momentarily stays his bow in delighted, jaw-dropped anticipation of the girl's sleight of hand; the old woman is egging on her young accomplice, while appearing ready to slip the purloined trinket into a bag squirreled away in the shadows (or is she actually picking the man's purse?). Clearly resembling the turbaned procuresses in analogous scenes by Van Honthorst and other Utrecht-based Caravaggesques, such as Dirck van Baburen (see **cat. n. II.4**), her raised finger draws attention to a leering gap-toothed expression which references a commonly understood emblem of lasciviousness: in the words of the lusty Wife of Bath from the *Canterbury Tales* by Geoffrey Chaucer, "Gat-tothed I was, and that becam me weel".[6]

The narrative of a young man feasting, flirting, and deriving little profit from the result probably relates to another biblical precedent, Jesus's parable, in the Gospel of Luke, of the prodigal son "who wasted his substance with riotous living".[7] But from the light which bathes Van Honthorst's scene, which is that of the late afternoon sun that "goeth down, and hasteth to his place where he arose", to the presence of the *vanitas* still-life basket of fruit and the designing confederacy of the two women, the *Concert* remains heavily influenced by the imagery of Ecclesiastes.[8] Of particular relevance is its caution that "more bitter than death the woman, whose heart is snares and nets, and her hands as bands".[9] Ecclesiastes's further remark that, "as the birds that are caught in the snare; so are the sons of men snared in an evil time" may also be recalled in one of the objects that has helped entrap the young victim: the wineglass on the table, which—although the detail is not wholly clear—has a stem apparently composed of a bird motif (the equivalent of the Dutch phrase to hunt birds, "vogelen", literally "to bird", was also common slang for copulation).[10] Van Honthorst's juxtaposition of youthful feminine allure alongside that of inevitable wizened old age (as in Pompeo Batoni's *Time Orders Old Age to Destroy Beauty*, **cat. n. III.8**) also responds to a pictorial tradition that peddled the impermanent, untrustworthy nature of female sexual power, and how death's presence in the world was contingent on Eve's role in the fall and susceptibility to the serpent (one notes the curiously reptilian, snake-eyed characterisation of Honthorst's procuress figure). Such misogynistic symbolism was a frequent theme in European painting, particularly in northern Europe, as most powerfully exemplified by the disturbing allegories of Hans Baldung Grien.[11]

It is Caravaggio's influence which is paramount, however: the *Concert* was painted a few years after Van Honthorst had returned to his native Utrecht following a successful early career in Rome where he had been directly exposed to Caravaggio's works, and had been supported by the same patrons. Although the daylight setting may seem surprising to viewers more familiar with Van Honthorst's earlier—supposedly more Caravaggesque—night-time scenes and dramatic candle-light effects (the Italians refer to him as 'Gherardo delle Notti'—'Gerard of the night scenes'), the *Concert* is also one of Van Honthorst's most authentic responses to Caravaggio's templates.[12] The sepulchral atmospherics of his mature work notwithstanding, Caravaggio painted few nocturnes, and studiously rejected artificial light sources. The *Concert's* dramatic realism, use of semi-obscured directed daylight, and half-length, foppishly-attired figures convened around a table, constitutes a careful mimicry of Caravaggio's early genre scenes. A particular inspiration was Caravaggio's hugely influen-

tial *Cardsharps* of ca.1595 in the Kimbell Art Museum, Fort Worth (AP 1987.06), with its analogous scene of *bravi* cheating a young gull (see also the copy after Manfredi's *Cardplayers* in this exhibition, **cat. n. IV.1**).[13] The fruit basket, with its arching sprig of vine leaves, is a direct quotation of another early Caravaggio genre scene, the *Basket of Fruit* of ca.1596 in the Pinacoteca Ambrosiana, Milan (inv. 151).[14] The *Concert's* motif of an alluring young woman in cahoots with an older, wizened companion is also reminiscent of Caravaggio's *Judith Beheading Holofernes* of ca. 1598 in the Palazzo Barberini, Rome (2533)—to one degree or another, the victims depicted in both works are each losing their head over a girl.[15]

Philip Cottrell

[1] For a detailed discussion of the work and its place in Van Honthorst's oeuvre, see JUDSON 1959, p. 241–242; JUDSON AND EKKART 1999, p. 209–210.

[2] Eccles. 8:15. All biblical quotations in this entry are taken from the KJV.

[3] See for example the "Merry Companies" by Van Honthorst in the Galleria degli Uffizi, Florence (inv. 1890.730) and the Alte Pinakothek, Munich (inv. 1312)—see PAPI 2010, p. 182; JUDSON AND EKKART 1999, p. 217–220.

[4] Eccles. 7:2.

[5] VASARI 1906, p. 373 and SHAKESPEARE 2016, p. 1829. The connection between love and music is also stressed with regard to common seventeenth-century expressions such as "Love makes one sing" in the discussion of this painting in JUDSON AND EKKART 1999, p. 210.

[6] CHAUCER 2008, p. 113. On the symbolic significance of teeth, extracted or merely missing, see GASH 2007. See also JUDSON AND EKKART 1999, p. 227. See Van Honthorst's *Procuress* in the Centraal Museum, Utrecht (inv. 10786) and also the picture of the same title by Van Baburen in the Museum of Fine Arts, Boston (inv. 50.2721). For an attempt to identify the *Concert* with a painting known as the *Theft of the Amulet*, which was retained by Van Honthorst's descendants until 1770, see BRAUN 1966, p. 240.

[7] Luke 15:13. On this interpretation of such scenes by Caravaggio and his followers see JUDSON AND EKKART 1999, p. 218; EDWARDS 2011, p. 183.

[8] Eccles. 1:5.

[9] Eccles. 7:26.

[10] Eccles. 9:12; GEER AND WIESEMAN 2007, p. 67.

[11] See for example Hans Baldung Grien, *Death and the Maiden*, Vienna, Kunsthistorisches Museum (inv. 2636), discussed in KOERNER 1985, p. 74–75.

[12] See for example the candlelit *Christ Before the High Priest* of ca. 1617 painted for Vincenzo Giustiniani (National Gallery, London, NG3679), the *Christ in the Carpenter's Shop* of ca. 1617 for Scipione Borghese (stolen in 1976 from the Convent of San Silvestro, Montecompatri), and the *Merry Company with a Lute Player* (now Galleria degli Uffizi, inv. 1890.730) which Van Honthorst completed for Cosimo II de' Medici, Grand Duke of Tuscany, just before departing Rome in the early summer of 1620. The first two of these commissioners were also patrons of Caravaggio. See JUDSON AND EKKART 1999, p. 6–7, 10–12, 14–15, 67–68, and 217–218.

[13] SPIKE 2010, p. 20–28. On the influence of the *Cardsharps*, see EDWARDS 2011 and LANGDON 2012.

[14] SPIKE 2010, p. 73–77.

[15] SPIKE 2010, p. 106–111.

Cat. n. IV.5*
Gerrit van Honthorst

Woman Playing a Lute

1624.
Oil on canvas, 106 × 90 cm (41.73 × 35.43 in.).
Inscription: *G. Honthorst fe. 1624.*
Fontainebleau (France), Château de Fontainebleau, inv. 1368.

Born in 1590, the son of a painter of tapestry cartoons, Gerrit van Honthorst was raised in the prosperous and well-populated city of Utrecht, a Catholic stronghold in the northern Netherlands (see also **cat. nos. II.7, IV.4**).[1] He was placed in the workshop of Abraham Bloemaert, a painter praised for his naturalistic landscapes and pastoral scenes by Karel van Mander in his very influential *Schilderboek* (*Book on Painting*), published in 1604.

At the beginning of the 1610s, Van Honthorst undertook the traditional trip to Italy, and he is documented there in 1616 where he signed a drawing after Caravaggio's masterful composition for the Cerasi Chapel in Santa Maria del Popolo, *The Martyrdom of St. Peter* (National Gallery, Oslo, Printroom, cat. D16).[2]

Rome was then a city bustling with artists and artistic activity. Moreover, the imprint of Caravaggio, who left the city in 1606 and died four years later, was particularly vivid. His innovations in the use of light, the choice of subjects, and the framing of the compositions were very influential on his local followers, such as Bartolomeo Manfredi and Orazio Gentileschi, as well as on Dutch artists active in Rome in the second decade of the seventeenth century, such as Gerrit van Honthorst, Hendrink ter Brugghen, and Dirk van Baburen. Many of Caravaggio's works were accessible in Roman churches or in the palaces of avid art collectors of the time. Van Honthorst was soon introduced into this *milieu* and received commissions from the three most important patrons of the time, the Marchese Vincenzo Giustiniani, Cardinal Scipione Borghese, and Cosimo II de' Medici (1590–1621), even taking up residence in the Giustiniani palace, near the church of San Luigi dei Francesi. The accessibility of his art collection, which counted paintings by Caravaggio, the Bassano painters, and Luca Cambiaso, undoubtedly exerted a strong influence upon the artist. Van Honthorst's Roman clients brought him great success, and he painted numerous altarpieces in the churches of Rome, and his taste for nocturnal scenes earned him the nickname "Gherardo delle Notti" ("Gerard of the night scenes").

He returned from Rome in 1620 and was enlisted as a master in the newly created Guild of Saint Luke in Utrecht, where he enjoyed an excellent reputation and continued to paint in an Italian manner with artificially lit religious scenes.[3] The introduction in Utrecht of the half-length single figure of a musician is a characteristic of this school of painting, typical of the Caravaggesque artists from Utrecht, which was established in the second decade of the seventeenth century, and dominated by Van Honthorst, Van Baburen, and Ter Brugghen.

Woman Playing a Lute is generally considered to come from the Noordeeinde Palace, Stadhouder Frederick-Hendrick of Orange-Nassau's residence in The Hague.[4] The Dutch court in The Hague seems to have had a great interest in the pictorial representation of short-lived pleasures, including musicians, courtesans, and popular figures in ravishing attires. In a court where etiquette was rigid, and during an era of strong Calvinist morality, these cheerful and luminous subjects must have provided a type of sweet escape.

These paintings were not cabinet paintings but much more often decoration pieces.[5] Indeed, we know that in 1622, Gerrit van Honthorst painted an illusionistic fresco ceiling, the *Musical Group on a Balcony* (Los Angeles, J. Paul Getty Museum, 70. PB 34) for a private house in Utrecht. In 1624, he painted the *Concert* (Musée du Louvre, inv. 1364) which is most likely the painting described in the 1632 inventory as "a painting for the mantelpiece".[6] It has been suggested that this painting was made as a pendant for the *Woman Playing Guitar* in the Musée du Louvre (inv 1369).[7] Though the appearance of the two figures is not similar when held in comparison, the paintings share the same format and could constitute a prelude to a duet as they depict one woman tuning a lute to give the note that will be played on the guitar by another woman. Paul de Mirimonde even proposed that both portraits were framing the 1624 *Concert* (see **cat. n. IV.4**) mentioned above.[8]

In this painting, the smiling woman presses her lute against her bosom and plucks its strings with one hand while adjusting the tone key with the other. She wears a rich costume of blue and yellow fabrics which recalls theatrical costumes of the Burgundian court, and is not reminiscent of the Netherlandish fashion of the period. Similar costumes are to be found in the *Smiling Girl Holding a Medallion* (Saint Louis Museum, inv. 63.1954), the *Guitar Player* in the Louvre (inv. 1368), and the *Woman Tuning a Lute* recently rediscovered at Sotheby's.[9] Indeed, Gerrit van Honthorst often used these revealing corsages of rich fabrics and feathered hats to depict women of ambiguous reputation (professional musicians or popular figures of little virtue) by using a 'visual pun'—the Dutch word for lute (*luit*) could also mean vagina. These feminine figures are often to be found in the repertoire of Van Honthorst: he painted at least twenty musician portraits from the first recorded *Merry Violonist* (Rijksmuseum, SK-A-180), which is dated 1623. The subject matter may be Italian in inspiration: Gerrit van Honthorst may have seen Caravaggio's *Lute Player*, commissioned by Vincenzo Giustiniani in

1595–1596, in his patron's palace in Rome. Nevertheless, the interpretation of it and the treatment of light and colors is very different from the sharp *chiaroscuro* of Caravaggio's compositions. Here, a strong natural daylight falls upon the sitter's face and bust. It literally models the contours of the wooden lute with its carved rosette and gives a shimmering effect to the ginger, curly hair, the yellow stripes of the dress, and the rosy cheekbones. The tight framing, which cuts to the left the hand of the musician and the sparkling eyes looking away, imbue this figure with great presence.

The symbolic interpretation of this painting remains mysterious. On the one hand, the lute has a traditional association with harmony and love.[10] On the other, the sensual appeal of the painting, the revealing costumes, and the seductive attitude lean toward a more licentious interpretation, a sort of exaltation of terrestrial and sensorial pleasures.

Oriane Beaufils

[1] Further bibliography on the subject may be found in *Corps et ombres* 2012, *Caravaggio in Holland* 2009, Judson and Ekkart 1999, *Peintures pour un château* 1998, *Princely Patrons* 1997, Nicolson 1990, p. 124, Moiso-Diekamp 1987, p. 172–173, 334–335, *Le siècle de Rembrandt* 1970, Pomme de Mirimonde 1960, p. 109–116.

[2] Judson and Ekkart 1999, p. 10.

[3] Judson 1959, p. 58.

[4] This is according to the inventory of 1632, where it is described as "A painting being a nymph playing on a lute with an ebony frame made by Hondthorst" in Broos 1997, p. 142.

[5] Cabinet paintings were small pictures, generally hung in a private art collections developed in Northern Europe especially during the seventeenth century. See Härting 1998.

[6] Judson and Ekkart 1999, p. 207.

[7] Pomme de Mirimonde 1960, p. 112–113.

[8] Ibid. Judson disproves this hypothesis in Judson and Ekkart 1999.

[9] Sotheby's, New York, January 31, 2013, lot 39.

[10] Millner Kahr 1998, p. 74.

This Ragge of *Death*, which thou shalt see,
Consider it; And Pious bee.

ILLVSTR. VIII.

Book. I

The Deceptiveness of Earthly Pleasures

Gifts from God, such as wealth and health, were to be enjoyed, but were also to be understood as short-lived, and not as a replacement for true treasure and joy, which could only be experienced in heaven. Some pastimes, however, were considered to be vices, and too much of a good thing was frowned upon, as was obsession with wealth.

These seventeenth- and eighteenth-century images reveal these concerns. Paintings that speak of accumulated wealth, or misspent evenings of drinking, gambling, and smoking, included *vanitas* references, such as skulls, smoldering ash, recently blown-out candles, and silent musical instruments, that were designed to reinforce moderation.

I said to myself, "Come now, I will make a test of pleasure; enjoy yourself." But again, this also was vanity. I said of laughter, "It is mad," and of pleasure, "What use is it?"

Sorrow is better than laughter, for by sadness of countenance the heart is made glad. The heart of the wise is in the house of mourning; but the heart of fools is in the house of mirth.

(Ecclesiastes 2:1–2, 7:3–4)

Cat. n. IV.6
Jan Fris

A Still-Life with a Stoneware Jug, a Glass of Beer, Playing Cards, and Smokers' Requisites

1665.
Oil on panel, 49 × 42 cm (19.29 × 16.53 in.).
Inscription: (on the stone) *J. Fris 1665*.
London (England), Richard Green Fine Paintings.

Very little is known about the life of Jan, or Johannes, Fris. He was born in Amsterdam in around 1627. The approximate year of his birth has been deduced from two documented declarations of his age.[1] He married in Amsterdam in 1649, and two years later he acquired citizenship there. He was buried in the same city on July 9, 1672. His work provides the best testament of his existence—he left a small oeuvre consisting almost exclusively of still-lifes, many of which are signed and dated, with dates ranging from 1647 to 1672.[2] His favorite subjects were still-lifes of smoking utensils, breakfast pieces, and *vanitas* still-lifes.

This painting is a fine and characteristic example of a still-life by Jan Fris. It depicts one of his favorite subjects—a still-life with smokers' requisites, or *toebackje*, as they were called in the seventeenth-century Netherlands. Food, drink, and smoking implements are displayed near the corner of a stone ledge. At the center of the composition are a stoneware jug and a tall pint of beer. Beside them appear a pewter plate with shrimp, a broken brazier of glowing coals, two white clay pipes, a paper wrapper containing tobacco, and a pack of playing cards: the six of hearts lies face up at the front of the ledge. Behind the brazier lies a bundle of *zwavelstokjes*—the predecessor of matches—and in front of it a small pile of ash, from which rises a thin wisp of smoke. While retaining a muted palette of browns, greys, ochre, terracotta, and white, the artist has paid great attention to the details of surfaces and textures, as is clearly visible in the sheen of the pewter, the sparkle of highlights on the glass and glazed ceramics, the cracked stone ledge, the crumpled paper. The upright format is typical of Fris.

Several of the objects depicted here, specifically the earthenware jug, the beer glass, the broken brazier, and the clay pipes, must have been studio props, since they recur in other works by Fris. The distinctive jug, bearing the coat of arms of Amsterdam, is of a type that was manufactured in the German Rhineland. An identical vessel forms the central motif in at least three other paintings, including a signed and dated still-life of 1650, in the Institut Néerlandais, Paris. In addition, there is a *Still-Life of Smoking Requisites* dated 1660, formerly in the Brod Gallery, London. Finally, an undated *Still-Life with an Earthenware Jug, a Glass, a Pipe, a Walnut, and other Objects on a Stone Ledge* that was sold at Christie's in London on November 30, 1973. The tall, cylindrical glass, with its distinctive spiral decoration, is called a *pasglas* and was used in drinking games. The glass was filled with beer and passed around a group of friends, each of whom was expected to drink down to the next ring in a single gulp. Anyone who failed to hit the mark had to drink a further measure. In Fris's day, such glasses often feature in depictions of bawdy tavern scenes. The long clay pipe is often referred to as a *Goudse pijp* in Dutch, owing to the fact that Gouda was for a long time the main center in the Netherlands for the manufacture of such pipes.

This type of tobacco still-life was an invention and specialty of the Dutch 'tonal' still-life painters, and can probably be traced to the Haarlem painter Pieter Claesz's work of the 1630s. The immediate inspiration for Jan Fris was, however, more likely the work of his slightly older Amsterdam colleagues Jan Jansz Treck and Jan Jansz van de Velde. In his choice and arrangement of objects, as well as in his coloring, Fris's style is especially close to that of Van de Velde's.

The theme of such paintings can probably be explained in several ways. Taken together, the objects depicted here suggest an evening of drinking, smoking, and playing cards. Enjoyable though such pastimes may be, they were also considered minor vices in the seventeenth century, and associated with idleness (smoking and drinking) and deceit (cards). Thus, still-lifes of this type could serve as a warning against excessive indulgence in such pleasures, with the *pasglas* referring to temperance, or keeping measure. In addition, such motifs as the broken brazier and the smoldering ash contain *vanitas* associations that allude to the transience of human existence: life is as fleeting as a wisp of smoke.

Pippa Cooper

[1] See BERGSTRÖM 1989, p. 121, and BREDIUS AND HIRSCHMANN 1919, p. 1990.

[2] He also painted a few portraits. See his *Portrait of the Tax Collector Marcellis Wttewael*, dated 1650, in DUTCH SEVENTEENTH CENTURY 1980.

Cat. n. IV.7

N. Le Peschier

Vanitas Still-Life

1660.
Oil on canvas, 57 × 70 cm (22.44 × 27.55 in.).
Amsterdam (the Netherlands), Rijksmuseum, SK-A-1686.

Little or nothing is known about this artist, not the year or place of his birth, not even his first name (Nicolaus? Norbertus?). He generally signed his canvases as "N. L. Peschier", as in this painting, but in some instances, such as that at the Philadelphia Museum of Art (see **figure 1**, p. 207), he signed as "N.us Le Peschier", which clarifies that the "L." in his signature stands for "Le" and is therefore part of his surname and not of his first name.[1] It is known that he was active between the years 1659 and 1661 because he signed and dated his artworks during that period.[2] The various sheets of paper represented in his paintings, displaying texts in French, suggest he may have been from a French-speaking region of Flanders, or a French painter active in that area.[3] As we know nothing about his life, consequently we do not have any information about the history of this painting—for whom it was carried out or who owned it through the centuries, except that it entered the collections of the Rijksmuseum in January 1897 after it was acquired from Michel van Gelder, who had it in his collection in Castle Zeecrabbe in Ukkel (Belgium).[4]

The painting illustrates a series of objects on a table in an interior setting: a quill, an inkwell, an open and crumpled letter bearing a seal, an hourglass, a semi-open book with earmarked pages, a cylindrical leather bag containing what appear to be paintbrushes and writing tools, a case with some letters and playing cards spilling out, a violin with broken strings, an open music score and, at the very center, a skull, which is the pivotal point around which all the objects are arranged.[5] On the left, hanging on a wall, there is an oil lamp whose wick exhales a thin line of smoke—a reference to Psalm 102:3 in which we read that our days "vanish in smoke" and our "bones burn like glowing embers" (KJV).[6] The objects on the canvas are not randomly distributed, rather their position is well thought through: the letter is by the skull's mouth, the book is next to the now empty eye sockets, while the violin and the score are by the ear—a subtle reference to the evanescent nature of our corporeality but also to the delights that come from that very corporeality.

The score on the painting is perfectly readable and the accuracy with which it is depicted not only highlights the importance of its message (hence the need for both music and verses to be readable), but it also allowed the present writer to identify both lyrics and music—hitherto undiscovered—which belong to the volume *Ghirlanda di madrigali a sei voci, di diversi eccellentissimi autori de' nostri tempi. Raccolta di giardini di fiori odoriferi musicali* (i.e., *Garland of six-voiced madrigals by several most excellent authors of our time. Collection of gardens of odoriferous mu-*

sical flowers), printed by Pierre Phalèse, in Antwerp, in 1601. As the title suggests, it is a miscellany of madrigals by different authors. The one visible in this painting is by one of the most famous Flemish musicians in Cinquecento Rome, Philippe de Monte.[7] The lyrics are by the famous Italian playwright, writer, and poet Battista Guarini. It is, in fact, the madrigal *Sì, mi dicesti, ed io*: a successful poetic text about fleeting love.[8] Therefore, in this painting, among all the symbols of vanity it is music that plays the leading role, as it is meant to warn the viewer against the vanity of transitory love, which—as the poem stipulates (see footnote 8 below)—was turned off with the same ease with which it was turned on. The artwork certainly is an exhortation to watch out for earthly vanities (as can be seen from the various objects on the table), but it is above all an invitation to be aware of the deceptiveness of fleeting love and sensual pleasures.

Corinna Ricasoli

[1] See also my companion piece on this painting in RICASOLI 2018, in press, and the bibliography therein.

[2] There are only about a dozen works attributed to N. Le Peschier today. About half of them are in public collections, while the other half has appeared with some cyclical regularity on the art market and their attribution is an issue due to the scarceness of Le Peschier's pictorial corpus, which makes comparisons on stylistic bases quite complex. The works in question, however, whether certain or uncertain, are all *vanitas* still-lifes, reminiscent of both those of the Leiden school and of the work of the painter Hendrick Andriessen from Antwerp. See CHONG AND KLOEK 1999, p. 296.

[3] However, he may have also been a Dutch painter who decided to translate his Dutch surname ("de Visser" or "Visscher"—"The Fisherman" or "Fisherman" in Dutch) into French ("Le Peschier" or "Peschier"— also "Fisherman"). Ibid.

[4] See DUMONT-WILDEN 1934.

[5] The decorations visible on the violin's tailpiece and fingerboard are typical of violins produced in the Flanders region in the seventeenth century. I wish to thank Dr. Giovanni Paolo Di Stefano, Curator of Musical Instruments at the Rijksmuseum, Amsterdam, for providing this information.

[6] SCHAMA 1987, p. 213.

[7] For Philippe de Monte's biography see LENAERTS 1989, p. 157–158, and also VAN DOORSLAER 1921.

[8] For the full Italian text of the poem, see GUARINI 1598, p. 111. The English translation (by the present writer) is the following: *"Yes", you*

told me, and I instantly sent that sweetest "yes" to my heart, and I burned from that most exquisite fire of love that none else could kindle: now that you've changed your mind, I did too, and just as a "yes" turned me on, a "no" put me out. This poem was put into music by no less than thirteen composers between 1588 and 1634. For the list of said composers, see POMPILIO 1997, p. 219. The list, however, does not include Michelangelo Rossi, who also put this madrigal into music. See Rossi's *Il secondo libro dei madrigali a cinque voci*, dated 1624–1629 and probably never printed. In this respect, see MANN 2002.

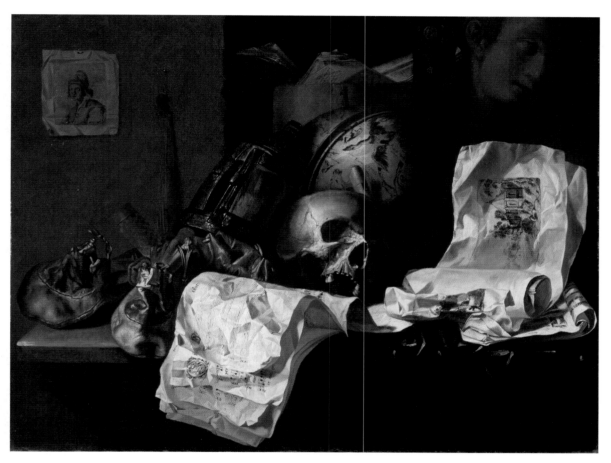

Figure 1:
N. Le Peschier, *Vanitas Still-Life*, 1661.
Oil on canvas, 80 × 101.6 cm (31.5 × 40 in.).
Philadelphia, PA (US), Philadelphia Museum of Art, inv. 1986-26-287.

Cat. n. IV.8
Jean-Baptiste Oudry
Allegory of the Arts

1713.
Oil on canvas 86 × 127 cm (33.85 × 50 in.).
Schwerin (Germany), Staatliches Museum, G188.

Jean-Baptiste Oudry is best known as a painter of animals, hunting scenes, and decorative compositions in which he specialized for most of his career, working for clients ranging from members of the middle class to the king of France. However, as a young artist, he had depicted a wider range of subjects, including a large number of portraits, few of which have survived. After receiving initial training from his father, a painter and picture dealer, he had been apprenticed to a portrait painter, Nicolas de Largillierre (1656–1746), for five years from about 1708.[1] After becoming a member of the Academy, in 1719, he received many royal commissions.[2] He also successfully sought patrons abroad, and even today the largest and most comprehensive collection of his work is at Schwerin, in northern Germany. Christian Ludwig, the Duke of Mecklenburg-Schwerin had commissioned paintings from him in 1732, but it was only in 1750 that he became Oudry's principal patron when he acquired thirteen paintings of animals at the king's menagerie at Versailles that had originally been commissioned by the king's surgeon, who died before being able to receive them. After Oudry's death, Christian Ludwig acquired another eighteen paintings, and the same number of drawings, in his estate sale. These included works from early in the artist's career that had remained in his studio all his life, including this painting, which is signed by the artist and dated 1713.[3]

The present artwork is arranged in a simple frieze, showing a bronzed plaster head identified as the god Apollo, a violin and its bow, a guitar placed on sheet music, a pot of amaranth flowers, a palette, and a candle with a mobile shade, allowing light from the candle to be directed to form specific shadows.[4] The candle has been extinguished. Like other still-lifes from this period, the objects are placed against a dark gray background that emphasizes the colors of the instruments and flowers.[5]

These objects refer to the arts of music, sculpture, and painting, with music occupying a central position. While the painting has been called an allegory of the arts, the prominent position of the amaranth, which is turning from dark green to bright red, apparently towering over the other objects, indicates its importance for the painting's meaning. A symbol of immortality since antiquity, it contrasts with the snuffed candle that, to the contrary, is a reflection of the transience of life. This is also symbolized by the silent musical instruments, whose immobility recalls the fleetingness of sound, thus offering a comparison between the impermanence of life and music. The amaranth, however, indicates an allegorical meaning for the painting—that an artist achieves immortality only through his or her art, as reflected in the maxim, *ars longa vita brevis* (art is long, life is short).[6] Other still-life paintings by Oudry from the same period have a *vanitas* connotation, such as the *Allegory of the Art of Painting* (Schwerin, Staatliches Museum, G263), which shows similar preoccupations and refers to the effort involved in creating art.[7]

The guitar reappears in an *Allegory of Europe* of 1722 at the Museum of Fine Arts, Houston, along with the same amaranth flowers.[8] They are accompanied by a violin and other musical instruments, but in this later painting they refer to the arts and culture of Europe. Oudry was himself an accomplished musician, and is known to have played the guitar quite well.[9] He seems to have identified closely with this instrument, as the frontispiece of his record book, or *Livre journal*, in which he kept a visual record of all his paintings for about five years, starting in 1713, includes a self-portrait playing the same guitar.[10]

Jane MacAvock

---

[1] For more about the precise timing of Oudry's apprenticeship, see BAILEY 2007, p. 2. See also GOUGENOT 1968, p. 365–403.

[2] See LE BAROQUE DES LUMIÈRES 2017.

[3] See ANIMAUX D'OUDRY 2003.

[4] See also JEAN-BAPTISTE OUDRY 2000.

[5] OPPERMAN 1977, vol. I, p. 23.

[6] Ibid., vol. II, p. 917.

[7] For more about this painting, see ibid., p. 917, and JEAN-BAPTISTE OUDRY 2000 (reproduced in color in entry no. 7).

[8] BF 1987.2. See J.-B. OUDRY 1982 for more about the painting, which had not been located at the time.

[9] GOUGENOT 1968, p. 379.

[10] Paris, Musée du Louvre, Département des arts graphiques, RF31045. For more about this, see JEAN-BAPTISTE OUDRY 2000, especially entry no. 8.

Cat. n. IV.9
Adriaen van Nieulandt

Vanitas Still-Life

1636.
Oil on panel, 40 × 37.2 cm (15.74 × 14.64 in.).
Haarlem (the Netherlands), Frans Hals Museum, OS 56-22.

Born in Antwerp, Adriaen van Nieulandt was a Flemish painter, engraver, and art dealer. His brother, Willem van Nieulandt, was also an artist. Adriaen was a pupil of Pieter Isaacsz and Frans Badens. He lived and worked in Amsterdam throughout his life. In 1628, he was also working as an art dealer. He was influenced in particular by Pieter Lastman and the Haarlem Mannerists.[1] This painting is an early example of the *vanitas* genre in Dutch art.

Vanitas Still-Life presents us with a striking and skillfully rendered ensemble of objects, each of which symbolizes the fleeting nature and vanity of life. The painting is dominated by a large skull whose vacant eye sockets and macabre grin imbue the painting with an eerie presence, a sense that its original occupant has a message to convey. The inscription below the skull *Ecquid Sunt aliud / quam breve gaudium?* (What do these things represent other than a brief joy?) delivers that message, lest we are in any doubt.[2] A Garden Tiger moth, and not a butterfly, as commonly thought, lies resting on the edge of a stone parapet, and is likely to relate to the Gospel of Matthew (6:19–21): "Do not store up for yourselves treasures on earth, where moth and rust consume and where thieves break in and steal; but store up for yourselves treasures in heaven, where neither moth nor rust consumes and where thieves do not break in and steal. For where your treasure is, there your heart will be also." In *vanitas* still-life paintings, the moth, a nocturnal insect that is attracted to light, represents the soul's quest for divine light, and therefore truth and enlightenment.[3] Next to the moth is a Turbo shell which has been polished down to reveal the exquisite, iridescent sheen of the nacre. Found only in the tropics, it would have been considered an expensive and exotic treasure. Its purpose was twofold—it was a symbol of resurrection and an allusion to the vanity of earthly possessions.[4] In addition, it provided the artist with an opportunity to demonstrate his skill in the realistic reproduction of form, texture, color, and reflected light. Similarly, the luster of the pearls, which in this instance is likely to be another reference to the Gospel of Matthew (13:45–46) "Again, the kingdom of heaven is like a merchant in search of fine pearls; on finding one pearl of great value, he went and sold all that he had and bought it". The biblical reference to merchants in search of fine pearls would undoubtedly have struck a chord in Amsterdam where the sale of gemstones was thriving. The coins scattered on the table are an obvious reference to the hoarding of wealth. The pile of books, well-thumbed, and by implication well-studied, are somewhat precariously placed and signify man's futile quest for knowledge in this life, as Ecclesiastes (2:15–16) points out "[...] 'What happens to the fool will happen to me also; why then have I been so very wise?' And I said to myself that this also is vanity. For there is no enduring remembrance of the wise or of fools, seeing that in the days to come all will have been long forgotten [...]." The vase of flowers on the left, which display five different varieties, represents the transience of life as their bloom is inevitably short-lived. Already, petals have fallen, demonstrating the onset of decay. The bouquet contains an iris, a rose, a columbine, and a marigold, which are attributes of the Virgin Mary, as well as a carnation which alluded to the passion of Christ.[5] A fly is prominently placed on the crown of the skull, and it acts as a *memento mori*— a vivid, repulsive reminder of the decay that follows death. In addition, the incessant and irritating buzzing of the fly led to it becoming a symbol of torment and torture and therefore a symbol of the passion of Christ.[6] The artist signed his name on the cover of the book at the bottom of the pile, where a makeshift bookmark displays the inscription *Mourir pour Vivre* (Die to Live), an obvious reference to the hope of life after death.

Audrey Nicholls

[1] ABELMANN 1998, p. 124. Among his important commissions were eleven works on copper for King Christian IV of Denmark, which were destroyed by fire in the nineteenth century. He also designed a frontispiece for Cesare Ripa's *Iconologia* (first printed in 1593).

[2] KÖHLER 2006, p. 564. Köhler suggests that Van Nieulandt derived the motif of the skull and the thighbone on a stone block with an inscription below from another early model, an allegorical print by Jan Saenredam after Abraham Bloemaert from around 1605/1607 (Rijksmuseum, RP-P-OB-10.533).

[3] KRITSKY AND CHERRY 2000, p. 19.

[4] IMPELLUSO 2004, p. 105.

[5] Ibid., p. 98, 115, 118–119. According to medieval legend, the tears shed by the Virgin Mary when she witnessed the crucifixion of her son fell to the ground and turned into carnations. In addition, in Italy the flower is known as *Chiodino* which means 'little nail' due to the shape of the bud, and because of this it came to be associated with the passion.

[6] Ibid., p. 337. See also **cat n. III.5.**

Index of Names

À Kempis, Thomas, German writer (1380–1471)

Alberti, Leon Battista, Italian architect and theorist (1404–1472)

Agostino Veneziano, see Agostino dei Musi

Albericus Londoniensis, see Londoniensis, Albericus

Alemán, Mateo, Spanish writer (1547–1614)

Alexander The Great, king of Macedonia (356–323 BCE, reign 336–323)

Antoninus Augustus Pius, Titus Aelius Hadrianus, Roman emperor (86–161 CE, reign 138–161 CE)

Antoninus Pius, see Pius, Titus Aelius Hadrianus Antoninus Augustus

Aristotle, ancient Greek philosopher and scientist (384–322 BCE)

Augustine, see Augustinus, Aurelius

Augustinus, Aurelius, bishop of Hippo, Doctor of the Church, philosopher, theologian, and saint (354–430 CE)

Auwera, see Von der Auwera, Johann Wolfgang

Azzolino, Giovanni Bernardino, Italian painter (ca. 1572–1645)

Baburen, see Van Baburen, Dirck

Bacon, Francis, English philosopher, statesman, and writer (1561–1626)

Badens, Frans, Flemish painter (1571–1618)

Bailly, David, Dutch painter (1584–1657)

Baldinucci, Filippo, Italian writer (1625–1696)

Baldung Grien, Hans, German painter (ca. 1484–1545)

Balthasar, Denner, German painter (1685–1749)

Barozzi, Jacopo, Italian architect and theorist (1507–1573)

Bassano family, see dal Ponte

Batoni, Pompeo Girolamo, Italian painter (1708–1787)

Bellotti, Pietro, Italian painter (1627–1700)

Bellotto, Bernardo, Italian painter (1721–1780)

Besborodko, Alexander Andréevitch, grand chancellor of Russia (1747–1799)

Beyeren, see Van Beyeren, Abraham

Bibbiena, see Galli Bibbiena, Ferdinando

Bizet d'Annonay, Charles Emmanuel, Flemish painter (1633–1691)

Bloemaert, Abraham, Dutch painter (1566–1651)

Boel, Pieter, Flemish painter (ca. 1622–1674)

Boel, Jan, Flemish printmaker (1592–1640)

Bonenberg, Bela, wife of Peter von Clapis (died 1528)

Borghese, see Caffarelli Borghese, Scipione

Bosch, Hieronymus, Netherlandish painter and draftsman (ca. 1450–1516)

Boscoli, Pier Paolo, Italian politician and conspirator (1481–1513)

Botticelli, see Filipepi, Sandro

Boulogne, see De Boulogne, Valentin

Bourbon, Christine Marie, duchess of Savoy and regent of Savoy (1606–1663, reign as duchess 1619–1637, reign as regent of Savoy 1637–1648)

Bracciolini, Poggio, Italian humanist and collector (1380–1459)

Bradstreet, Anne, English poet (1612–1672)

Brant, Sebastian, German humanist (ca. 1457–1521)

Bredael, see Van Bredael, Pierre

Brenz, Johannes, German theologian and Protestant Reformer (1499–1570)

Bronzino, see Di Cosimo, Agnolo

Brunelleschi, Filippo, Italian architect and sculptor (1377–1446)

Bruyn, Bartholomaeus, the Elder, German painter (1493–1555)

Bunyan, John, English writer (1628–1688)

Buonarroti, Michelangelo, Italian artist, architect, and poet (1475–1564)

Caffarelli Borghese, Scipione, Italian cardinal and patron (1576–1633)

Callot, Jacques, French draftsman and printmaker (1592–1635)

Cambiaso, Luca, Italian painter and printmaker (1527–1585)

Campin, Robert, Flemish painter (ca.1378/1379–1444)

Canal, Giovanni Antonio, Italian painter (1697–1768)

Canaletto, see Canal, Giovanni Antonio

Capponi, Agostino, Italian politician and conspirator (1471–1513)

Caravaggio, see Merisi, Michelangelo

Carneo, Antonio, Italian painter (1637–1692)

Caroselli, Angelo, Italian painter (1585–1652)

Cartari, Vincenzo, Italian writer (ca. 1531–after 1569)

Carucci, Jacopo, Italian painter (1494–1557)

Cassana, Niccolò, Italian painter (1659–1714)

Castellani, Castellano, Italian poet and playwright (1461–ca.1519)

Cavalier d'Arpino, see Cesari, Giuseppe

Cerrini, Giovanni Domenico, Italian painter (1609–1681)

Ceruti, Giacomo, Italian painter (1698–1767)

Cesari, Giuseppe, Italian painter (1568–1640)

Cézanne, Paul, French painter (1839–1906)

Charles I, see Stuart, Charles I

Charles V, see Habsburg, Charles V

Charron, Pierre, French theologian, writer, and philosopher (1541–1603)

Chaucer, Geoffrey, English writer (ca. 1343–1400)

Chigi, Flavio, cardinal (1631–1693)

Chigi, Fabio, pope of the Catholic Church (1599–1667, reign 1655–1667)

Christine of Savoy, see Bourbon, Christine Marie

Chrysostom, John, bishop and Doctor of the Church (ca. 349–407)

Cicero, Marcus Tullius, Roman attorney, politician, and writer (106–43 BCE)

Cifrondi, Antonio, Italian painter (1656–1730)

Cipper, Giacomo Francesco, Austrian painter (1664–1736)

Claesz, Pieter, Dutch painter (1597–1661)

Clapis, see Von Clapis, Peter

ISAACSZ, Pieter Fransz, Danish painter (1569–1625)

James I, see Stuart, James Charles

JANSSENS, Abraham, Flemish painter (ca. 1575–1632)

JERMIN, Michael, English scholar (1591–1659)

Jerome, see Hieronymus, Eusebius Sophronius

JOEST, Jan, German painter (ca. 1455–1519)

JUVARRA, Filippo, Italian architect and scenographer (1678–1736)

LAGNEAU, Nicolas, French painter (ca. 1590–ca. 1666)

LANDI, Stefano, Italian composer (1587–1639)

LASTMAN, Pieter, Dutch painter (1583–1633)

LÁSZÓ PYRKER, János, bishop of Eger (1772–1847)

LE BRUN, Charles, French designer and painter (1619–1690)

LE PESCHIER, N., Flemish or Dutch painter (active 1659–1661)

LEOPARDI, Giacomo, Italian poet, philosopher, writer, and scholar (1798–1837)

LIEVENS, Jan, Dutch painter (1607–1674)

LIGOZZI, Jacopo, Italian painter (1547–1627)

LILY, William, English writer and scholar (ca. 1468–1522)

Lint, see Van Lint, Hendrik Frans

Lint, see Van Lint, Peter

LUTTICHUIJS, Simon, Dutch painter (1610–1661)

LONDONIENSIS, Albericus, English monk and writer (12th century)

Lorrain, see Gellée, Claude

LOSCHI, Antonio, Italian humanist and diplomat (ca. 1365–1441)

LUTHER, Martin, German theologian (1483–1546)

MACHIAVELLI, Niccolò, Italian statesman and writer (1469–1527)

MAGNASCO, Alessandro, Italian painter (1667–1749)

Mander, see Van Mander, Karel

MANFREDI, Bartolomeo, Italian painter (1582–1622)

MARTINELLI, Giovanni, Italian painter (1600–1659)

MASTERS, Edgar Lee, American attorney, poet, writer, and dramatist (1868–1950)

MATTIOLI, Pietro Andrea, Italian physician and naturalist (ca. 1501–1578)

MAZZARINO, Giulio, Italian cardinal (1602–1661)

MELANCHTHON, Philip, German theologian and Protestant Reformer (1497–1560)

MERISI, Michelangelo, Italian painter (1571–1610)

Michelangelo, see Buonarroti, Michelangelo

Montaigne, see De Montaigne, Michel

MORE, Thomas, English attorney, philosopher, writer, and saint (1478–1535)

MORGAN, Sydney, Irish novelist (ca. 1781–1859)

MORONI, Giovanni Battista, Italian painter (ca. 1525–ca. 1580)

Nettesheim, see von Nettesheim

NEVILLE, William, English poet (1497–ca. 1545)

Nieulandt, see Van Nieulandt, Adriaen, the Younger

NUVOLONE, Panfilo, Italian painter (1581–ca. 1651)

Oost, see Van Oost, Jacob, the Elder

OOSTERLINCK, Gregorius, Dutch painter (active 17th–18th centuries)

OUDRY, Jean-Baptiste, French painter (1686–1755)

PALLADIO, Andrea, Italian architect, draftsman, and author (1508–1580)

PAMMACHIUS, Roman senator and saint (died ca. 409)

Panderen, see Van Panderen, Egbert

PANNINI, Giovanni Paolo, Italian painter and architect (1691–1765)

PASCOLI, Lione, Italian lawyer, economist, collector, and writer (1674–1744)

Passe, see Van de Passe, Crispijn, the Elder

Passe, see Van de Passe, Crispijn, the Younger

PASSERI, Giovanni Battista, Italian painter and author (1610–1679)

PERETTI, Felice, pope of the Catholic Church (ca. 1520–1590, reign 1585–1590)

Perugino, see Vannucci, Pietro

PETRARCA, Francesco, Italian poet and humanist (1304–1374)

Petrarch, see Petrarca, Francesco

PIPPI, Giulio, Italian painter and architect (ca. 1499–1546)

PIRANESI, Giovanni Battista, Italian printmaker (1720–1778)

Pitocchetto, see Ceruti, Giacomo

PITTONI, Giovanni Battista, the Younger, Italian painter (1687–1767)

PLATO, ancient Greek philosopher (ca. 428–348 BCE)

Pontormo, see Carucci, Jacopo

Pope Alexander VII, see Chigi, Fabio

Pope Clement VII, see de' Medici, Giulio

Pope Clement XII, see Corsini, Lorenzo

Pope Innocent III, see Dei Conti di Segni, Lotario

Pope Julius II, see Della Rovere, Giuliano

Pope Leo X, see de' Medici, Giovanni

Pope Sixtus IV, see Della Rovere, Francesco

Pope Sixtus V, see Peretti, Felice

PREISLER, Daniel, German painter (1627–1665)

Prosper of Aquitaine, see Tiro, Prosper

QUARLES, Francis, English poet (1592–1644)

RAHNER, Karl, German theologian (1904–1984)

RAIMONDI, Marcantonio, Italian printmaker (ca. 1470/1482–ca. 1527/1534)

Raphael, see Santi, Raffaello

RÉGNIER, Nicolas, French painter (1591–1667)

Rembrandt, see Van Rijn, Rembrandt Harmensz

RENI, Guido, Italian painter (1575–1642)

Ribera, see De Ribera, Jusepe

RICCI, Marco, Italian painter (1676–1730)

RICCI, Sebastiano, Italian painter (1659–1734)

RICCIARDI, Giovanni Battista, Italian philosopher and poet (1623–1686)

RIPA, Cesare, Italian scholar and writer (ca. 1555–1622)

ROBERT, Hubert, French painter (1733–1808)

ROCCA, Angelo, Italian scholar and monk (1545–1620)

Romano, see Pippi, Giulio

ROMBOUTS, Theodoor, Flemish painter and printmaker (1597–1637)

ROSA, Salvator, Italian painter and printmaker (1615–1673)

Rosso Fiorentino, see Di Jacopo, Giovanni Battista

RUBENS, Peter Paul, Flemish painter (1577–1640)

SADELER, Raphael, I, Flemish painter and printmaker (ca. 1560–ca. 1628)

SAENREDAM, Jan, Dutch draftsman (1565–1607)

Saint Augustine, see Augustinus, Aurelius

Sandrart, see Von Sandrart, Joachim

SANTI, Raffaello, Italian painter and architect (1483–1520)

SAVOLDO, Giovanni Girolamo, Italian painter (ca. 1480–after 1548)

SCHIEBLING, Christian, German painter (1603–1663)

Schönborn, Friedrich Karl, see Von Schönborn, Friedrich Karl

Schönborn, Lothar Franz, see Von Schönborn, Lothar Franz

SCHWARZ, Hans, German sculptor and medalist (1492–after 1521)

Scorel, see Van Scorel, Jan

Bibliography

1853 un musée est né 2003
1853, un musée est né! hommage à Antoine et Françoise Lorin, premiers donateurs du Musée de Brou, exh. cat. edited by B. Deloche et al., Bourg-en-Bresse (Musée de Brou), Bourg-en-Bresse: Monastère royal de Brou Église & musée, 2003.

À Kempis 2008
Thomas à Kempis, *The Imitation of Christ*, edited by H. McElwaine Helms and R. J. Edmonson, Brewster: Paraclete Press, 2008.

A Summary Catalog 1991
Museum of Fine Arts Budapest: Old Masters' Gallery: A Summary Catalog of Italian, French, Spanish and Greek Paintings, edited by V. Tátrai, Budapest: Museum of Fine Arts, 1991.

Abelmann 1998
Annelies M. Abelmann, ad vocem "Nieulandt, Adriaen van", *The Dictionary of Art*, Oxford: Grove, vol. XXIII, 34 vols., 1998.

Ait 2002
Ivana Ait, *San Lorenzo de' Speziali in Miranda: A.D. 1602–2002*, Roma: Delfino, 2002.

Alberti 1966
Leon Battista Alberti, *On Painting*, translated by J. R. Spencer, New Haven: Yale University Press, 1966.

Album wystawy Grzech 2015
Album wystawy Grzech. Obrazy grzechu w sztuce europejskiej od XV do początku XX wieku, exh. cat. edited by B. Purc-Stępniak, Gdańsk (Muzeum Narodowe w Gdańsku), Gdańsk: Muzeum Narodowe w Gdańsku, 2015.

Lexikon der christlichen Ikonographie 1994
Allgemeine Ikonographie: Saba, Königin von - Zypresse, Lexikon der christlichen Ikonographie, edited by E. Kirschbaum and W. Braunfels, Roma & Freiburg & Basel & Wien: Herder, 1994, vol. IV, 8 vols.

Anders 2014
Selena Anders, "Patronage in the Golden Age of the 'Capriccio'", *The Architectural Capriccio: Memory, Fantasy and Invention*, edited by L. Steil, Farnham: Ashgate, 2014, p. 41–60.

Anelli 1996
Luciano Anelli, "Bellotti e Nicolini: un pennello ed una penna a confronto sul tema di "Esculapio" nella Venezia del Seicento", *Civiltà bresciana*, vol. V, 1 (1996), p. 5–27.

Anelli and Bonomi 1996
Luciano Anelli and Alfredo Bonomi, *Pietro Bellotti: 1625–1700*, Brescia: Grafo, 1996.

Animaux d'Oudry 2003
Animaux d'Oudry: Collection des ducs de Mecklembourg-Schwerin, exh. cat. edited by V. Droguet et al., Versailles (Musée national des châteaux de Versailles et de Trianon), Fontainebleau (Musée national du château de Fontainebleau), Paris: Éditions de la réunion des Musées Nationaux, 2003.

Arasse 2006
Daniel Arasse, *L'ambizione di Vermeer*, translated by V. Zini, Biblioteca Einaudi (217), Torino: Einaudi, 2006.

Argan and Contardi 1983
Giulio Carlo Argan and Bruno Contardi, *Da Leonardo a Canova*, Storia dell'arte classica e italiana, Firenze: Sansoni, 1983, vol. IV, 5 vols.

Ariès 1980
Philippe Ariès, *L'uomo e la morte dal Medioevo ad oggi*, Storia e società, Bari: Laterza, 1980.

Arnold and Olsen 2003
Ken Arnold and Danielle Olsen, *Medicine Man: The Forgotten Museum of Henry Wellcome*, London: The British Museum Press, 2003.

Asemissen and Schweikhart 1994
Hermann Ulrich Asemissen and Gunter Schweikhart, *Malerei als Thema der Malerei*, Acta humaniora. Schriften zur kunstwissenschaft und Philosophie, Berlin: Akademie Verlag, 1994.

Auffret 1989
Isabelle Auffret, "De David de Heem à Johannes Hannot: un cas de maquillage de signature, ou comment l'imitateur passe pour le maître", *Anonymat et signature*, Collection Études et travaux, École du Louvre. École du Patrimoine (2) (1989), p. 139–147.

Augustinus 1838
Aurelius Augustinus, *Sancti Aurelii Augustini Hipponensis Episcopi Opera Omnia*, Paris: Bibliopolas, 1838, vol. X (pars altera).

Bacon 1730
Francis Bacon, *Francisci Baconi Baronis de Verulamio, Vicecomitis Sancti Albani, Magni Angliae Cancellarii, Opera Omnia, Quatuor Voluminibus Comprehensa: Hactenus Edita, ad Autographorum Maxime Fidem, emendantur; Nonnulla Etiam, ex Mss Codicibus Deprompta, Nunc Primum Prodeunt*, Londini: Impensis R. Gosling ad Insigne Mitrae & Coronae in Vico vulgo vocato Fleet-Street, 1730, vol. II, 4 vols.

Bailey 2007
Colin B. Bailey, "'A Long Working Life, Considerable Research and Much Thought': An Introduction to the Art and Career of Jean-Baptiste Oudry (1686–1755)", *Oudry's Painted Menagerie*, exh. cat. edited by M. Morton, Los Angeles (The J. Paul Getty Museum), Los Angeles: J. Paul Getty Museum, 2007, p. 1–29.

Baldasso 2005
Renzo Baldasso, ad vocem "Garzoni, Giovanna (1600–1670)", *Great Lives from History. The 17th Century, 1601-1700*, Pasadena: Salem Press, 2005.

Baldinucci 1830
Filippo Baldinucci, *La vita di Salvatore Rosa scritta da Filippo Baldinucci fiorentino con varie aggiunte*, edited by B. Gamba, Venezia: Tipografia di Alvisopoli, 1830.

Bandera 2009
Sandrina Bandera, "Invito alla Pinacoteca", *Brera: la Pinacoteca: storia e capolavori*, edited by S. Bandera, Milano: Skira, 2009, p. 53–165.

Barbour 1974
Ian Graeme Barbour, *Myths, Models, and Paradigms: A Comparative Study in Science and Religion*, New York: Harper & Row, 1974.

Barnes and Rose 2002
Donna R. Barnes and Peter G. Rose, *Matters of Taste: Food and Drink in Seventeenth-Century Dutch Art and Life*, Syracuse: Syracuse University Press, 2002.

Barnet 1997
Peter Barnet, "New Developments in Ivory and Bone Carving" (catalog entry), *Images in Ivory: Precious Objects of the Gothic Age*, exh. cat. edited by P. Barnet, Detroit (The Detroit Institute of Arts), Baltimore (The Walters Art Gallery), Princeton: Princeton University Press, 1997.

BARSANTI AND BECCALONI 2013
Claudia Barsanti and Marika Beccaloni, "La chiesa di Santa Maria Liberatrice: dal Foro Romano al Testaccio", *Miti antichi e moderni: studi in onore di Edo Bellingeri*, edited by D. Gavrilovich *et al.*, Arti dello spettacolo (2), Roma: UniversItalia, 2013, p. 253–269.

BARTHOLOMEW 2009
Craig G. Bartholomew, *Ecclesiastes*, Baker Commentary on the Old Testament, Wisdom and Psalms, Grand Rapids: Baker Academic, 2009.

BARZMAN 1985
Karen Edis Barzman, *The Università, Compagnia, ed Accademia del Disegno*, Ph.D. Thesis, Baltimore: John Hopkins University, 1985.

Bassifondi del Barocco 2014
I bassifondi del Barocco: la Roma del vizio e della miseria, exh. cat. edited by F. Cappelletti and A. Lemoine, Roma (Villa Medici), Paris (Petit Palais), Milano: Officina Libraria, 2014.

BATTAGLIA 2006
Roberta Battaglia, "A First Collection of the 'Vedute di Roma': Some New Elements on the States", *Memoirs of the American Academy in Rome. Supplementary Volumes*, vol. IV (2006), p. 93–119.

BATTERSBY 1974
Martin Battersby, *Trompe l'oeil. The Eye Deceived*, London: St. Martin's Academy Editions, 1974.

BATTISTINI 2004
Matilde Battistini, *Astrologia, magia e alchimia*, I dizionari dell'arte, Milano: Electa, 2004.

BERGEZ 2004
Daniel Bergez, *Littérature et peinture*, Paris: A. Colin, 2004.

BERGSTRÖM 1989
Ingvar Bergström, "Tobacco Still Life" (catalog entry), *Still Lifes of the Golden Age: Northern European Paintings from the Heinz Family Collection*, exh. cat. edited by A. K. Wheelock, Washington, DC (National Gallery of Art), Boston (Museum of Fine Arts), Washington, DC: National Gallery of Art, 1989, p. 121.

BERGSTRÖM 1956
Ingvar Bergström, *Dutch Still-Life Painting in the Seventeenth Century*, translated by C. Hedström and G. Taylor, London: Faber & Faber, 1956.

Bernardo Bellotto 2001
Bernardo Bellotto and the Capitals of Europe, exh. cat. edited by E. P. Bowron, Venezia (Museo Correr), Houston (Museum of Fine Arts), New Haven: Yale University Press, 2001.

BERNHARD 1976
Marianne Bernhard, *Rembrandt. Druckgraphik*, München: Südwest Verlag, 1976, vol. I, 2 vols.

BIAŁOSTOCKI 1982
Jan Białostocki, *Symbole i obrazy w swiecie sztuki*, Studia i rozprawy z dziejów sztuki i myśli o sztuce, Warszawa: Panstwowe Wydawnictwo Naukowe, 1982, 2 vols.

BLANKERT 1978
Albert Blankert, *Vermeer of Delft: Complete Edition of the Paintings*, Oxford: Phaidon, 1978.

BOREA 1970a
Evelina Borea, "Giocatori di carte" (catalog entry), *Caravaggio e Caravaggeschi nelle gallerie di Firenze*, exh. cat. edited by E. Borea, Firenze (Palazzo Pitti), Firenze: Sansoni, 1970a, p. 17–18.

BOREA 1970b
Evelina Borea, "Concerto" (catalog entry), *Caravaggio e Caravaggeschi nelle gallerie di Firenze*, exh. cat. edited by E. Borea, Firenze (Palazzo Pitti), Firenze: Sansoni, 1970b, p. 19.

BORZELLO 2000
Frances Borzello, *A World of Our Own: Women as Artists*, London: Thames & Hudson, 2000.

BOSCH 1990
Lynette M. F. Bosch, "Bronzino's London 'Allegory': Love versus Time", *Notes in the History of Art*, vol. IX, 2 (1990), p. 30–35.

BOSING 1994
Walter Bosing, *Hieronymus Bosch, c. 1450–1516: Between Heaven and Hell*, Basic Art series (11), Köln: Taschen, 1994.

BOWRON 2000
Edgar Peters Bowron, "Hendrik Frans Van Lint called Monsu Studio" (catalog entry), *Art in Rome in the Eighteenth Century*, exh. cat. edited by E. P. Bowron, Philadelphia (Philadelphia Museum of Art), Houston (Museum of Fine Arts), London: Merrell, 2000, p. 388.

BOWRON 2016
Edgar Peters Bowron, *Pompeo Batoni: A Complete Catalogue of His Paintings*, New Haven: Yale University Press, 2016, vol. I, 2 vols.

BRANT 1498
Sebastian Brant, *Carmina varia*, Basel: Johann Bergmann de Olpe, 1498.

BRAUN 1966
Hermann Braun, *Gerard und Willem van Honthorst*, Ph.D. Thesis, Göttingen: Georg-August-Universität Göttingen, 1966.

BREDIUS AND HIRSCHMANN 1919
Abraham Bredius and Otto Hirschmann, *Künstler-Inventare: Urkunden zur Geschichte der holländischen Kunst des XVIten, XVIIten und XVIIIten Jahrhunderts*, Den Haag: Nijhoff, 1919, vol. VI, 8 vols.

BREJON DE LAVERGNÉE 1993
Arnauld Brejon de Lavergnée, "Le caravagisme en Europe: à propos de la réédition du Nicolson", *Gazette des Beaux-Arts*, vol. CXXII, 1498 (1993), p. 191–222.

BROOS 1987
Ben Broos, *Meesterwerken in het Mauritshuis*, Den Haag: Staatsuitgeverij, 1987.

BROOS 1997
Bernardus Petrus Jozef Broos, "Young Woman Playing the Lute" (catalog entry), *Princely Patrons: The Collection of Frederick Henry of Orange and Amalia of Solms in The Hague*, exh. cat. edited by P. van der Ploeg and C. Vermeeren, Zwolle: Waanders, 1997, p. 142–145.

BRUNATI 1837
Giuseppe Brunati, *Dizionarietto degli uomini illustri della Riviera di Salò considerata qual era sotto la Rep. veneta cioè formata dalle sei quadre o distretti antichi di Gargnano, Maderno, Salò, Montagna, Valtenese, e Campagna*, Milano: Pogliani, 1837.

BRUNNER-BULST 2004
Martina Brunner-Bulst, *Pieter Claesz.: der Hauptmeister des Haarlemer Stillebens im 17. Jahrhundert. Kritischer Oeuvrekatalog*, Lingen: Luca-Verlag, 2004.

BRUSATI 1990/1991
Celeste Brusati, "Stilled Lives: Self-Portraiture and Self-Reflection in Seventeenth-Century Netherlandish Still-Life Painting", *Simiolus*, 20 (1990/1991), p. 168–182.

BRUSATI 1999
Celeste Brusati, "Capitalizing on the Counterfeit: Trompe L'Oeil Negotiations", *Het Nederlandse stilleven, 1550–1720*, exh. cat. edited by A. Chong, Amsterdam (Rijksmuseum), Cleveland (Cleveland Museum of Art), Amsterdam: Rijksmuseum, 1999, p. 59–71.

BRUYN AND PEESE BINKHORST 1982
J. Bruyn and Lideke Peese Binkhorst, *A Corpus of Rembrandt Paintings: 1625–1631*, Den Haag: Nijhoff Publishers, 1982, vol. I, 6 vols.

BUIJS AND VAN BERGE-GERBAUD 1991
Hans Buijs and Mària van Berge-Gerbaud, *Tableaux flamands et hollandais du Musée des Beaux-Arts de Lyon*, introduction by Philippe Durey, Collections flamandes et hollandaises des musées de province, Zwolle: Waanders, 1991.

BUIJSEN 1994
Edwin Buijsen, "Lute Player" (catalog entry), *The Hoogsteder Exhibition of Music and Painting in the Golden Age*, exh. cat. edited by E. Buijsen and L. P. Grijp, Den Haag (Hoogsteder & Hoogsteder), Antwerpen (Hessenhuis), Zwolle: Waanders, 1994, p. 128–131.

BUNYAN 1967
John Bunyan, *The Pilgrim's Progress from This World to That Which Is to Come, Under The Similitude of a Dream*, Clarion Classics, Grand Rapids: Zondervan Pub. House, 1967.

BUSIRI VICI 1987
Andrea Busiri Vici, *Peter, Hendrik e Giacomo van Lint: tre pittori di Anversa del '600 e '700 lavorano a Roma*, Roma: Ugo Bozzi, 1987.

BUVELOT 1995
Quentin Buvelot, "Jacob van Campen als schilder en tekenaar", *Jacob van Campen: het klassieke ideaal in de Gouden Eeuw*, exh. cat. edited by J. Huisken and K. A. Ottenheym, Amsterdam (Koninklijk Paleis), Amsterdam: Architectura & Natura, 1995, p. 53–120.

BUVELOT AND BUIJS 2002
Quentin Buvelot and Hans Buijs, "Notes to the Catalogue Entries", *A Choice Collection: Seventeenth-Century Dutch Paintings from the Frits Lugt Collection*, exh. cat. edited by Q. Buvelot and H. Buijs, Den Haag (Mauritshuis), Zwolle: Waanders, 2002, p. 193–225.

BUVELOT 2002
Quentin Buvelot, "Still-Life with Books" (catalog entry), *A Choice Collection: Seventeenth-Century Dutch Paintings from the Frits Lugt Collection*, exh. cat. edited by Q. Buvelot *et al.*, Den Haag (Mauritshuis), Zwolle: Waanders, 2002, p. 96–101.

BUVELOT 2008a
Quentin Buvelot, "Stilleven met boeken en een globe" (catalog entry), *Niederländische Malerei: die Sammlung Kremer*, exh. cat. edited by P. van der Ploeg *et al.*, Köln (Wallraff-Richartz Museum), Kassel (Staatliche Museen, Gemäldegalerie Alte Meister), Haarlem (Frans Hals Museum), München: Hirmer, 2008, p. 84-87.

BUVELOT 2008b
Quentin Buvelot, "Oude vrouw die een munt bekijkt bij kaarslicht" (catalog entry), *Niederländische Malerei: die Sammlung Kremer*, exh. cat. edited by P. van der Ploeg *et al.*, Köln (Wallraff-Richartz Museum), Kassel (Staatliche Museen, Gemäldegalerie Alte Meister), Haarlem (Frans Hals Museum), München: Hirmer, 2008, p. 96–101.

CACIORGNA 2004
Marilena Caciorgna, "La navata centrale", *Il pavimento del Duomo di Siena: l'arte della tarsia marmorea dal XIV al XIX secolo. Fonti e simbologia*, edited by M. Caciorgna and R. Guerrini, Cinisello Balsamo: Silvana, 2004.

CAMERON 2001
Euan Cameron, *Early Modern Europe: An Oxford History*, Oxford: Oxford University Press, 2001.

CAMPBELL 1974
Lorne Campbell, "Robert Campin, the Master of Flémalle and the Master of Mérode", *The Burlington Magazine*, vol. CXVI, 860 (1974), p. 634–646.

CANEVA 2001
Caterina Caneva, "La Gioventù e la Morte" (catalog entry), *I mai visti: capolavori dai depositi degli Uffizi*, exh. cat. edited by A. Petrioli Tofani and C. Caneva, Firenze (Galleria degli Uffizi), Firenze: Giunti, 2001, p. 96.

CANISIUS 1833
Petrus Canisius, *Summa doctrinae christianae*, Augsburg: Karl Kollmann, 1833, vol. IV, 4 vols.

CAPITELLI 2016
Giovanna Capitelli, "Dutch Caravaggists in Rome", *Caravaggio and the Painters of the North*, exh. cat. edited by G. J. van der Sman, Madrid (Thyssen-Bornemisza Museum), Madrid: Fundación Colección Thyssen-Bornemisza, 2016, p. 33–41.

CAPPELLETTI 1998
Francesca Cappelletti, "A Roma, dopo Caravaggio. Le 'figure moderne', qualche pittore straniero", *Da Caravaggio a Ceruti. La scena di genere e l'immagine dei pitocchi nella pittura italiana*, exh. cat. edited by F. Porzio and M. Bona Castellotti, Brescia (Museo civico di Santa Giulia), Milano: Skira, 1998, p. 295–305.

CAPRARA 1980
Vittorio Caprara, ad vocem "Ceruti, Giacomo Antonio, detto il Pitocchetto", *Dizionario Biografico degli Italiani*, Roma: Istituto della Enciclopedia Italiana, vol. XXIV, 1980.

***Caravaggio in Holland* 2009**
Caravaggio in Holland: Musik und Genre bei Caravaggio und den Utrechter Caravaggisten, exh. cat. edited by J. Sander, Frankfurt am Main (Städel Museum), München: Hirmer, 2009.

CARMINATI 2000
Marco Carminati, "Giacomo Ceruti, il Pitocchetto", *Pittura in Lombardia. Dall'età spagnola al Neoclassicismo*, edited by S. Zuffi, Milano: Electa, 2000, p. 193–203.

CARRARA 2008
Eliana Carrara, "La nascita dell'Accademia del Disegno di Firenze: il ruolo di Borghini, Torelli e Vasari", *Les Académies dans l'Europe humaniste. Idéaux et pratiques. Actes d'un colloque international*, edited by M. Deramaix *et al.*, Genève: Droz, 2008, p. 129–162.

CARTARI 1647
Vincenzo Cartari, *Imagini delli Dei de gl'Antichi*, Venezia: Presso il Tomasini, 1647.

CASWELL 1998
Jean M. Caswell, ad vocem " Bruyn, Bartholomaeus I", *The Dictionary of Art*, Oxford: Grove, vol. V, 34 vols., 1998.

CAVALLI-BJÖRKMAN 1998
Görel Cavalli-Björkman, "Vanitas-Stilleben als Phänomen des Krisenbewusstseins", *1648: Krieg und Frieden in Europa*, exh. cat. edited by K. Bussmann and H. Schilling, Münster (Westfälischen Landesmuseum für Kunst und Kulturgeschichte) and Osnabrück (Kulturgeschichtlichen Museum sowie in der Kunsthalle Dominikanerkirche), München: Bruckmann, 1998, vol. II (Kunst und Kultur), 2 vols., p. 501–50

CHADWICK 1964
Owen Chadwick, *The Reformation*, The Pelican History of the Church (3), Baltimore: Penguin Books, 1964.

CHAIX 1977
Pierre Henri Chaix, *La Bresse protestante au XVIIème siècle*, Bourg-en-Bresse: P. H. Chaix, 1977.

CHARRON 1640
Pierre Charron, *Of Wisdome: Three Books*, translated by S. Lennard, London: R. B. for William Aspley, 1640.

CHAUCER 2008
Geoffrey Chaucer, *The Riverside Chaucer*, edited by L. D. Benson, Oxford: Oxford University Press, 2008.

CHIOCCIONI 1963
Pietro Chioccioni, *La Basilica e il Convento dei Santi Cosma e Damiano in Roma*, Roma: Curia Generalizia dell'Ordine, 1963.

CHONG AND KLOEK 1999
Alan Chong and Wouter Kloek, "N. Le Peschier" (catalog entry), *Still-Life Paintings from the Netherlands, 1550–1720*, exh. cat. edited by A. Chong and W. Kloek, Amsterdam (Rijksmuseum), Cleveland (Cleveland Museum of Art), Zwolle: Waanders, 1999, p. 296.

CHRISTIANSON 1998
Eric S. Christianson, *A Time to Tell: Narrative Strategies in Ecclesiastes*, Journal for the Study of the Old Testament Supplement Series (280), Sheffield: Sheffield Academic Press, 1998.

CHRISTIANSON 2007
Eric S. Christianson, *Ecclesiastes Through the Centuries*, Blackwell Bible Commentaries, Malden & Oxford: Blackwell, 2007.

CHRISTIANSON 2012
Eric S. Christianson, *Ecclesiastes Through the Centuries*, Malden & Oxford: Wiley-Blackwell, 2012.

CLARIDGE *et al.* 2010
Amanda Claridge *et al.*, *Rome: An Oxford Archaeological Guide*, Oxford: Oxford University Press, 2010.

CLARK 1959
Anthony M. Clark, "Some Early Subject Pictures by P. G. Batoni", *The Burlington Magazine*, vol. CI, 675 (1959), p. 232–243.

COARELLI AND USAI 1975
Filippo Coarelli and Luisanna Usai, *Guida archeologica di Roma*, Milano: Mondadori, 1975.

COHEN 1973
Kathleen Cohen, *Metamorphosis of a Death Symbol. The Transi Tomb in the Late Middle Ages and the Renaissance*, California Studies in the History of Art (15), Berkeley: University of California Press, 1973.

COLLOP 1667
John Collop, *Charity commended, or, a Catholick Christian soberly instructed*, London, 1667.

COOK 2010
Christopher Cook, "An Allegory with Venus and Cupid: A Story of Syphilis", *Journal of the Royal Society of Medicine*, vol. CIII, 11 (2010), p. 458–460.

Corps et ombres **2012**
Corps et ombres: Caravage et le caravagisme européen, exh. cat. edited by M. Hilaire *et al.*, Montpelier (Musée Fabre), Toulouse (Musée des Augustins), Los Angeles (Los Angeles County Museum of Art), Hartford (Wadsworth Atheneum), Milano: 5 Continents, 2012.

CRAGG 1960
Gerald R. Cragg, *The Church and The Age of Reason, 1648–1789*, The Penguin History of the Church (4), Harmondsworth: Penguin Books, 1960.

CRENSHAW 1987
James L. Crenshaw, *Ecclesiastes: A Commentary*, The Old Testament Library, Philadelphia: Westminster Press, 1987.

CRENSHAW 2007
James L. Crenshaw, "Qoheleth in Historical Context", *Biblica*, vol. LXXXVIII, 2 (2007), p. 285–299.

CUZIN 1980
Jean-Pierre Cuzin, "Manfredi's 'Fortune Teller' and Some Problems of 'Manfrediana Methodus'", *Bulletin of the Detroit Institute of Arts*, vol. LVIII, 1 (1980), p. 14–25.

CUZIN 1988
Jean-Pierre Cuzin, "Manfredi e i francesi", *Dopo Caravaggio: Bartolomeo Manfredi e la Manfrediana methodus*, Cremona (Santa Maria della Pietà), Milano: Mondadori, 1988, p. 42–49.

The Cyclopaedia **1819**
The Cyclopaedia; or, Universal Dictionary of Arts, Sciences and Literature, edited by A. Rees, London: Longman, Hurst, Rees, Orme and Brown, 1819, vol. XXI, 39 vols.

D'ADDA 2002
Roberta D'Adda, "The Porter" (catalog entry), *Titian to Tiepolo: Three Centuries of Italian Art*, exh. cat. edited by G. Algranti and J. Anderson, Canberra (National Gallery of Australia), Melbourne (Melbourne Museum), Firenze: ArtificioSkira, 2002, p. 228–229.

D'AFFLITTO 2008
Chiara D'Afflitto, ad vocem "Martinelli, Giovanni", *Dizionario Biografico degli Italiani*, Roma: Istituto della Enciclopedia Italiana, vol. LXXI, 2008.

D'ALVERNY 1965
Marie-Thérèse D'Alverny, *Alain de Lille: textes inédits*, Paris: J. Vrin, 1965.

D'ARCY WOOD 2001
Gillen D'Arcy Wood, *The Shock of the Real: Romanticism and Visual Culture, 1760–1860*, New York: Palgrave, 2001.

D'ONOFRIO 1989
Cesare D'Onofrio, *Visitiamo Roma nel Quattrocento: la città degli umanisti*, Collana di studi e testi per la storia della città di Roma (9), Roma: Romana società editrice, 1989.

DANESI SQUARZINA 2003
Silvia Danesi Squarzina, "Introduzione", *Decorazione e collezionismo a Roma nel Seicento. Vicende di artisti, committenti, mercanti*, edited by F. Cappelletti, Artisti opere committenti (1), Roma: Gangemi, 2003, p. 3–8.

DE BONI 1840
Filippo De Boni, *Biografia degli artisti*, Venezia: co' tipi del Gondoliere, 1840.

DE CAYEUX 1998
Jean de Cayeux, ad vocem " Robert, Hubert", *The Dictionary of Art*, Oxford: Grove, vol. XXVI, 34 vols., 1998.

DE DOMINICI 1742
Bernardo De Dominici, *Vite de' pittori, scultori ed architetti napoletani*, Napoli: Per Francesco e Cristoforo Ricciardo, Stampatori del Real Palazzo, 1742, vol. III, 3 vols.

DE GIROLAMI CHENEY 1992
Liana De Girolami Cheney, "Dutch Vanitas Paintings: the Skull", *The Symbolism of Vanitas in the Arts, Literature, and Music: Comparative and Historical Studies*, edited by L. De Girolami Cheney, Lewiston: E. Mellen Press, 1992, p. 113–133.

DE GIROLAMI CHENEY 2007
Liana De Girolami Cheney, *Giorgio Vasari's Teachers: Sacred & Profane Art*, New York: Peter Lang, 2007.

DE LASTIC SAINT-JAL 1955
Georges de Lastic Saint-Jal, "Les devants de cheminée", *Connaissance des arts*, 39 (1955), p. 26–31.

DE MAERE AND WABBES 1994
Jan de Maere and Marie Wabbes, *Illustrated Dictionary of 17th Century Flemish Painters*, edited by J. A. Martin, Brussels: La Renaissance du Livre, 1994, vol. III, 3 vols.

DE MONTAIGNE 1991
Michel de Montaigne, *The Complete Essays*, translated by M. A. Screech, edited by M. A. Screech, introduction by M. A. Screech, Penguin Classics, London: Penguin Books, 1991.

DE TOLNAY 1939
Charles De Tolnay, *Le Maître de Flémalle et les frères Van Eyck*, Bruxelles: Éditions de La Connaissance, 1939.

DE VORAGINE 2012
Jacobus De Voragine, *The Golden Legend: Readings on the Saints*, Princeton: Princeton University Press, 2012.

Death **2012**
Death: A Picture Album, London (Wellcome Collection), London: Wellcome Collection, 2012.

DEBAISIEUX 1994
Françoise Debaisieux, *Caen: Musée des Beaux Arts. Peintures des écoles étrangères*, Inventaire des collections publiques françaises (36), Paris: Réunion des Musées Nationaux, 1994.

DELL 2013
Katharine Julia Dell, *Interpreting Ecclesiastes: Readers Old and New*, Critical Studies in the Hebrew Bible (3), Winona Lake: Eisenbrauns, 2013.

DELLA PERGOLA 1955
Paola della Pergola, *Galleria Borghese: i dipinti*, Cataloghi dei musei e gallerie d'Italia, Roma: Istituto poligrafico dello Stato, 1955, vol. II, 2 vols.

DEWITT 2011
Lloyd DeWitt, "Testing Tradition Against Nature: Rembrandt's Radical New Image of Jesus", *Rembrandt and the Face of Jesus*, exh. cat. edited by L. DeWitt and S. Slive, Paris (Musée du Louvre), Philadelphia (Philadelphia Museum of Art), Detroit (Detroit Institute of Arts), Philadelphia, Paris, Detroit & New Haven: in association with Yale University Press, 2011, p. 109–145.

DI NOLA 1995
Alfonso Maria Di Nola, *La nera signora. Antropologia della morte e del lutto*, Magia e religioni (32), Roma: Newton Compton, 1995.

Donation d'Antoine Brasseur **1981**
Donation d'Antoine Brasseur, exh. cat. edited by M. P. Baudienville *et al.*, Lille (Musée des Beaux-Arts), Arras: Imprimerie Centrale de l'Artois, 1981.

DU MOULIN 1652
Pierre Du Moulin, *Heraclitus, or, Mans looking-glass and survey of life*, London: Printed for Henry Seile, 1652.

DUBIN 2010
Nina L. Dubin, *Futures and Ruins: Eighteenth-Century Paris and the Art of Hubert Robert*, Los Angeles: Getty Research Institute, 2010.

DUCHESNE AND RÉVEIL 1830
Jean Duchesne and Achille Réveil, *Musée de peinture et de sculpture ou recueil des principaux tableaux, statues et bas reliefs des collections publiques et particulières de l'Europe*, Paris: Audot, 1830, vol. VII, 16 vols.

DUCOS 2011
Blaise Ducos, "The Orient and Rembrandt's Redefinition of Christ Iconography", *Rembrandt and the Face of Jesus*, exh. cat. edited by L. DeWitt and S. Slive, Paris (Musée du Louvre), Philadelphia (Philadelphia Museum of Art), Detroit (Detroit Institute of Arts), Philadelphia, Paris, Detroit & New Haven: in association with Yale University Press, 2011, p. 161–177.

DULLES 1980
Avery Dulles, "The Symbolic Structure of Revelation", *Theological Studies*, vol. XLI, 1 (1980), p. 51–73.

DUMONT-WILDEN 1934
Louis Dumont-Wilden, *La collection Michel van Gelder au Château Zeecrabbe, Uccle*, Bruxelles: Helio, S. A. R., 1934.

Dutch and Flemish Old Masters 2002
Dutch and Flemish Old Masters from the Kremer Collection, edited by P. van der Ploeg *et al.*, Den Haag: Fondation Aetas Aurea, 2002.

Dutch Seventeenth Century 1980
Dutch Seventeenth Century Portraiture: The Golden Age, exh. cat. edited by W. H. Wilson, Sarasota (John and Mable Ringling Museum of Art), Sarasota: John and Mable Ringling Museum of Art, 1980.

EBERT-SCHIFFERER 1999
Sybille Ebert-Schifferer, *Natures mortes*, Les Phares, Paris: Citadelles & Mazenod, 1999.

EBERT-SCHIFFERER 2010
Sybille Ebert-Schifferer, "Il tempo infante: un disegno poetico-allegorico di Salvator Rosa", *Salvator Rosa e il suo tempo 1615–1673*, edited by S. Ebert-Schifferer *et al.*, Roma: Campisano, 2010, p. 289–298.

EBERT 2009
Bernd Ebert, *Simon und Isaack Luttichuys. Monographie mit kritischem Werkverzeichnis*, Berlin & München: Deutscher Kunstverlag, 2009.

EDWARDS 2011
Nancy E. Edwards, "The Cardsharps", *Caravaggio and His Followers in Rome*, exh. cat. edited by D. Franklin and S. Schütze, Ottawa (National Gallery of Canada), Fort Worth (The Kimbell Art Museum), New Haven: Yale University Press, 2011, p. 180–209.

EKSERDJIAN 2007
David Ekserdjian, *Alle origini della natura morta*, Milano: Electa, 2007.

El joven Ribera 2011
El joven Ribera, exh. cat. edited by J. Milicua *et al.*, Madrid (Museo del Prado), Madrid: Museo del Prado, 2011.

ELIASON 1989
Eric Jon Eliason, *Vanitas vanitatum: Piers Plowman, Ecclesiastes, and Contempt of the World*, Ph.D. Thesis, Charlottesville: University of Virginia, 1989.

ELLUL 1990
Jacques Ellul, *Reason for Being: A Meditation on Ecclesiastes*, translated by J. M. Hanks, Grand Rapids: William B. Eerdmans, 1990.

ERIKSEN 2014
Anne Eriksen, *From Antiquities to Heritage: Transformations of Cultural Memory*, New York: Berghahn Books, 2014.

ETTLINGER 1985
Gerard H. Ettlinger, "The Form and Method of the Commentary on Ecclesiastes by Gregory of Agrigentum", *Papers of the Ninth International Conference on Patristic Studies, Oxford, 1983*, edited by E. A. Livingstone, Studia Patristica (19), Kalamazoo: Cistercian Publ., 1985, p. 317–320.

FAGIOLO AND SCHEZEN 2001
Marcello Fagiolo and Roberto Schezen, *Roman Gardens: Villas of the City*, New York: Monacelli Press, 2001.

FAIETTI 2011
Marzia Faietti, "Il disegno padre delle arti, i disegni degli artisti, il disegno delle 'Vite': intersecazioni semantiche in Vasari scrittore", *Figure, memorie, spazio. La grafica del Quattrocento. Appunti di teoria, conoscenza e gusto*, exh. cat. edited by M. Faietti *et al.*, Firenze (Galleria degli Uffizi), Firenze: Giunti, 2011, p. 13–37.

FARÉ 1962
Michel Faré, *La Nature morte en France. Son histoire et son évolution du XVIIIe au XXe siècle*, Genève: P. Cailler, 1962, 2 vols.

FARÉ AND FARÉ 1976
Michel Faré and Fabrice Faré, *La vie silencieuse en France. La nature morte au XVIIIème siècle*, Fribourg: Office du livre, 1976.

FAWCETT 1971
Thomas Fawcett, *The Symbolic Language of Religion*, Minneapolis: Augsburg Publishing House, 1971.

FISCH 1988
Harold Fisch, "Qohelet: A Hebrew Ironist", *Poetry with a Purpose: Biblical Poetics and Interpretation*, Bloomington: Indiana University Press, 1988, p. 158–178.

For Your Eyes Only 2014
For Your Eyes Only: A Private Collection, from Mannerism to Surrealism, exh. cat. edited by A. Beyer, Venezia (Fondazione Peggy Guggenheim), Basel (Kunstmuseum Basel), Ostfildern: Hantje Cantz, 2014.

FOUCART-WALTER 2001
Élisabeth Foucart-Walter, "Pieter Boel (1622-1674), peintre des animaux de Louis XIV. Le fonds des études peintres des Gobelins", *Pieter Boel (1622-1674), peintre des animaux de Louis XIV. Le fonds des études peintres des Gobelins*, exh. cat. edited by É. Foucart-Walter, Paris (Musée du Louvre), Paris: Réunion des Musées Nationaux, 2001, p. 13–59.

FOUCART 1990
Jacques Foucart, "La peinture hollandaise et flamande de vanité: une réussite dans la diversité", *Les vanités dans la peinture au XVIIe siècle méditation sur la richesse, le dénuement et la rédemption*, exh. cat. edited by A. Tapié *et al.*, Caen (Musée des Beaux-Arts) and Paris (Musée du Petit Palais), Paris & Caen: A. Michel & Musée des Beaux-Arts, 1990, p. 55–68.

FOX 1989
Michael V. Fox, *Qohelet and His Contradictions*, Journal for the Study of the Old Testament. Supplement Series (71), Sheffield: Almond Press, 1989.

FOX 1999
Michael V. Fox, *A Time to Tear Down and a Time to Build Up: A Rereading of Ecclesiastes*, Grand Rapids: William B. Eerdmans, 1999.

FRANGI 1987
Francesco Frangi, "Portarolo" (catalog entry), *Giacomo Ceruti il Pitocchetto*, exh.

cat. edited by M. Gregori *et al.*, Brescia (Monastero di Santa Giulia), Milano: Mazzotta, 1987, p. 179–180.

FRANGI 1993
Francesco Frangi, "Pietro Bellotti" (catalog entry), *Un museo da scoprire: dipinti antichi della Pinacoteca del Castello Sforzesco*, exh. cat. edited by M. T. Fiorio and M. Bona Castellotti, Milano (Museo Archeologico ed Artistico nel Castello Sforzesco), Milano: Electa, 1993, p. 96–97.

FRANGI 1998
Francesco Frangi, "L'immagine dei poveri tra genere, realtà e cultura assistenziale: riflessioni in argine al ciclo di Padernello di Giacomo Ceruti", *Da Caravaggio a Ceruti. La scena di genere e l'immagine dei pitocchi nella pittura italiana*, exh. cat. edited by F. Porzio and M. Bona Castellotti, Brescia (Museo civico di Santa Giulia), Milano: Skira, 1998, p. 43–61.

FRANITS 2004
Wayne E. Franits, *Dutch Seventeenth-Century Genre Painting: Its Stylistic and Thematic Evolution*, New Haven: Yale University Press, 2004.

FRANITS 2009
Wayne E. Franits, "Laboratorium Utrecht: Baburen, Honthorst und Terbrugghen im künstlerischen Austausch", *Caravaggio in Holland: Musik und Genre bei Caravaggio und den Utrechter Caravaggisten*, exh. cat. edited by J. Sander *et al.*, Frankfurt am Main (Städel Museum), München: Hirmer, 2009, p. 37–53.

FREEDBERG 1960
Anne B. Freedberg, "Some Recent Accessions, 'Made Mortal They Must Die': An Allegory", *Bulletin of the Museum of Fine Arts*, vol. LVIII, 313/314 (1960), p. 84–110.

FRIEDLÄNDER 1956
Max Julius Friedländer, *Early Netherlandish Painting: From van Eyck to Bruegel*, translated by M. Kay, edited by F. Grossmann, London: Phaidon, 1956.

FRIEDRICH 2004
Verena Friedrich, *Rokoko in der Residenz Würzburg. Studien zu Ornament und Dekoration des Rokoko in der ehemaligen fürstbischöflichen Residenz zu Würzburg*, Forschungen zur Kunst- und Kulturgeschichte (9), München: Bayerische Schlösserverwaltung, 2004.

Galleria Nazionale di Parma 2000
Galleria Nazionale di Parma. Catalogo delle opere: il Settecento, edited by L. Fornari Schianchi *et al.*, Milano: Ricci, 2000.

GALLO 2010
Marco Gallo, "Il Maestro del Giudizio di Salomone e il giovane Ribera: un problema ancora aperto", *I Caravaggeschi. Percorsi e protagonisti*, edited by A. Zuccari and C. Strinati, Milano: Skira, 2010, vol. II, 2 vols., p. 483–488.

GARMS 1982
Jörg Garms, "Piranesi e la scenografia", *La scenografia barocca*, edited by A. Schnapper, Atti del XXIV Congresso Internazionale di Storia dell'Arte (5), Bologna: Editrice Clueb, 1982, p. 117–122.

GARRIGOU-LAGRANGE 1991
Réginald Garrigou-Lagrange, *Life Everlasting and the Immensity of the Soul: A Theological Treatise on the Four Last Things: Death, Judgment, Heaven, Hell*, Rockford: Tan Books, 1991.

GASCOIGNE 1910
George Gascoigne, *The Complete Works of George Gascoigne*, edited by J. W. Cunliffe, Cambridge: Cambridge University Press, 1910, vol. II, 2 vols.

GASH 2007
John Gash, "The Caravagesque Toothpuller", *Others and Outcasts in Early Modern Europe: Picturing the Social Margins*, edited by T. Nichols, Aldershot: Ashgate, 2007, p. 134–155.

GAUK-ROGER 1998
Nigel Gauk-Roger, ad vocem " Bellotto, Bernardo", *The Dictionary of Art*, Oxford: Grove, vol. III, 34 vols., 1998.

GAVUZZO-STEWART 1999
Silvia Gavuzzo-Stewart, *Nelle carceri di G. B. Piranesi*, Italian perspectives (2), Leeds: Northern Universities Press, 1999.

GEER AND WIESEMAN 2007
Elena J. Geer and Marjorie E. Wieseman, *Dutch Painting: The National Gallery*, London: National Gallery, 2007.

GERRA 1937
Ferdinando Gerra, *Salvator Rosa e la sua vita romana dal 1650 al 1672 in un carteggio inedito con Giovan Battista Ricciardi*, Roma: Studio d'Autografi, 1937.

GIANFRANCESCHI 2011
Michela Gianfranceschi, *Le incisioni da Caravaggio e caravaggeschi: musici, giocatori e indovine nelle scene di genere*, edited by S. Macioce, Roma: Logart Press, 2011.

GIANTO 1992
Agustinus Gianto, "The Theme of Enjoyment in Qohelet", *Biblica*, vol. LXXIII, 4 (1992), p. 528–532.

GILMAN 1980
Ernest B. Gilman, "Word and Image in Quarles' 'Emblemes'", *Critical Inquiry*, vol. VI, 3 (1980), p. 385–410.

GOLDSCHEIDER 1958
Ludwig Goldscheider, *Jan Vermeer: The Paintings*, London: Phaidon, 1958.

GOLDSTEIN 1975
Carl Goldstein, "Vasari and the Florentine Accademia del Disegno", *Zeitschrift für Kunstgeschichte*, 38 (1975), p. 145–152.

GORDIS 1978
Robert Gordis, *Koheleth—The Man and His World: A Study of Ecclesiastes*, Schocken Books, New York: Schocken Books, 1978.

GÓRECKA-PETRAJTIS AND SZWED 1993
Krystyna Górecka-Petrajtis and Jerzy Szwed, *Malarstwo flamandzkie i holenderskie, XVII w. w zbiorach Muzeum Narodowego w Gdańsku*, Gdańsk: Muzeum Narodowe w Gdańsku, 1993.

GOUGENOT 1968
Louis Gougenot, "Vie de M. Oudry", *Mémoires inédits sur la vie et les ouvrages des membres de l'Académie royale de peinture et de sculpture*, edited by L. E. Dussieux, Paris: F. de Nobele, 1968, p. 365–403.

GOULD 1838
John Gould, *Biographical Dictionary of Painters, Sculptors, Engravers, and Architects*, London: G. and A. Greenland, 1838, vol. II, 2 vols.

GOVIER 2009
Louise Govier, *The National Gallery, guida per i visitatori*, London: Louise Rice, 2009.

GRANGER 1621
Thomas Granger, *A Familiar Exposition or Commentarie on Ecclesiastes. Wherein the worlds vanity, and the true felicitie are plainely deciphered*, London: T. S., for Thomas Pauier, 1621.

GREGORI 1982
Mina Gregori, *Giacomo Ceruti*, Monumenta Bergomensia (58), Cinisello Balsamo: Pizzi, 1982.

GREGORI 1988
Mina Gregori, "Dal Caravaggio al Manfredi", *Dopo Caravaggio: Bartolomeo Manfredi e la Manfrediana methodus*, Cremona (Santa Maria della Pietà), Milano: Mondadori, 1988, p. 13–25.

GREGORIUS 1924
Papa Gregorius, *Gregorii Magni Dialogi. Libri IV*, edited by U. Moricca, Fonti per la storia d'Italia (57), Roma: Tip. del Senato di G. Bardi, 1924.

GREINDL 1956
Edith Greindl, *Les peintres flamands de nature morte au XVIIe siècle*, Bruxelles: Elsevier, 1956.

GREVILLE 1633
Fulke Greville, *Certaine learned and elegant workes of the Right Honourable Fulke, Lord Brooke, written in his youth and familiar exercise with Sir P. Sidney*, London: E. P. for H. Seyle, 1633.

GRÜNDLER 1989
Otto Gründler, "Devotio Moderna", *Christian Spirituality: High Middle Ages and Reformation*, edited by J. Raitt et al., World Spirituality (17), New York: Crossroad, 1989, vol. II, 3 vols., p. 176–193.

GUARINI 1598
Battista Guarini, *Rime del molto illustre Signor cavaliere Battista Guarini dedicate all'illustrissimo, et reverendissimo Signor Cardinale Pietro Aldobrandini*, Venezia: Giovanni Battista Ciotti, 1598.

HAAK 1984
Bob Haak, *The Golden Age: Dutch Painters of the Seventeenth Century*, translated by E. Willems-Treeman, New York: H. N. Abrams, 1984.

HÄRTING 1998
Ursula Härting, ad vocem "Cabinet Picture", *The Dictionary of Art*, Oxford: Grove, vol. V, 34 vols., 1998.

HARTJE 2004
Nicole Hartje, *Bartolomeo Manfredi (1582–1622): Ein Nachfolger Caravaggios und seine europäische Wirkung. Monographie und Werkverzeichnis*, Weimar: Verlag und Datenbank für Geisteswissenschaften, 2004.

HARTLAUB 1951
Gustav Friedrich Hartlaub, *Zauber des Spiegels. Geschichte und Bedeutung des Spiegels in der Kunst*, München: Piper, 1951.

HARTT AND WILKINS 2006
Frederick Hartt and David G. Wilkins, *History of Italian Renaissance Art: Painting, Sculpture, Architecture*, Upper Saddle River: Pearson Prentice Hall, 2006.

HATTAWAY 1968
Michael Hattaway, "Paradoxes of Solomon: Learning in the English Renaissance", *Journal of the History of Ideas*, vol. XXIX, 4 (1968), p. 499–530.

HELMUS 2005
Liesbeth M. Helmus, "Il carattere olandese del caravaggismo di Utrecht", *Caravaggio e l'Europa: il movimento caravaggesco internazionale da Caravaggio a Mattia Preti*, exh. cat. edited by L. Spezzaferro and B. Calzavara, Milano: Skira, 2005, p. 87–97.

HENKEL AND SCHÖNE 1967
Arthur Henkel and Albrecht Schöne, *Emblemata. Handbuch zur Sinnbildkunst des XVI. und XVII. Jahrhunderts*, Stuttgart: Metzler, 1967, vol. I, 2 vols.

HIND 1914
Arthur M. Hind, "Giovanni Battista Piranesi: Some Further Notes and a List of His Works-(Concluded)", *The Burlington Magazine for Connoisseurs*, vol. XXIV, 131 (1914), p. 262–264.

HIND 1922
Arthur M. Hind, *Giovanni Battista Piranesi. A Critical Study with a List of his Published Works and Detailed Catalogues of the Prisons and the Views of Rome*, London: Cotswold Gallery, 1922.

HOLLÄNDER 1923
Eugen Holländer, *Die Medizin in der Klassischen Malerei*, Beiträge aus dem Grenzgebiet zwischen Medizingeschichte und Kunst, Kultur, Literatur (1), Stuttgart: Enke, 1923.

HOLLSTEIN 1964
Friedrich W. H. Hollstein and Karel G. Boon, *Hollstein's Dutch and Flemish Etchings, Engravings, and Woodcuts: ca. 1450–1700*, Amsterdam: Hertzberger, 1964, vol. XV, 72 vols.

HOLM-NIELSEN 1975-1976
Svend Holm-Nielsen, "The Book of Ecclesiastes and the Interpretation of It in Jewish and Christian Theology", *Annual of the Swedish Theological Institute*, 10 (1975–1976), p. 38–96.

HÖLTGEN 2004
Karl Josef Höltgen, ad vocem "Quarles, Francis (1592–1644)", *Oxford Dictionary of National Biography*, Oxford: Oxford University Press, vol. XLV, 2004.

IMBELLONE 2008
Alessandra Imbellone, "Il Tempo ordina alla Vecchiaia di distruggere la Bellezza" (catalog entry), *Pompeo Batoni, 1708–1787. L'Europa delle Corti e il Grand Tour*, exh. cat. edited by L. Barroero and F. Mazzocca, Lucca (Palazzo Ducale), Cinisello Balsamo: Silvana Editoriale, 2008, p. 208–209.

IMPELLUSO 2004
Lucia Impelluso, *Nature and Its Symbols: A Guide to Imagery*, translated by S. Sartarelli, Los Angeles: J. Paul Getty Museum, 2004.

INNOCENTIUS III 1978
Innocentius III, *De miseria condicionis humane*, edited by R. E. Lewis, The Chaucer Library, Athens: The University of Georgia Press, 1978.

J.-B. Oudry 1982
J.-B. Oudry: 1686–1755, exh. cat. edited by H. N. Opperman, Paris (Galeries Nationales d'Exposition du Grand Palais), Paris: Réunion des Musées Nationaux, 1982.

JACK WARD 1972
Mary Ann Jack Ward, *The Accademia del Disegno In Sixteenth Century Florence: A Study of An Artist's Institution*, Ph.D. Thesis, Chicago: University of Chicago, 1972.

JACK WARD 1976
Mary Ann Jack Ward, "The Accademia del Disegno in Late Renaissance Florence", *The Sixteenth Century Journal*, vol. VII, 2 (1976), p. 3–20.

JANSSEN 2005
Anouk Janssen, "De iconografie van de ouderdom en het werk van de jonge Rembrandt", *Rembrandts moeder: mythe en werkelijkheid*, exh. cat. edited by C. Vogelaar *et al.*, Leiden (Stedelijk Museum De Lakenhal), Zwolle: Waanders, 2005, p. 53–66.

Jean-Baptiste Oudry 2000
Jean-Baptiste Oudry, Jean-Antoine Houdon: Vermächtnis der Aufklärung, exh. cat. edited by K. Berswordt-Wallrabe *et al.*, Schwerin (Staatliches Museum), Schwerin: Staatliches Museum, 2000.

JERMIN 1639
Michael Jermin, *A Commentary upon the Whole Booke of Ecclesiastes or the Preacher. Wherein the Originall Hebrew Text Is Carefully Examined, Our Owne English Translation and Others Are Duely Viewed and Compared, in which also the Literall Sense Is Chiefly Considered, Other Senses as Usefull Are Not Omitted*, London: Ric. Hodgkinsonne, for John Clark, 1639.

JEROME 1954
Jerome, *Letters and Select Works*, translated by W. H. Fremantle, Grand Rapids: William B. Eerdmans, 1954.

JEROME 2000
Jerome, *Commentary on Ecclesiastes*, translated by R. MacGregor Lane, Unpublished, 2000.

José de Ribera 2005
José de Ribera: bajo el signo de Caravaggio (1613–1633), exh. cat. edited by N. Spinosa and J. Carrete Parrondo, Salamanca (Sala de Exposiciones de San Eloy), Salamanca: Caja Duero, 2005.

JUDSON 1959
Jay Richard Judson, *Gerrit van Honthorst: A Discussion of His Position in Dutch Art*, Utrechtse bijdragen tot de kunstgeschiedenis (6), Den Haag: Nijhoff, 1959.

JUDSON AND EKKART 1999
Jay Richard Judson and Rudolf E. O. Ekkart, *Gerrit van Honthorst, 1592–1656*, Aetas aurea (14), Doornspijk: Davaco, 1999.

Jusepe de Ribera 1992
Jusepe de Ribera 1591–1652, exh. cat. edited by A. E. Pérez Sánchez and N. Spinosa, Napoli (Castel Sant'Elmo, Certosa di San Martino, Cappella del Tesoro di San Gennaro), Napoli: Electa Napoli, 1992.

Jusepe de Ribera 2003
Jusepe de Ribera, el Españoleto, exh. cat. edited by A. E. Pérez Sánchez and N. Spinosa, Ciudad de México (Museo Nacional de San Carlos), Barcelona: Lunwerg, 2003.

KEYES 2011
George S. Keyes, "Perception and Belief: The Image of Christ and the Meditative Turn in Rembrandt's Religious Art", *Rembrandt and the Face of Jesus*, exh. cat. edited by L. DeWitt and S. Slive, Paris (Musée du Louvre), Philadelphia (Philadelphia Museum of Art), Detroit (Detroit Institute of Arts), Philadelphia, Paris, Detroit & New Haven: in association with Yale University Press, 2011, p. 1–29.

KOERNER 1985
Joseph Leo Koerner, "The Mortification of the Image: Death as a Hermeneutic in Hans Baldung Grien", *Representations*, 10 (1985), p. 52–101.

KÖHLER 2006
Neeltje Köhler, "Adriaen van Nieulandt", *Painting in Haarlem 1500–1850. The Collection of the Frans Hals Museum*, edited by P. Biesboer and N. Köhler, Ghent: Ludion, 2006, p. 564.

KOREVAAR 2005
Gerbrand Korevaar, "Rembrandt van Rijn: Oude man die zijn geld telt", *Rembrandts moeder: mythe en werkelijkheid*, exh. cat. edited by C. Vogelaar *et al.*, Leiden (Stedelijk Museum De Lakenhal), Zwolle: Waanders, 2005, p. 150–151.

KRANZBÜHLER 1932
Mechthild Kranzbühler, "Johann Wolfgang von Auwera: ein fränkischer Bildhauer des 18. Jahrhunderts", *Städel-Jahrbuch*, 7/8 (1932), p. 182–219.

KREISEL 1953
Heinrich Kreisel, *Der Rokokogarten zu Veitshöchheim*, München: Hirmer Verlag, 1953.

KREN 1980
Thomas Kren, "Chi non vuol Baccho: Roeland van Laer's Burlesque Painting about Dutch Artists in Rome", *Simiolus: Netherlands Quarterly for the History of Art*, vol. XI, 2 (1980), p. 63–80.

KRITSKY AND CHERRY 2000
Gene Kritsky and Ron H. Cherry, *Insect Mythology*, San Jose: Writers Club Press, 2000.

L'Âge d'or 1991
L'Âge d'or de la nature morte, exh. cat. edited by M. Taeckens *et al.*, Marcq-en-Baroeul (Fondation Anne et Albert Prouvost), Marcq-en-Baroeul: Fondation Septentrion, 1991.

LA COSTA 2005
Isabella La Costa, "La Gioventù sorpresa dalla Morte" (catalog entry), *Il Male. Esercizi di pittura crudele*, exh. cat. edited by S. Moriggi and V. Sgarbi, Torino (Palazzina di Caccia di Stupinigi), Milano: Skira, 2005, vol. I, 2 vols., p. 331.

LANGDON 1998
Helen Langdon, ad vocem "Rosa, Salvator", *The Dictionary of Art*, Oxford: Grove, vol. XXVII, 34 vols., 1998.

LANGDON 2010
Helen Langdon, "The Art and Life of Salvator Rosa", *Salvator Rosa (1615–1673): Bandits, Wilderness and Magic*, exh. cat. edited by H. Langdon, London (Dulwich Picture Gallery), Fort Worth (Kimbell Art Museum), London: Holberton, 2010, p. 11–49.

LANGDON 2012
Helen Langdon, *Caravaggio's "Cardsharps": Trickery and Illusion*, Kimbell Masterpiece Series (6), Fort Worth: Kimbell Art Museum, 2012.

LANGENBACH 2014
Randolph Langenbach, "The Building of a Symbolic Image", *Real Virtuality about the Destruction and Multiplication of World*, edited by U. Gehmann and M. Reiche, Bielefeld: Transcript, 2014, p. 91–118.

LANGMUIR 2006
Erika Langmuir, *The National Gallery Companion Guide*, London: National Gallery Company, 2006.

LASSELS 1670
Richard Lassels, *The Voyage of Italy, or, A Compleat Journey through Italy*, Paris: to be sold in London, by John Starkey, 1670, vol. I, 2 vols.

LAUREATI 2005
Laura Laureati, "Un percorso tra vedutisti e paesisti attivi a Roma nel Settecento", *Il Settecento a Roma*, exh. cat. edited by A. Lo Bianco and A. Negro, Roma (Museo Nazionale del Palazzo di Venezia), Cinisello Balsamo: Silvana Editoriale, 2005, p. 83–87.

LAVOIE 1995
Jean-Jacques Lavoie, *Qohélet: une critique moderne de la Bible*, Montréal: Médiaspaul, 1995.

***Le baroque des Lumières* 2017**
Le baroque des Lumières: chefs d'oeuvre des églises parisiennes au XVIIIe siècle, exh. cat. edited by C. Gouzi and C. Leribault, Paris (Musée du Petit Palais), Paris: Paris Musées Editions, 2017.

***Le livre* 1972**
Le Livre, exh. cat. edited by R. Pierrot and M. Thomas, Paris (Bibliothèque nationale), Paris: Bibliothèque nationale, 1972.

***Le siècle de Rembrandt* 1970**
Le siècle de Rembrandt: tableaux hollandais des collections publiques françaises, exh. cat. edited by A. Bréjon de Lavergnée, Paris (Musée du Petit Palais), Paris: Réunion des Musées Nationaux, 1970.

***Le siècle de Rubens* 1977**
Le siècle de Rubens dans les collections publiques françaises, exh. cat. edited by J. Foucart and J. Lacambre, Paris (Grand Palais), Paris: Éditions des Musées Nationaux, 1977.

***Le trompe-l'oeil* 2005**
Le trompe-l'oeil plus vrai que nature?, exh. cat. edited by M. Milman *et al.*, Bourg-en-Bresse (Monastère royal de Brou), Bourg-en-Bresse & Versailles: Musée de Brou & Éd. Artlys, 2005.

LEMOINE 2016
Annick Lemoine, "The Art of Invention after Caravaggio: 'dal naturale' Audacity in the Work of the 'Forestieri' in Rome", *Caravaggio and the Painters of the North*, exh. cat. edited by G. J. van der Sman, Madrid (Thyssen-Bornemisza Museum), Madrid: Fundación Colección Thyssen-Bornemisza, 2016, p. 43–51.

LENAERTS 1989
René-Bernard Lenaerts, ad vocem "De Monte, Philippus", *Dizionario enciclopedico universale della musica e dei musicisti. Le biografie*, Torino: UTET, vol. V, 8 vols., 1989.

LEOPARDI 1923
Giacomo Leopardi, *The Poems of Leopardi*, edited and translated by G. L. Bickersteth, Cambridge: Cambridge University Press, 1923.

***Les Peintres de la réalité* 1934**
Les Peintres de la réalité en France au XVIIe siècle, exh. cat. edited by C. Sterling and P. Jamot, Paris (Musée national de l'Orangerie), Paris: Édition des Musées Nationaux, 1934.

***Les vanités* 1990**
Les vanités dans la peinture au XVIIe siècle. Méditation sur la richesse, le dénuement et la rédemption, exh. cat. edited by A. Tapié *et al.*, Caen (Musée des Beaux-Arts), Paris (Musée du Petit Palais), Paris & Caen: A. Michel & Musée des Beaux-Arts, 1990.

LEVEY 1971
Michael Levey, *National Gallery Catalogues: The Seventeenth and Eighteenth Century Italian Schools*, London: National Gallery, 1971.

LIEDTKE 1993
Walter Liedtke, "An Allegory of Worldly Vanity" (catalog entry), *Masterworks from the Musée Des Beaux-arts, Lille*, exh. cat. edited by A. Brejon de Lavergnée, New York (The Metropolitan Museum of Art), New York: The Metropolitan Museum of Art, 1993, p. 79–83.

LINDEMANN 1985
Bernd Wolfgang Lindemann, "Ultima Schönborniana: unpublizierte Entwürfe zu nicht ausgeführten Epitaphien für Franz Georg von Schönborn, Kurfürst zu Trier", *Wiener Jahrbuch für Kunstgeschichte*, 38 (1985), p. 247–259.

LIPPMANN 1895
Friedrich Lippmann, *The Seven Planets*, translated by F. Simmonds, London: Asher & Co., 1895.

LOHFINK 2003
Norbert Lohfink, *Qoheleth*, translated by S. McEvenue, A Continental Commentary, Minneapolis: Fortress Press, 2003.

LONGHI 1928
Roberto Longhi, *R. Galleria Borghese*, Precisioni nelle gallerie italiane (1), Roma: Pinacotheca, 1928.

LOYOLA 1687
Ignatius of Loyola, *Notitie appartenenti à gli Esercitij spirituali di S. Ignatio Loiola indirizzate alle persone, che vogliono impiegarsi in essi la prima volta*, Bologna: per l'Erede di Vittorio Benacci, 1687.

LUTHER 1972
Martin Luther, *Notes on Ecclesiastes; Lectures on the Song of Solomon; Treatise on the Last Words of David*, edited by J. Pelikan and H. C. Oswald, Luther's Works (15), Saint Louis: Concordia, 1972.

MACEY 1987
Samuel L. Macey, *Patriarchs of Time: Dualism in Saturn-Cronus, Father Time, the Watchmaker God, and Father Christmas*, Athens: University of Georgia Press, 1987.

MACHIAVELLI 1961
Niccolò Machiavelli, *Lettere*, edited by F. Gaeta, Universale economica. Biblioteca di classici italiani (6), Milano: Feltrinelli, 1961, vol. VI, 8 vols.

MACLAREN 1991
Neil MacLaren, *The Dutch School, 1600–1900*, edited by C. Brown, National Gallery catalogues, London: The National Gallery London, 1991.

MAETZKE 1986
Gabriella Maetzke, "Area Nord-occidentale del Foro Romano", *Bullettino della Commissione Archeologica di Roma*, vol. XCI, 2 (1986), p. 372–379.

MAHONEY 1977
Michael Mahoney, *The Drawings of Salvator Rosa*, Outstanding Dissertations in the Fine Arts, New York: Garland, 1977, vol. I, 2 vols.

MALASPINA DI SANNAZARO 1824
Luigi Malaspina di Sannazaro, *Catalogo di una raccolta di stampe antiche compilato dallo stesso possessore* Milano: dai tipi di Giovanni Bernardoni, 1824, vol. III, 5 vols.

MÂLE 1984
Emile Mâle, *L'arte religiosa nel '600. Italia, Francia, Spagna, Fiandra*, translated by M. Donvito, Le grandi stagioni, Milano: Jaca Book, 1984.

MANN 2002
Brian Richard Mann, *The Madrigals of Michelangelo Rossi*, Monuments of Renaissance Music (10), Chicago: University of Chicago Press, 2002.

MANTZ 1872
Paul Mantz, "La galerie de Maurice Cottier", *Gazette des Beaux-Arts*, vol. V (1872), p. 375–397.

MARANDEL 1987
J. Patrice Marandel, "Introduction", *Europe in the Age of Enlightenment and Revolution*, New York: The Metropolitan Museum of Art, 1987, p. 6–17.

MARCON AND CASOLI 2007
Loretta Marcon and Giovanni Casoli, *Qohélet e Leopardi: l'infinita vanità del tutto*, Napoli: Guida, 2007.

MARSHALL 1991
David Ryley Marshall, "The Roman Baths Theme from Viviano Codazzi to G. P. Panini: Transmission and Transformation", *Artibus et Historiae*, vol. XII, 23 (1991), p. 129–159.

MARSHALL 2014
David Ryley Marshall, "The Campo Vaccino: Order and the Fragment from Palladio to Piranesi", *The Site of Rome: Studies in the Art and Topography of Rome, 1400–1750*, edited by D. R. Marshall, Roma: "L'Erma" di Bretschneider, 2014, p. 140–161.

MARTIN 1913
Wilhelm Martin, *Gerard Dou: des Meisters Gemälde in 247 Abbildungen*, Klassiker der Kunst in Gesamtausgaben (24), Stuttgart; Berlin: Deutsche Verlags-Anstalt, 1913.

***Masterpieces of Ivory* 1985**
Masterpieces of Ivory from the Walters Art Gallery, edited by R. H. J. Randall, New York: Hudson Hills Press, 1985.

MASTERS 1992
Edgar Lee Masters, *Antologia di Spoon River*, edited by A. Porta, Oscar classici moderni (52), Milano: Mondadori, 1992.

Masters of Light 1998
Masters of Light: Dutch Painters in Utrecht During the Golden Age, exh. cat. edited by J. A. Spicer *et al.*, San Francisco (Fine Arts Museums of San Francisco), Baltimore (Walters Art Gallery), London (The National Gallery), New Haven: Yale University Press, 1998.

MÁTRAY 1846
Gábor Mátray, *Pyrker János László egri patriarcha-érsek képtára a Magyar Nemzeti Múzeum Képcsarnokában*, Pest: Trattner és Károlyi Intézete, 1846.

MAUÉ 1983
Claudia Maué, "Wiener Skulpturen in Zeichnungen des Würzburger Bildhauers Johann Wolfgang van der Auwera (1708–1756)", *Mainfränkisches Jahrbuch für Geschichte und Kunst*, 35 (1983), p. 52–94.

MAYER 1653
John Mayer, *A Commentary upon the Holy Writings of Job, David, and Solomon That Is, These Five, Job, Psalmes, Proverbs, Ecclesiastes, and the Song of Songs, Being Part of Those which by the Antients Were Called Hagiographa Wherein the Diverse Translations and Expositions, Both Literall and Mysticall, of All the Most Famous Commentators, Both Ancient and Modern, Are Propounded, Examined and Censured, and the Texts from the Originall Much Illustrated, for the Singular Benefit of All That Bee Studious of the Holy Scriptures*, London: Robert and William Leybourn, 1653.

MAZZINGHI 2002
Luca Mazzinghi, "Qohelet and Enochism: A Critical Relationship", *The Origins of Enochic Judaism: Proceedings of the First Enoch Seminar*, edited by G. Boccaccini, Torino: Silvio Zamorani, 2002, p. 157–168.

MAZZINGHI 2009a
Luca Mazzinghi, *Ho cercato e ho esplorato. Studi sul Qohelet*, Bologna: EDB, 2009a.

MAZZINGHI 2009b
Luca Mazzinghi, "The Divine Violence in the Book of Qoheleth", *Biblica*, vol. XC, 4 (2009b), p. 545–558.

MEIJER 1994
Fred G. Meijer, "Vanitas Still Life with Books and Manuscripts, a Skull and a Shawm" (catalog entry), *The Hoogsteder Exhibition of Music & Painting in the Golden Age*, exh. cat. edited by E. Buijsen and L. P. Grijp, Den Haag (Hoogsteder & Hoogsteder), Antwerpen (Hessenhuis), Zwolle: Waanders, 1994, p. 178–181.

MEIJER 2003
Fred G. Meijer, *The Collection of Dutch and Flemish Still-Life Paintings Bequeathed by Daisy Linda Ward*, Zwolle: Waanders, 2003.

MEISS 1976
Millard Meiss, "Light as Form and Symbol in Some Fifteenth-Century Paintings", *The Painter's Choice: Problems in the Interpretation of Renaissance Art*, New York: Harper & Row, 1976, p. 3–18.

Meisterzeichnungen 1987
Meisterzeichnungen / Master Drawings: 1500–1900, exh. cat. edited by K. Krass, München (Kunsthandel Bellinger), London (Harari and Johns), München: Harari and Johns, 1987.

MENOZZI 1980
Daniele Menozzi, *Chiesa, poveri, società nell'età moderna e contemporanea*, Dipartimento di scienze religiose (13), Brescia: Queriniana, 1980.

MEULEMEESTER 1984
Jean Luc Meulemeester, *Jacob van Oost de Oudere en het zeventiende-eeuwse Brugge*, Brugge: Westvlaamse Gidsenkring, 1984.

MILLER 1977
Dwight C. Miller, "A Preparatory Study for Salvator Rosa's L'Umana Fragilità", *The Burlington Magazine*, vol. CIXX, 889 (1977), p. 272–273.

MILLNER KAHR 1998
Madlyn Millner Kahr, *La peinture hollandaise du siècle d'or*, translated by J. Bosser, Paris: Librairie générale française, 1998.

MILLS 2003
Mary E. Mills, *Reading Ecclesiastes: A Literary and Cultural Exegesis*, Burlington: Ashgate, 2003.

MINERVINI 1879
Giulio Minervini, "Appendice. Relazione letta nell'adunanza generale della Società Reale di Napoli il dì 6 gennaio 1878", *Atti della Reale Accademia di archeologia, lettere e belle arti*, Napoli: Stamperia della Regia Università, 1879, vol. IX, 40 vols., p. 3–43.

MOISO-DIEKAMP 1987
Cornelia Moiso-Diekamp, *Das Pendant in der holländischen Malerei des 17. Jahrhunderts*, Frankfurt am Main: Lang, 1987.

MONTIAS 1989
John Michael Montias, *Vermeer and His Milieu: A Web of Social History*, Princeton: Princeton University Press, 1989.

MORGAN 1824
Sydney Morgan, *The Life and Times of Salvator Rosa*, London: Printed for Henry Colburn, 1824, vol. I, 2 vols.

MURPHY 1992
Roland E. Murphy, *Ecclesiastes*, Word Biblical Commentary (23A), Dallas: Word Books, 1992.

MYERS 1991
Mary L. Myers, "Project for a Triumphal Arch" (catalog entry), *French Architectural and Ornament Drawings of the Eighteenth Century* exh. cat. edited by M. L. Myers, New York (The Metropolitan Museum of Art), New York: The Metropolitan Museum of Art, 1991, p. 172–174.

Natures mortes 1954
Natures mortes de l'antiquité au XVIIIe siècle, exh. cat. edited by M. Allemand, Saint-Etienne (Musée d'art et d'industrie), Saint-Etienne: Le Musée, 1954.

Natures mortes 1956
Natures mortes d'hier et d'aujourd'hui, exh. cat. edited by J. Vergnet-Ruiz, Besançon (Musée des Beaux-Arts et, d'archéologie), Besançon: Musée des Beaux-Arts, 1956.

Natures mortes françaises 1951
Natures mortes françaises du XVIIe siècle à nos jours, exh. cat. edited by J. -L. Vaudoyer, Paris (Galerie Charpentier), Paris: La Galerie, 1951.

NEHAMES AND WOODRUFF 1997
Alexander Nehames and Paul Woodruff, "Phaedrus", *Plato: Complete Works*, edited by J. M. Cooper, Indianapolis: Hackett Publishing Company, 1997, p. 506–556.

NEUBERT 2007
Michaela Neubert, "Der Arion-Brunnen des ehemaligen Gerhardschen Hofs zu Würzburg von Johann Wolfgang van der Auwera", *Architektur und Figur*, edited by N. Riegel *et al.*, München: Deutsche Kunstverlag, 2007, p. 405–424.

NICOLSON 1957
Benedict Nicolson, "Terbrugghen repeating himself", *Miscellanea Prof. Dr. D. Roggen*, Antwerpen: Uitgeverij de Sikkel, 1957, p. 193–203.

NICOLSON 1958
Benedict Nicolson, *Hendrick Terbrugghen*, Den Haag: Nijhoff, 1958.

NICOLSON 1979
Benedict Nicolson, *The International Caravaggesque Movement: Lists of Pictures by Caravaggio and His Followers throughout Europe from 1590 to 1650*, Oxford: Phaidon, 1979.

NICOLSON 1990
Benedict Nicolson, *Caravaggism in Europe*, edited by L. Vertova, Archivi di storia dell'arte, Torino: Allemandi, 1990, vol. I, 3 vols.

Nieuw licht op de Gouden Eeuw 1986
Nieuw licht op de Gouden Eeuw: Hendrick ter Brugghen en tijdgenoten, exh. cat. edited by A. Blankert and L. J. Slatkes, Utrecht (Centraal Museum), Utrecht: Centraal Museum, 1986.

NISSEN 1914
Benedikt Momme Nissen, "Rembrandt und Honthorst", *Oud-Holland*, 32 (1914), p. 73–80.

Old Master Paintings 2004
Old Master Paintings: Part One, London (Sotheby's, 8 December 2004), London: Sotheby's, 2004.

One Hundred Master Paintings 2007
One Hundred Master Paintings, exh. cat. edited by E. Schavemaker, Maastricht (Noortman Master Paintings), Maastricht: Noortman Master Paintings, 2007.

OPPERMAN 1977
Hal N. Opperman, *Jean-Baptiste Oudry*, Outstanding Dissertations in the Fine Arts, New York: Garland, 1977, 2 vols.

Orangerie 2006
Orangerie, 1934: les "Peintres de la réalité", exh. cat. edited by P. Georgel *et al.*, Paris (Musée de l'Orangerie), Paris: Réunion des Musées Nationaux, 2006.

OVIDIUS NASO 1844
Publius Ovidius Naso, *Opere di Publio Ovidio Nasone tradotte ed illustrate*, Venezia: dalla Tip. di Giuseppe Antonelli editore, 1844.

PALLUCCHINI 1981
Rodolfo Pallucchini, *La pittura veneziana del seicento*, Milano: Electa, 1981, vol. I, 2 vols.

PANOFSKY 1939
Erwin Panofsky, *Studies in Iconology. Humanistic Themes in the Art of the Renaissance*, New York: Oxford University Press, 1939.

PANOFSKY 1953
Erwin Panofsky, *Early Netherlandish Painting: Its Origins and Character*, Charles Eliot Norton lectures 1947/48, Cambridge: Harvard University Press, 1953, 2 vols.

PAPI 2002
Gianni Papi, "Jusepe de Ribera a Roma e il Maestro del Giudizio di Salomone", *Paragone. Arte*, vol. LIII, 44 (2002), p. 21–43.

PAPI 2003
Gianni Papi, "Ancora su Ribera a Roma", *Les cahiers d'histoire de l'art*, 1 (2003), p. 63–74.

PAPI 2005
Gianni Papi, "Mendicante" (catalog entry), *Caravaggio e l'Europa: il movimento caravaggesco internazionale da Caravaggio a Mattia Preti*, exh. cat. edited by L. Spezzaferro and B. Calzavara, Milano (Palazzo Reale), Wien (Liechtenstein-Museum), Milano: Skira, 2005, p. 250.

PAPI 2010
Gianni Papi, "Cena con suonatore di liuto" (catalog entry), *Caravaggio e caravaggeschi a Firenze*, exh. cat. edited by G. Papi, Firenze (Palazzo Pitti), Livorno: Sillabe, 2010, p. 182.

PAPI 2014
Gianni Papi, "Mendicante" (catalog entry), *I bassifondi del Barocco: la Roma del vizio e della miseria*, exh. cat. edited by F. Cappelletti and A. Lemoine, Roma (Villa Medici), Paris (Petit Palais), Milano: Officina Libraria, 2014, p. 202.

PASCOLI 1730
Lione Pascoli, *Vite de' pittori, scultori ed architetti moderni*, Roma: Antonio de' Rossi nella strada del Seminario Romano, 1730, vol. I, 2 vols.

PASSERI 1772
Giovanni Battista Passeri, *Vite de' pittori, scultori, ed architetti che anno lavorato in Roma, morti dal 1641 fino al 1673*, Roma: Vittorio Settari, 1772.

PAUCCI 1751
Domenico Maria Paucci, *Esercizi spirituali proposti alli ecclesiastici così secolari come regolari, tanto per commodo de' missionari in tempo, che li dovranno proporre quanto per quelli, che si vorranno ridurre in santa solitudine, a farseli privatamente. Opera del p. fr. Domenico Maria Paucci predicatore generale, e missionario dell'Ordine de' Predicatori. Seconda edizione*, Napoli & Messina: Stamperia di Francesco Gaipa, 1751.

PAUL 2012
Carole Paul, *The First Modern Museums of Art: The Birth of an Institution in 18th- and Early 19th-Century Europe*, Los Angeles: J. Paul Getty Museum, 2012.

Peintures françaises et italiennes 1999
Peintures françaises et italiennes, XVIe-XVIIIe siècles, exh. cat. edited by M. -D. Nivière, Bourg-en-Bresse (Musée de Brou), Bourg-en-Bresse: Musée de Brou, 1999.

Peintures pour un château 1998
Peintures pour un château: cinquante tableaux (XVIe–XIXe siècle) des collections du château de Fontainebleau, exh. cat. edited by D. Véron-Denise and V. Droguet, Fontainebleau (Musée National du Château de Fontainebleau), Paris: Réunion des Musées Nationaux, 1998.

Peinture religieuse en Bresse 1984
Peinture religieuse en Bresse au XVIIème siècle, Bourg-en-Bresse (Musée de Brou), Bourg-en-Bresse: Musée de Brou, 1984.

PERRY 1993a
Theodore Anthony Perry, "Montaigne y Kohelet sobre las vanidades de este mundo: hacia una filosofía sefardí", *Actes del Simposi Internacional sobre Cultura Sefardita*, edited by J. Ribera, Barcelona: Facultat de Filologia, Secció d'Hebreu i Arameu, 1993a, p. 263–278.

PERRY 1993b
Theodore Anthony Perry, *Dialogues with Kohelet: The Book of Ecclesiastes, Translation and Commentary*, University Park: Pennsylvania State University Press, 1993b.

PESCIO 2015
Claudio Pescio, *La pittura olandese del secolo d'oro*, Firenze: Giunti, 2015.

PIESKE 1964
Christa Pieske, "Eine barocke Lebens- und Todesallegorie", *Jahrbuch der Hamburger Kunstsammlungen*, 9 (1964), p. 7–16.

PIGLER 1954
Andor Pigler, *A Régi Képtár katalógusa*, Budapest: Akadémiai Kiadó, 1954, vol. I, 2 vols.

PIGLER 1967
Andor Pigler, *Museum der Bildenden Künste Budapest. Katalog der Galerie alter Meister*, Budapest: Akadémiai Kiadó, 1967.

PINÇON 2008
Bertrand Pinçon, *L'énigme du bonheur. Étude sur le sujet du bien dans le livre de Qohélet*, Supplements to Vetus Testamentum (119), Leiden: Brill, 2008.

PINELLI 2010
Antonio Pinelli, *Souvenir. L'industria dell'antico e il Grand Tour a Roma*, Roma: Laterza, 2010.

Piranesi e la veduta 1989
Piranesi e la veduta del Settecento a Roma, exh. cat. edited by L. Angelucci, Roma (Palazzo Braschi), Mogliano Veneto (Villa La Marignana-Benetton), Roma: Artemide Edizioni, 1989.

PIRANESI 1756
Giovanni Battista Piranesi, *Le antichità romane*, Roma: Nella stamperia di Angelo Rotilj, nel Palazzo de' Massimi, 1756.

POLANYI AND PROSCH 1975
Michael Polanyi and Harry Prosch, *Meaning*, Chicago: University of Chicago Press, 1975.

POMME DE MIRIMONDE 1960
Albert Pomme de Mirimonde, "'L' accord retrouvé' de Gerrit van Honthorst", *La Revue des arts*, vol. X, 3 (1960), p. 109–116.

POMME DE MIRIMONDE 1964
Albert Pomme de Mirimonde, "Les natures mortes à instruments de musique de Pieter Boel", *Jaarboek van het Koninklijk Museum voor Schone Kunsten Antwerpen* (1964), p. 107–143.

POMME DE MIRIMONDE 1965
Albert Pomme de Mirimonde, "Les oeuvres françaises à sujet de musique au musée du Louvre. II. Natures mortes des XVIIIe et XIXe siècles", *La Revue du Louvre et des musées de France*, vol. XV, 3 (1965), p. 111–124.

Pompeo Batoni 2007
Pompeo Batoni: Prince of Painters in Eighteenth-Century Rome, exh. cat. edited by E. Peters Bowron and P. B. Kerber, Houston (Museum of Fine Arts) and London (National Gallery), New Haven: Yale University Press, 2007.

POMPILIO 1997
Angelo Pompilio, *Guarini, la musica, i musicisti*, ConNotazioni (3), Lucca: Libreria Musicale Italiana, 1997.

PORZIO 1989
Francesco Porzio, "Giacomo Ceruti detto il Pitocchetto: Portarolo seduto su una cesta; Portarolo seduto con cesta a tracolla, uova e pollame ", *Pinacoteca di Brera. Scuole lombarda, ligure e piemontese 1535–1796*, edited by P. Slavich, Musei e gallerie di Milano, Milano: Electa, 1989, p. 116–120.

PRAZ 1964
Mario Praz, *I volti del tempo*, Collana di saggi (25), Napoli: Edizioni Scientifiche Italiane, 1964.

Princely Patrons 1997
Princely Patrons: The Collection of Frederick Henry of Orange and Amalia of Solms in The Hague, exh. cat. edited by P. Ploeg and C. Vermeeren, Zwolle: Waanders, 1997.

Purc-Stępniak 2002
Beata Purc-Stępniak, "Still Life with Skull" (catalog entry), *Leonardo da Vinci and the Splendor of Poland: A History of Collecting and Patronage*, exh. cat. edited by L. Winters and D. Folga-Januszewska, Milwaukee (Milwaukee Art Museum), Houston (Museum of Fine Arts), San Francisco (California Palace of the Legion of Honor), New Haven: Yale University Press, 2002, p. 80.

Purc-Stępniak 2003
Beata Purc-Stępniak, "Martwa natura z czaszka z Muzeum Narodowego w Gdansku: z badan nad symbolika kuli jako Vanitas", *Studia z historii sztuki i kultury Gdanska i Europy Pólnocnej* (2003), p. 279–300.

Purc-Stępniak 2004a
Beata Purc-Stępniak, *Kula jako symbol vanitas: z kregu badan nad malarstwem XVII wieku*, Gdansk: Słowo, 2004a.

Purc-Stępniak 2004b
Beata Purc-Stępniak, "Martwa natura z czaszką" (catalog entry), *Transalpinum: od Giorgiona i Dürera do Tycjana i Rubensa. Dziela malarstwa europejskiego ze zbiorów Kunsthistorisches Museum w Wiedniu, Muzeum Narodowego w Warszawie i Muzeum Narodowego w Gdańsku*, exh. cat. edited by D. Folga-Januszewska and A. Ziemba, Warszawa (Muzeum Narodowe), Gdańsk (Muzeum Narodowe), Olszanica: Bosz, 2004b, p. 136.

Purc-Stępniak 2005
Beata Purc-Stępniak, "Martwa natura z czaszką" (catalog entry), *Uczony i jego pracownia*, exh. cat. edited by M. Reklewska, Kraków (Muzeum Uniwersytetu Jagiellońskiego), Krakow: Muzeum Uniwersytetu Jagiellonskiego, 2005, p. 140–142.

Puyvelde and Puyvelde 1971
Leo van Puyvelde and Thierry van Puyvelde, *Flemish Painting: The Age of Rubens and Van Dyck*, translated by A. Kendall, London: Weidenfeld and Nicolson, 1971.

Pyrker emlékkönyv 1987
Pyrker emlékkönyv, edited by G. Hölvényi, Eger: Egyetemi Nyomda, 1987.

Pyrker érsek képtára 2002
Pyrker érsek képtára. Válogatás a budapesti Szépművészeti Múzeum gyűjteményéből, exh. cat. edited by Á. Szigethi, Eger (Dobó István Vármúzeum), Eger: Dobó István Vármúzeum, 2002.

Quarles 1635
Francis Quarles, *Emblemes*, London: Printed by G. M. and sold at Iohn Marriots shope, 1635.

Ragaller 1979
Heinrich Ragaller, *Johann Wolfgang van der Auwera: ein Skizzenbuch. Dokumente zur Gartenplastik für den Prinzen Eugen*, Würzburg: Echter, 1979.

Rahner 1966
Karl Rahner, "The Theology of the Symbol", *Theological Investigations: More Recent Writings*, translated by K. Smyth, Baltimore: Helicon, 1966, vol. IV, 16 vols., p. 221–252.

Raupp 1984
Hans-Joachim Raupp, *Untersuchungen zu Künstlerbildnis und Künstlerdarstellung in den Niederlanden im 17. Jahrhundert*, Studien zur Kunstgeschichte (25), Hildesheim: Olms, 1984, vol. 25.

Renzi 1999
Lorenzo Renzi, *Proust e Vermeer: apologia dell'imprecisione*, Intersezioni (190), Bologna: il Mulino, 1999.

Ricasoli 2011
Corinna Ricasoli, "'It may well be that he dabbles in daubing'. Notes on a Drawing Attributed to Caravaggio and the Career of Tommaso Salini", *Artefact. Journal of the Irish Association of Art Historians*, 5 (2011), p. 63–77.

Ricasoli 2014
Corinna Ricasoli, *'Non Omnis Moriar': Artists' Funerary Monuments in Baroque Rome*, Ph.D. Thesis, Dublin: University College Dublin, 2014.

Ricasoli 2015
Corinna Ricasoli, "Memento mori in Baroque Rome", *Studies: an Irish Quarterly Review*, vol. CIV, 416 (2015), p. 456–467.

Ricasoli 2018
Corinna Ricasoli, "Quel foco bellissimo d'amore: Qohelet, Le Peschier, Guarini, De Monte e la vanità dell'amore fugace", *Il libro aperto e divorato. Bibbia, traduzioni, arte e culture*, edited by G. Benzi, in press, 2018.

Ricoeur 1962
Paul Ricoeur, "The Hermeneutics of Symbols and Philosophical Reflection", *International Philosophical Quarterly*, vol. II, 2 (1962), p. 191–218.

Ripa and Orlandi 1765
Cesare Ripa and Cesare Orlandi, *Iconologia del cavaliere Cesare Ripa perugino. Notabilmente accresciuta d'Immagini, di Annotazioni, e di Fatti dall'Abate Cesare Orlandi patrizio di Città della Pieve Accademico Augusto*, Perugia: Nella stamperia di Piergiovanni Costantini, 1765, vol. II, 5 vols.

Rollenhagen 1611
Gabriel Rollenhagen, *Nucleus emblematum selectissimorum quea quae Itali vulgo impressas vacant*, Les Recueils d'emblèmes et les traités de physiognomonie de la Bibliothèque Interuniversitaire de Lille (3), Paris: Aux Amateurs de Livres, 1611, 2 vols.

Rollenhagen 1983
Gabriel Rollenhagen, *Sinn-Bilder: ein Tugendspiegel*, edited by C. -P. Warncke, Die bibliophilen Taschenbücher (378), Dortmund: Harenberg, 1983.

Roma 1999
Roma, Guida d'Italia, Milano: Touring Club, 1999.

Rosa 1695
Salvatore Rosa, *Satire di Salvator Rosa dedicate a Settano*, In Amsterdam [i.e. Roma]: presso Sevo Prothomastix, 1695.

Rosa and Salvini 1833
Salvatore Rosa and Anton Maria Salvini, *Satire e vita di Salvator Rosa*, edited by A. M. Salvini, Firenze: Attilio Tofani, 1833.

Rosa and Cesareo 1892
Salvatore Rosa and Giovanni Alfredo Cesareo, *Poesie e lettere edite e inedite di Salvator Rosa, pubblicate criticamente e precedute dalla vita dell'Autore rifatta su nuovi documenti*, Napoli: Real Accademia di archeologia, lettere e belle arti, Tipografia della Regia Università, 1892, vol. II, 2 vols.

Rosenberg *et al.* 1966
Jakob Rosenberg *et al.*, *Dutch Art and Architecture, 1600–1800*, The Pelican History of Art, Harmondsworth: Penguin, 1966.

Rosin 1997
Robert Rosin, *Reformers, the Preacher and Skepticism: Luther, Brenz, Melanchthon and Ecclesiastes*, Veröffentlichungen des Instituts für Europäische Geschichte Mainz (171), Mainz: P. von Zabern, 1997.

Röttgen 1962
Herwarth Röttgen, "Ein barockes Bild von Vergänglichkeit und Hoffnung zum Selbstbildnis Daniel Preisslers mit seiner Familie", *Das Münster*, 15 (1962), p. 48–49.

Rowell 2012
Diana Rowell, *Paris: The 'New Rome' of Napoleon I*, London: Bloomsbury, 2012.

Ruffini 2011
Marco Ruffini, *Art Without an Author: Vasari's Lives and Michelangelo's Death*, New York: Fordham University Press, 2011.

Rupp 2002
Michael Rupp, *"Narrenschiff" und "Stultifera navis": deutsche und lateinische Moralsatire von Sebastian Brant und Jakob Locher in Basel 1494 - 1498*, Studien und Texte zum Mittelalter und zur frühen Neuzeit, Münster: Waxmann, 2002, vol. III.

Safarik 1973
Eduard A. Safarik, "Per la pittura veneta del Seicento: Girolamo Forabosco", *Arte illustrata*, 6 (1973), p. 353–363.

Salerno 1963
Luigi Salerno, *Salvator Rosa*, Collana d'arte del Club del Libro (5), Firenze: Club del Libro, 1963.

Salvagni 2008
Isabella Salvagni, "Architettura ed «Aequa potestas». Filippo Juvarra, l'Accademia di San Luca e gli architetti", *La forma del pensiero. Filippo Juvarra. La costruzione del ricordo attraverso la celebrazione della memoria*, edited by C. Ruggero and T. Caserta, Roma: Campisano Editore, 2008, p. 33–53.

Salvator Rosa 2008
Salvator Rosa tra mito e magia, exh. cat.
edited by N. Spinosa, Napoli (Museo e
Gallerie Nazionali di Capodimonte), Napoli:
Electa Napoli, 2008.

Santa Maria Antiqua 2016
Santa Maria Antiqua tra Roma e Bisanzio,
exh. cat. edited by M. Andaloro *et al.*, Roma
(Santa Maria Antiqua), Milano: Electa, 2016.

SCARAMELLA 2002
Pierroberto Scaramella, "The Italy of
Triumphs and of Contrasts", *Humana
Fragilitas: The Themes of Death in Europe
from the 13th Century to the 18th Century*,
edited by P. Scaramella and A. Tenenti,
Clusone: Ferrari Editrice, 2002,
p. 25–98.

SCHAAR 1983
Eckhard Schaar, "Calvinismus und Kunst in
den nördlichen Niederlanden", *Luther und
die Folgen für die Kunst*, exh. cat. edited by
W. Hofmann *et al.*, Hamburg (Hamburger
Kunsthalle), München: Prestel, 1983,
p. 348–374.

SCHAMA 1987
Simon Schama, *The Embarrassment of
Riches: an Interpretation of Dutch Culture in
the Golden Age*, New York: Knopf, 1987.

SCHAMA 1991
Simon Schama, *The Embarrassment of
Riches: An Interpretation of Dutch Culture in
the Golden Age*, London: Fontana, 1991.

SCHILLING 1979
Michael Schilling, *Imagines mundi.
Metaphorische Darstellung der Welt in der
Emblematik*, Mikrokosmos (4), Frankfurt am
Main: Lang, 1979.

SCHOORS 2013
Antoon Schoors, *Ecclesiastes*, Historical
Commentary on the Old Testament, Leuven
& Paris: Peeters, 2013.

SCHREUDER 1997
Marc Schreuder, "A Newly Discovered Early
Barn Interior by Jan Davidsz. de Heem
(1606–1683/84)", *Oud-Holland*, 111 (1997),
p. 13–18.

SCHWIENHORST-SCHÖNBERGER 2004
Ludger Schwienhorst-Schönberger, *Kohelet*,
Herders Theologischer Kommentar zum
Alten Testament, Freiburg im Breisgau:
Herder, 2004.

SCIOLLA 1981
Gianni Carlo Sciolla, "Pittori caravaggeschi
olandesi a Roma 1610–1630 e una proposta
per la cerchia di Dirck van Baburen",
*Bollettino del Centro Interuniversitario di
Ricerche sul Viaggio in Italia* vol. III, 2 (1981),
p. 5–18.

SECKER 1913
Hans Friedrich Secker, *Die Städtische
Gemäldegalerie im Franziskanerkloster.
Führer durch die öffentlichen
Kunstsammlungen in Danzig: Burau*, 1913.

SEDLMAIER AND VON FREEDEN 1955
Richard Sedlmaier and Max H. Von Freeden,
*Wolfgang von der Auveras Schönborn-
Grabmäler im Mainfränkischen Museum und
die Grabmalkunst der Schönborn-Bischöfe*,
Mainfränkische Hefte (23), Würzburg:
Freunde Mainfränkischer Kunst und
Geschichte, 1955.

SEGAL 1991
Sam Segal, "Interieur: Een man in gedachten
verzonken" (catalog entry), *Jan Davidsz de
Heem en zijn kring*, exh. cat. edited by S.
Segal, Utrecht (Centraal Museum Utrecht),
Braunschweig (Herzog-Anton-Ulrich-
Museum), Braunschweig: Herzog Anton
Ulrich-Museum, 1991, p. 127–128.

SEGAL 1998
Sam Segal, ad vocem "Heem, Jan Davidsz
de", *The Dictionary of Art*, Oxford: Grove,
vol. VIII, 34 vols., 1998.

SELLINK 2000
Manfred Sellink, *Cornelis Cort*, edited by H.
Leeflang, The New Hollstein Dutch and
Flemish Etchings, Engravings and
Woodcuts, 1450–1700, Rotterdam: Sound &
Vision Publishers, 2000, vol. XVI, 81 vols.

SHAKESPEARE 2016
William Shakespeare, *The New Oxford
Shakespeare: The Complete Works*, edited by
G. Taylor *et al.*, Oxford: Oxford University
Press, 2016.

SILVER AND PERLOVE 2011
Larry Silver and Shelley Perlove,
"Rembrandt's Jesus", *Rembrandt and the Face
of Jesus*, exh. cat. edited by L. DeWitt and S.
Slive, Paris (Musée du Louvre), Philadelphia
(Philadelphia Museum of Art), Detroit
(Detroit Institute of Arts), Philadelphia,
Paris, Detroit & New Haven: in association
with Yale University Press, 2011, p. 75–107.

SKIRA 1989
Pierre Skira, *Still Life: A History*, New York:
Rizzoli, 1989.

SLATKES 1966
Leonard Joseph Slatkes, "David de Haen and
Dirk van Baburen in Rome", *Oud-Holland*,
81 (1966), p. 173–186.

SLATKES 1998
Leonard Joseph Slatkes, ad vocem "Baburen,
Dirck van", *The Dictionary of Art*, Oxford:
Grove, vol. III, 34 vols., 1998.

SLATKES AND FRANITS 2007
Leonard Joseph Slatkes and Wayne E.
Franits, *The Paintings of Hendrick ter
Brugghen (1588–1629). Catalogue Raisonné*,
Amsterdam: John Benjamins Pub. Co., 2007.

SMITS 1933
Karel Smits, *De iconografie van de
Nederlandsche primitieven*, Amsterdam: De
Spieghel, 1933.

SPIKE 1984
John Thomas Spike, "Portrait of Giovanni
Battista Ricciardi" (catalog entry), *Baroque

*Portraiture in Italy: Works from North
American Collections*, exh. cat. edited by J. T.
Spike, Sarasota (John and Mable Ringling
Museum of Art), Hartford (Wadsworth
Atheneum), Sarasota: John and Mable
Ringling Museum of Art, 1984, p. 158–159.

SPIKE 2010
John Thomas Spike, *Caravaggio*, New York
and London: Abbeville Press, 2010.

SPINELLI 2011
Riccardo Spinelli, "Giovanni Martinelli: alla
ricerca di una 'difficile' biografia", *Giovanni
Martinelli pittore di Montevarchi. Maestro
del Seicento fiorentino*, edited by A.
Baldinotti *et al.*, Firenze: Maschietto Editore,
2011, p. 23–55.

SPINOSA 2003
Nicola Spinosa, *Ribera: l'opera completa*,
Napoli: Electa, 2003.

SPINOSA 2008
Nicola Spinosa, *Ribera: la obra completa*,
Madrid: Fundación Arte Hispánico, 2008.

Stadtmuseum zu Danzig 1902
*Stadtmuseum zu Danzig: Gemälde-
Verzeichnis*, S. L., 1902.

STERLING 1959
Charles Sterling, *Still Life Painting from
Antiquity to the Present Time*, New York:
Universe Books, 1959.

STROCCHI 2003
Maria Letizia Strocchi, "Giovanna Garzoni"
(catalog entry), *La natura morta italiana da
Caravaggio al Settecento*, exh. cat. edited by
M. Gregori, Firenze (Palazzo Strozzi),
Milano: Electa, 2003, p. 487.

SUMMERS 1969
David Summers, "The Sculptural Program of
the Cappella di San Luca in the Santissima
Annunziata", *Mitteilungen des
Kunsthistorischen Institutes in Florenz*, 14
(1969), p. 67–90.

SUMOWSKI 1983
Werner Sumowski, ad vocem "Anonymous
Rembrandt School", *Gemälde der
Rembrandt-Schüler*, Landau/Pfalz: Ed. PVA,
vol. III (B. Keil-J. Ovens), 6 vols., 1983.

TACKE 1995
Andreas Tacke, *Die Gemälde des 17.
Jahrhunderts im Germanischen
Nationalmuseum*, Mainz: von Zabern, 1995.

TARABRA 2008
Daniela Tarabra, *European Art of the
Eighteenth Century*, translated by R. M.
Giammanco Frongia, Los Angeles: J. Paul
Getty Museum, 2008.

TEMPLE 1690
William Temple, *Miscellanea. The Second
Part in Four Essays. I. Upon Ancient and
Modern Learning, II. Upon the Gardens of
Epicurus, III. Upon Heroick Vertue, IV. Upon
Poetry*, London: Printed by J. R. for Ri. and
Ra. Simpson, 1690.

Tenenti 1989
Alberto Tenenti, *Il senso della morte e l'amore della vita nel Rinascimento*, edited by A. Tenenti, Biblioteca di cultura storica (175), Torino: Einaudi, 1989.

The Jerusalem Talmud 2008
The Jerusalem Talmud: Third Order: Našim. Tractate Qiddušin, edited by H. W. Guggenheimer, Berlin: De Gruyter, 2008.

The Kunstkammer 2016
The Kunstkammer. Wonders Are Collectable, Kunstkammer Edition (1), edited by G. Laue, München, 2016.

The New Testament 1972
The New Testament in Modern English, London: Harper Collins Publishers, 1972.

The Paradise of Dainty Devices 1927
The Paradise of Dainty Devices (1576–1606), edited by H. E. Rollins, Cambridge: Harvard University Press, 1927.

The Splendid Century 1960
The Splendid Century: French Art, 1600–1715, exh. cat. edited by M. Laclotte, Washington, DC (The National Gallery of Art), Toledo (The Toledo Museum of Art), New York (The Metropolitan Museum of Art), New York: The Metropolitan Museum of Art, 1960.

Thieme *et al.* 1922
Ulrich Thieme *et al.*, ad vocem "Hannot, Johannes", *Allgemeines Lexikon der bildenden Künstler von der Antike bis zur Gegenwartn*, Leipzig: Seemann, vol. XV, 37 vols., 1922.

Thürlemann 2002
Felix Thürlemann, *Robert Campin: A Monographic Study with Critical Catalogue*, London: Prestel, 2002.

Tiberia 2010
Vitaliano Tiberia, *La Compagnia di S. Giuseppe di Terrasanta da Clemente XI a Pio VI*, Fonti medievali e moderne / Università degli studi di Lecce, Dipartimento dei beni delle arti e della storia (14), Galatina: M. Congedo, 2010.

Tillich 1960
Paul Tillich, "Art and Ultimate Reality", *CrossCurrents*, vol. X, 1 (1960), p. 1–14.

Timmers 1947
Jan Joseph Marie Timmers, *Symboliek en iconographie der Christelijke kunst*, Romen's compendia Roermond: J. J. Romen & Zonen-Uitgevers, 1947.

Prosper 1972
Prosper Tiro, *Expositio Psalmorum a centesimo usque ad centesimum quinquagesimum; Sententiae ex operibus s. Augustini*, edited by M. Gastaldo, Corpus christianorum. Series latina (68A), Turnholti: Brepols, 1972.

Tongiorgi Tomasi 2002
Lucia Tongiorgi Tomasi, "The Flowering of Florence: Botanical Art for the Medici", *The Flowering of Florence: Botanical Art for the Medici*, exh. cat. edited by L. Tongiorgi Tomasi and G. A. Hirschauer, Washington, DC (The National Gallery of Art), Aldershot: Lund Humphries, 2002, p. 75–109.

Tragicomedia 2004
Tragicomedia, *Vanitas vanitatum: Rome 1650*, London: Warner Classics, 2004.

Trenschel 1986
Hans-Peter Trenschel, "Zur Rolle der Vorstudien bei Johann Wolfgang von der Auwera und Johann Peter Wagner", *Entwurf und Ausführung in der europäischen Barockplastik. Beiträge zum internationalen Kolloquium des Bayerischen Nationalmuseums und des Zentralinstituts für Kunstgeschichte*, edited by P. Volk, München: Schnell & Steiner, 1986, p. 215–238.

Trevor-Roper 1967
Hugh Redwald Trevor-Roper, *Religion, the Reformation and Social Change and Other Essays*, London & Melbourne: Macmillan, 1967.

Trezzani 1998
Ludovico Trezzani, ad vocem "Codazzi, Viviano", *The Dictionary of Art*, Oxford: Grove, vol. VII, 34 vols., 1998.

Trois siècles de peinture française 1949
Trois siècles de peinture française - XVIe–XVIIIe siècles. Choix d'œuvres des Musées de France, exh. cat. edited by J. Vergnet-Ruiz, Genève (Musée Rath), Genève, 1949.

Tümpel 1971
Christian Tümpel, "Ikonographische Beiträge zu Rembrandt", *Jahrbuch der Hamburger Kunstsammlungen*, 16 (1971), p. 20–38.

Tümpel 1983
Christian Tümpel, "Die Reformation und die Kunst der Niederlande", *Luther und die Folgen für die Kunst*, exh. cat. edited by W. Hofmann *et al.*, Hamburg (Hamburger Kunsthalle), München: Prestel, 1983, p. 309–321.

Tuominen 2014
Minna Tuominen, *The Still Lifes of Edwaert Collier (1642–1708)*, Ph.D. Thesis, Helsinki: University of Helsinki, 2014.

Van der Haeghen 1906
Victor van der Haeghen, *La Corporation des Peintres et des Sculpteurs de Gand. Matricule, comptes et documents, 16e–18e siècles*, Bruxelles: Librairie Nationale d'Art et d'Histoire, 1906.

Van der Stighelen 1998
Katlijne Van der Stighelen, ad vocem "Panderen, Egbert van", *The Dictionary of Art*, Oxford: Grove, vol. XXIII, 34 vols., 1998.

Van Doorslaer 1921
George Van Doorslaer, *La vie et les oeuvres de Philippe de Monte*, Bruxelles: Maurice Lamertin, 1921.

van Haemstede 1634
Adriaan Van Haemstede, *Historien der Vromer Martelaren die om het getuychenis des H. Evangeliums haer bloet gestort hebben vande tijden Christi af tot desen tegenwoordigen tijt en Iaere 1633*, Amsterdam: Ian Evertsz Cloppenburg, 1634.

Van Miegroet 1998
Hans J. Van Miegroet, ad vocem "Vanitas", *The Dictionary of Art*, Oxford: Grove, vol. XXXI, 1998.

Van Straten 1992
Roelof Van Straten, "Early Works by Lievens and Rembrandt in Two Unknown Still Lifes", *Artibus et Historiae*, vol. XIII, 26 (1992), p. 121–142.

Vanitas: Meditations on Life 2000
Vanitas: Meditations on Life and Death in Contemporary Art, exh. cat. edited by J. B. Ravenal, Richmond (Virginia Museum of Fine Arts), Richmond: Virginia Museum of Fine Arts, 2000.

Vasari 1906
Giorgio Vasari, *Le opere di Giorgio Vasari*, edited by G. Milanesi, Firenze: G. C. Sansoni, 1906, vol. VI, 9 vols.

Venturi 1893
Adolfo Venturi, *Il museo e la Galleria Borghese*, Collezione Edelweiss (4), Roma: Società Laziale, 1893.

Verdon 1996
Timothy Verdon, "'Colui che dà le leggi alla natura': norma, novità, stravaganza e solitudine in Pontormo", *Pontormo e Rosso: atti del convegno di Empoli e Volterra*, edited by R. P. Ciardi and A. Natali, Venezia: Marsilio, 1996, p. 47–51.

Verdon 2005a
Timothy Verdon, *La Basilica di San Pietro: i papi e gli artisti*, Uomini e religioni. Saggi, Milano: Mondadori, 2005a.

Verdon 2005b
Timothy Verdon, *Mary in Western Art*, New York: Hudson Hills Press, 2005b.

Le XVIIe siècle français 1958
Le XVIIe siècle français: chefs-d'oeuvre des musées de province, Paris (Musée du Petit Palais), Paris: Presses artistiques, 1958.

Vergnet-Ruiz and Laclotte 1962
Jean Vergnet-Ruiz and Michel Laclotte, *Petits et grands musées de France, la peinture française des primitifs à nos jours*, Paris: Éditions Cercle D'art, 1962.

Verstegen and Ceen 2013
Ian Verstegen and Allan Ceen, *Giambattista Nolli and Rome: Mapping the City before and after the Pianta Grande*, Roma: Studium Urbis, 2013.

Vertova 1992
Luisa Vertova, "La Morte Secca", *Mitteilungen des Kunsthistorischen Institutes in Florenz*, vol. XXXVI, 1/2 (1992), p. 103–128.

Verzeichniss eines Thieles 1856
Verzeichniss eines Thieles der Kabrun`schen Bildgallerie in Danzig aufgestellt in dem Hause Hundegasse No 10, Preis 2 Sgr. Vermehrte, verbesserte Auflage, Danzig: Wedelsche Hofbuchdruckerei, 1856.

Vílchez Líndez 1994
José Vílchez Líndez, *Eclesiastés o Qohélet*, Nueva Biblia Española: Comentario Teológico y Literario, Sapienciales (3), Estella (Navarra): Editorial Verbo Divino, 1994.

Villari 1895
Pasquale Villari, *Niccolò Macchiavelli e i suoi tempi: illustrati con nuovi documenti*, Milano: Ulrico Hoepli, 1895, vol. II, 2 vols.

Villis 2000
Carl Villis, "Bernardo Bellotto's Seven Large Views of Rome, c. 1743", *The Burlington Magazine*, vol. CXLII, 1163 (2000), p. 76–81.

Volpi 2008
Caterina Volpi, "Salvator Rosa, nuovi documenti e riflessioni sul primo periodo romano e su quello fiorentino", *Storia dell'Arte*, 20 (2008), p. 85–116.

Volpi 2010
Caterina Volpi, "The Frailty of Human Life" (catalog entry), *Salvator Rosa (1615–1673): Bandits, Wilderness and Magic*, exh. cat. edited by H. Langdon, London (Dulwich Picture Gallery), Fort Wort (Kimbell Art Museum), London: Holberton, 2010, vol. 2010, p. 220–223.

Von Bartsch 1801–1821
Adam Von Bartsch, *Le peintre graveur*, Wien: J. V. Degen, 1801–1821, vol. XV, 21 vols.

Von Goethe 1885
Johann Wolfgang von Goethe, *Goethe's Travels in Italy Together with his Second Residence in Rome and Fragments on Italy*, translated by C. Nisbet, London: Bell, 1885.

Von Sandrart 1925
Joachim Von Sandrart, *Joachim von Sandrarts Academie der Bau-, Bild- und Mahlerey-Künste von 1675. Leben der berühmten Maler, Bildhauer und Baumeister*, edited by A. R. Peltzer, München: Hirth, 1925.

Wagenaar-Burgemeister 2016
Wendela Wagenaar-Burgemeister, "Vanitas Still Life with a Skull, Musical Instruments, a Globe, Books and Writing Paraphernalia", *Salomon Lilian Old masters 2016*, Amsterdam: Salomon Lilian, 2016, p. 12–15.

Wahrman 2012
Dror Wahrman, *Mr. Collier's Letter Racks: A Tale of Art & Illusion at the Threshold of the Modern Information Age*, New York & Oxford: Oxford University Press, 2012.

Wallace 1968
Richard W. Wallace, "Salvator Rosa's Democritus and L'Umana Fragilità", *The Art Bulletin*, vol. L, 1 (1968), p. 21–32.

Wallace 1979
Richard W. Wallace, "Self-Portrait" (catalog entry), *Salvator Rosa in America*, exh. cat. edited by R. W. Wallace, Wellesley (Wellesley College Museum), Wellesley: Burton, 1979, p. 11–13, 21.

Warner 2000
Marina Warner, *Monuments and Maidens: The Allegory of the Female Form*, Berkeley: University of California Press, 2000.

Wassyng Roworth 1988
Wendy Wassyng Roworth, "The Consolations of Friendship: Salvator Rosa's Self-Portrait for Giovanni Battista Ricciardi", *Metropolitan Museum Journal*, vol. XXIII (1988), p. 103–124.

Waźbiński 1987
Zygmunt Waźbiński, *L'Accademia medicea del disegno a Firenze nel Cinquecento: idea e istituzione*, Accademia toscana di scienze e lettere "La Colombaria": Studi (84), Firenze: Olschki, 1987, 2 vols.

Welu 1979
James A. Welu, "Johannes Hannot" (catalog entry), *17th Century Dutch Painting: Raising the Curtain on New England Private Collections*, exh. cat. edited by J. A. Welu, Worcester (Worcester Art Museum), Worcester: Worcester Art Museum, 1979, p. 35–37.

Werness 2004
Hope B. Werness, *The Continuum Encyclopedia of Animal Symbolism in Art*, New York & London: Continuum, 2004.

Wescher 1954
Paul Wescher, *A Catalogue of Italian, French and Spanish Paintings, XIV–XVIII Century*, Los Angeles: Los Angeles County Museum of Art, 1954.

Westermann 1996
Mariët Westermann, *A Worldly Art: The Dutch Republic, 1585–1718*, Perspectives, New York: Harry Abrams, 1996.

Wheelwright 1962
Philip Ellis Wheelwright, *Metaphor and Reality*, Bloomington: Indiana University Press, 1962.

Whinney 1968
Margaret Dickens Whinney, *Early Flemish Painting*, Books That Matter, New York: Praeger, 1968.

Whybray 1982
Roger Norman Whybray, "Qoheleth, Preacher of Joy", *Journal for the Study of the Old Testament*, vol. VII, 23 (1982), p. 87–98.

Wieseman 1999
Betsy Wieseman, "Boeken en een luit op een tafel" (catalog entry), *Het Nederlandse stilleven, 1550–1720*, exh. cat. edited by A. Chong, Amsterdam (Rijksmuseum), Cleveland (Cleveland Museum of Art), Amsterdam: Rijksmuseum, 1999, p. 168–169.

Wilton-Ely 1994
John Wilton-Ely, *Giovanni Battista Piranesi: The Complete Etchings*, San Francisco: Alan Wolfsy Fine Arts, 1994, 2 vols.

Winston 1993
Anne Winston, "Tracing the Origins of the Rosary: German Vernacular Texts", *Speculum*, vol. LXVIII, 3 (1993), p. 619–636.

Witcombe 1998
Christopher L. C. E. Witcombe, ad vocem "Musi, Agostino dei", *The Dictionary of Art*, Oxford: Grove, vol. XXII, 34 vols., 1998.

Wither 1635
George Wither, *A Collection of Emblemes Ancient and Modern, Quickened with Metricall Illustrations, Both Morall and Divine and Disposed Into Lotteries*, London: Printed by A. M[athewes] for H. Taunton, 1635.

Wittkower and Wittkower 2007
Rudolf Wittkower and Margot Wittkower, *Nati sotto Saturno. La figura dell'artista dall'antichita alla rivoluzione francese*, translated by F. Salvatorelli, Einaudi (353), Torino: Einaudi, 2007.

Wurfbain 1998
Maarten Wurfbain, ad vocem "Collier, Edwaert", *The Dictionary of Art*, Oxford: Grove, vol. VII, 34 vols., 1998.

Zani 1820
Pietro Zani, *Enciclopedia metodica critico-ragionata delle belle arti, parte seconda*, Parma: Tipografia Ducale, 1820, vol. IV, 9 vols.

Zauber der Medusa 1987
Zauber der Medusa. Europäische Manierismen, exh. cat. edited by W. Hofmann, Wien (Künstlerhaus), Wien: Löcker, 1987.

Zeri and Dolcetta 1998
Federico Zeri and Marco Dolcetta, *Bronzino: Allegoria del trionfo di Venere*, Cento dipinti, Milano: Rizzoli, 1998.

Zsámboky 1564
János Zsámboky, *Emblemata*, Antwerp: ex officina Christophori Plantini, 1564.

Zuccari 2009
Alessandro Zuccari, "Angelo Caroselli e il 'Giudizio di Salomone' della Galleria Borghese", *Da Caravaggio ai caravaggeschi*, edited by M. Calvesi and A. Zuccari, Roma: CAM, 2009, p. 345–363.

Zum Sterben schön 2006
Zum Sterben schön! Alter, Totentanz und Sterbekunst von 1500 bis heute, exh. cat. edited by A. Hülsen-Esch and H. Westermann-Angerhausen, Köln (Museum Schnütgen), Düsseldorf (Goethe-Museum), Recklinghausen (Städtische Kunsthalle), Regensburg: Schnell & Steiner, 2006, vol. II, 2 vols.